Bloom's Modern Critical Views

Bloom's Modern Critical Views

Bloom's Modern Critical Views

WALT WHITMAN
Updated Edition

Edited and with an introduction by
Harold Bloom
Sterling Professor of the Humanities
Yale University

CHELSEA HOUSE
P U B L I S H E R S
An imprint of Infobase Publishing

Bloom's Modern Critical Views: Walt Whitman, Updated Edition

Copyright © 2006 by Infobase Publishing
Introduction © 2006 by Harold Bloom

Chelsea House
An imprint of Infobase Publishing
132 West 31st Street
New York NY 10001

Library of Congress Cataloging-in-Publication Data
Walt Whitman / Harold Bloom, editor.— Updated ed.
    p. cm. — (Bloom's modern critical views)
  Updated edition of Walt Whitman, in the Modern critical views series,
published in 1985.
  Includes bibliographical references and index.
  ISBN 0-7910-9252-6 (hardcover)
  1. Whitman, Walt, 1819-1892—Criticism and interpretation. I. Bloom,
Harold. II. Series.
  PS3238.W365 2006
  811'.3—dc22   2005038040

Contributing Editor: Jesse Zuba
Cover design by Keith Trego

Printed in the United States of America

Bang EJB 10 9 8 7 6 5 4 3 2 1

This book is printed on acid-free paper.

All links and web addresses were checked and verified to be correct at the time of
publication. Because of the dynamic nature of the web, some addresses and links may have
changed since publication and may no longer be valid.

Contents

Editor's Note

This book revises *Walt Whitman: Modern Critical Views* (1985) which I edited twenty years ago. The revision is substantial, as only four of the twelve essays now included were in the earlier volume (Lawrence, Burke, Lewis, Bloom). My Introduction is the same, but the book closes with a new Afterthought, which expresses something of my current thinking about the greatest writer yet to come forth in the four centuries of Western literature composed in the New World, whether in English, Spanish, Portuguese, or French.

The Introduction meditates upon Whitman's original and still unassimilated psychic cartography. D.H. Lawrence's prophetic essay, really a prose poem, ambivalently celebrates the American Bard as the pioneer poet who broke the new road since followed by so many, Lawrence included.

In Kenneth Burke's superb evocation, Whitman's personalization of his democratic vision is traced throughout his prose and poetry, while R.W.B. Lewis usefully details the poet's progress through the major editions of *Leaves of Grass*.

My essay studies what Whitman called "the tally" as his central trope for his own image of voice.

Kerry C. Larson gives us his useful insights into Whitman's catalogs, while David Bromwich superbly illuminates what Whitman meant by "immortality."

Whitman's idiom, with its 1855 to 1860 movement from confidence in language to a wariness of its entrapments, is shrewdly analyzed by Mark Bauerlein, after which John Hollander gives us the best sustained account we have of why Whitman's poetry initially looks easy, but is wonderfully difficult.

Helen Vendler, our major Formalist critic, masterfully surveys the

Lincoln elegies of Whitman, whom I would categorize as our greatest Formalist poet.

The Orphic critical seer, Angus Fletcher, sublimely attempts to displace Whitman's High Romanticism into the older Picturesque that blends into the American environment poem.

My Afterthought presents Whitman as the poet of the American Religion, who ventured to give us *Leaves of Grass* as the American Bible.

HAROLD BLOOM

Introduction

I

As poet and as person, Walt Whitman remains large and evasive. We cannot know, even now, much that he desired us not to know, despite the best efforts of many devoted and scholarly biographers. The relation between the life and the poetry is far more uncertain than most of his readers believe it to be. Yet Whitman is so important to us, so crucial to an American mythology, so absolutely central to our literary culture, that we need to go on trying to bring his life and his work together. Our need might have delighted Whitman, and might have troubled him also. Like his master, Emerson, Whitman prophesied an American religion that is post-Christian, but while Emerson dared to suggest that the Crucifixion was a defeat and that Americans demand victory, Whitman dared further, and suggested that he himself had satisfied the demand. Here is Emerson:

> The history of Christ is the best document of the power of character which we have. A youth who owed nothing to fortune and who was "hanged at Tyburn"—by the pure quality of his nature has shed this epic splendor around the facts of his death which has transfigured every particular into a grand universal symbol for the eyes of all mankind ever since.
>
> He did well. This great Defeat is hitherto the highest fact we have. But he that shall come shall do better. The mind requires a far higher exhibition of character, one which shall make itself good to the senses as well as to the soul; a success to the senses as well as to the soul. This was a great Defeat; we demand Victory....
> *Journal*, April 1842

This grand journal entry concludes, magnificently: "I am *Defeated* all the time; yet to Victory I am born." And here is Whitman, "he that shall come," doing better:

> That I could forget the mockers and insults!
> That I could forget the trickling tears and the blows of the
>   bludgeons and hammers!
> That I could look with a separate look on my own crucifixion and
>   bloody crowning.
>
> I remember now,
> I resume the overstaid fraction,
> The grave of rock multiplies what has been confided to it, or to
>   any graves,
> Corpses rise, gashes heal, fastenings roll from me.
>
> I troop forth replenish'd with supreme power....
> ("Song of Myself," 963-970)

This is Walt Whitman "singing and chanting the things that are part of him, / The worlds that were and will be, death and day," in the words of his involuntary heir, Wallace Stevens. But which Walt Whitman is it? His central poem is what he finally entitled "Song of Myself," rather than, say, "Song of My Soul." But which self? There are two in the poem, besides his soul, and the true difficulties of reading Whitman begin (or ought to begin) with his unnervingly original psychic cartography, which resists assimilation to the Freudian maps of the mind. Freud's later system divides us into the "I" or ego, the "above-I" or superego, and the "it" or id. Whitman divided himself (or recognized himself as divided) into my self, my soul, and the "real Me" or "Me myself," where the self is a kind of ego, the soul not quite a superego, and the real Me not at all an id. Or to use a vocabulary known to Whitman, and still known to us, the self is personality, the soul is character, and again the real Me is a mystery. Lest these difficulties seem merely my own, and not truly Whitman's, I turn to the text of "Song of Myself." Here is Walt Whitman, my self, the persona or mask, the personality of the poet:

> Walt Whitman, a kosmos, of Manhattan the son,
> Turbulent, fleshy, sensual, eating, drinking and breeding,
> No sentimentalist, no stander above men and women or apart
>   from them,

No more modest than immodest.
("Song of Myself," 497-500)

That is Walt Whitman, one of the roughs, an American, but hardly
Walter Whitman, Jr., whose true personality, real Me or Me myself, is
presented in the passage I love best in the poem:

These come to me days and nights and go from me again,
But they are not the Me myself.

Apart from the pulling and hauling stands what I am,
Stands amused, complacent, com- passionating, idle, unitary,
Looks down, is erect, or bends an arm on an impalpable certain rest,
Looking with side-curved head curious what will come next,
Both in and out of the game and watching and wondering at it.
("Song of Myself," 73-79)

This "Me myself" is not exactly "hankering, gross, mystical, nude," nor is it
quite "turbulent, fleshy, sensual, eating, drinking and breeding." Graceful
and apart, cunningly balanced, charming beyond measure, this curious real
Me is boylike and girl-like, very American yet not one of the roughs,
provocative, at one with itself. Whatever the Whitmanian soul may be, this
Me myself evidently can have no equal relation with it. When the
Whitmanian "I" addresses the soul, we hear a warning:

I believe in you my soul, the other I am must not abase itself to you,
And you must not be abased to the other.
("Song of Myself," 82-83)

The "I" here is the "Myself" of "Song of Myself," poetic personality,
robust and rough. "The other I am" is the Me myself, in and out of the game,
and clearly not suited for embraces with the soul. Whitman's wariness, his
fear of abasement, whether of his soul or of his true, inner personality, one
to the other, remains the enigma of his poetry, as of his life, and largely
accounts for his intricate evasions both as poet and as a person.

II

Whitman's critics thus commence with a formidable disadvantage as they
attempt to receive and comprehend his work. The largest puzzle about the

continuing reception of Whitman's poetry is the still prevalent notion that we ought to take him at his word, whether about his self (or selves) or about his art. No other poet insists so vehemently and so continuously that he will tell us all, and tell us all without artifice, and yet tells us so little, and so cunningly. Except for Dickinson (the only American poet comparable to him in magnitude), there is no other nineteenth-century poet as difficult and hermetic as Whitman; not Blake, not Browning, not Mallarmé. Only an elite can read Whitman, despite the poet's insistence that he wrote for the people, for "powerful uneducated persons" as his "By Blue Ontario's Shore" proclaims. His more accurate "Poets to Come" is closer to his readers' experience of him:

> I am a man who, sauntering along without fully stopping, turns a
>   casual look upon you and then averts his face….

Whitman was surely too sly to deceive himself, or at least both of his selves, on this matter of his actual poetic evasiveness and esotericism. Humanly, he had much to evade, in order to keep going, in order to start writing and then to keep writing. His biographers cannot give us a clear image of his childhood, which certainly was rather miserable. His numerous siblings had mostly melancholy life histories: madness, retardation, marriage to a prostitute, depressiveness, hypochondria figure among their fates. The extraordinary obsessiveness with health and cleanliness that oddly marks Whitman's poetry had a poignant origin in his early circumstances. Of his uneasy relationship to his father we know a little, but not much. But we know nothing really of his mother, and how he was toward her. Perhaps the central fact about Whitman's psyche we know well enough: he needed, quite early, to become the true father of all his siblings, and perhaps of his mother, also. Certainly he fathered and mothered as many of his siblings as he could, even as he so beautifully became a surrogate father and mother for thousands of wounded and sick soldiers, Union and Confederate, white and black, in the hospitals of Washington, DC, throughout the Civil War.

The extraordinary and truthful image of Whitman that haunts our country, the vision of the compassionate, unpaid, volunteer wound-dresser, comforting young men in pain, soothing the dying, is the climax of Paul Zweig's new book on how the man Walter Whitman, Jr., became the poet Walt Whitman. This vision informs the finest pages of Zweig's uneven but moving study; I cannot recall any previous Whitman biographer or critic so vividly and humanely portraying Whitman's hospital service. Searching for the authentic Whitman, as Zweig shows, is a hopeless quest; our greatest poet will always be our most evasive, and perhaps our most self-contradictory. Whitman, at his strongest, has overwhelming pathos as a poet, equal I think to any in the language. The *Drum-Taps* poem called "The Wound-Dresser" is far from Whitman at his astonishing best, and yet its concluding lines carry the persuasive force of his poetic and human images unified for once:

> Returning, resuming, I thread my way through the hospitals,
> The hurt and wounded I pacify with soothing hand,
> I sit by the restless all the dark night, some are so young,
> Some suffer so much, I recall the experience sweet and sad,
> (Many a soldier's loving arms about this neck have cross'd and rested,
> Many a soldier's kiss dwells on these bearded lips).

Zweig is admirably sensitive in exploring the ambiguities in the intensities of Whitman's hospital experience, and more admirable still in his restraint at not voicing how much all of us are touched by Whitman's pragmatic saintliness during those years of service. I cannot think of a Western writer of anything like Whitman's achievement who ever gave himself or herself up so directly to meeting the agonized needs of the most desperate. There are a handful of American poets comparable to Whitman in stature: Emily Dickinson certainly, Wallace Stevens and Robert Frost perhaps, and perhaps even one or two others. Our image of them, or of our greatest novelists, or even of Whitman's master, Emerson, can move us sometimes, but not as the image of the wound-dresser Whitman must move us. Like the Lincoln whom he celebrated and lamented, Whitman is American legend, a figure who has a kind of religious aura even for secular intellectuals. If Emerson founded the American literary religion, Whitman alone permanently holds the place most emblematic of the life of the spirit in America.

These religious terms are not Zweig's, yet his book's enterprise usefully traces the winding paths that led Whitman on to his apotheosis as healer and comforter. Whitman's psychosexuality, labyrinthine in its perplexities, may be the central drive that bewildered the poet into those ways, but it was not the solitary, over-whelming determinant that many readers judge it to be. Zweig refreshingly is not one of these overdetermined readers. He surmises that Whitman might have experienced little actual homosexual intercourse. I suspect none, though Whitman evidently was intensely in love with some unnamed man in 1859, and rather more gently in love again with Peter Doyle about five years later. Zweig accurately observes: "Few poets have written as erotically as Whitman, while having so little to say about sex. For the most part, his erotic poetry is intransitive, self-delighting." Indeed, it is precisely autoerotic, rather more than it is homoerotic; Whitman overtly celebrates masturbation, and his most authentic sexual passion is always for himself. One would hardly know this from reading many of Whitman's critics, but one certainly knows it by closely reading Whitman's major poems. Here is part of a crucial crisis-passage from "Song of Myself," resolved through successful masturbation:

> I merely stir, press, feel with my fingers, and am happy,
> To touch my person to some one else's is about as much as I can
>   stand.
>
> Is this then a touch? quivering me to a new identity,
> Flames and ether making a rush for my veins,
> Treacherous tip of me reaching and crowding to help them,
> My flesh and blood playing out lightning to strike what is hardly
>   different from myself....
>
> I went myself first to the headland, my own hands carried me there.
>
> You villain touch! what are you doing? my breath is tight in its
>   throat,
> Unclench your floodgates, you are too much for me.
>
> Blind loving wrestling touch, sheath'd hooded sharp-tooth'd touch!
> Did it make you ache so, leaving me?
>
> Parting track'd by arriving, perpetual payment of perpetual loan,
> Rich showering rain, and recom- pense richer afterward.
>
> Sprouts take and accumulate, stand by the curb prolific and vital,
> Landscapes projected masculine, full-sized and golden.
> ("Song of Myself," 617-622, 639-647)

I take it that this celebratory mode of masturbation, whether read metaphorically or literally, remains the genuine scandal of Whitman's poetry. This may indeed be one of the kernel passages in Whitman, expanded and elaborated as it is from an early notebook passage that invented the remarkable trope of "I went myself first to the headland," the headland being the psychic place of *extravagance*, of wandering beyond limits, where you cannot scramble back to the shore, place of the father, and where you may topple over into the sea, identical with night, death, and the fierce old mother. "My own hands carried me there," as they fail to carry Whitman in "When Lilacs Last in the Dooryard Bloom'd":

> O great star disappear'd — O the black murk that hides the star!
> O cruel hands that hold me powerless—O helpless soul of me!

These can be only Whitman's own hands, pragmatically cruel because they cannot hold him potently, disabled as he is by a return of repressed guilt. Lincoln's death sets going memories of filial guilt, the guilt that the mortal sickness of Walter Whitman, Sr., should have liberated his son into the full flood of creativity that resulted in the 1855 first edition of *Leaves of Grass* (the father died a week after the book's publication). What Whitman's poetry does not express are any reservations about autoeroticism, which more than sadomasochism remains the last Western taboo. It is a peculiar paradox that Whitman, who proclaims his love for all men, women, and children, should have been profoundly solipsistic, narcissistic, and self-delighting, but that paradox returns us to the Whitmanian self or rather selves, the cosmological persona as opposed to the daemonic "real Me."

III

The most vivid manifestation of the "real Me" in Whitman comes in the shattering "Sea-Drift" poem, "As I Ebb'd with the Ocean of Life":

> O baffled, balk'd, bent to the very earth,
> Oppress'd with myself that I have dared to open my mouth,
> Aware now that amid all that blab whose echoes recoil upon me I
>   have not once had the least idea who or what I am,
> But that before all my arrogant poems the real Me stands yet
>   untouch'd, untold, altogether unreach'd,
> Withdrawn far, mocking me with mock-congratulatory signs and
>   bows,
> With peals of distant ironical laughter at every word I have
>   written,
> Pointing in silence to these songs, and then to the sand beneath.
> I perceive I have not really under- stood any thing, not a single
>   object, and that no man ever can,

Nature here in sight of the sea taking advantage of me to dart
    upon me and sting me,
Because I have dared to open my mouth to sing at all.

It is Walt Whitman, kosmos, American, rough, who is mocked here by
his real self, a self that knows itself to be a mystery, because it is neither
mother, nor father, nor child; neither quite female nor quite male; neither
voice nor voicelessness. Whitman's "real Me" is what is best and oldest in
him, and like the faculty Emerson called "Spontaneity" it is no part of the
creation, meaning both nature's creation and Whitman's verbal cosmos. It is
like a surviving fragment of the original Abyss preceding nature, not Adamic
but pre-Adamic. This "real Me" is thus also presexual, and so plays no role
either in the homoerotic "Calamus" poems or in the dubiously heterosexual
"Children of Adam" group. Yet it seems to me pervasive in the six long or
longer poems that indisputably are Whitman's masterpieces: "The Sleepers,"
"Song of Myself," "Crossing Brooklyn Ferry," "As I Ebb'd with the Ocean of
Life," "Out of the Cradle Endlessly Rocking," "When Lilacs Last in the
Dooryard Bloom'd."

Though only the last of these is overtly an elegy, all six are in covert
ways elegies for the real Me, for that Me myself that Whitman could not
hope to celebrate, as a poet, and could not hope to fulfill, as a sexual being.
This "real Me" is not a spirit that denies, but rather one that always remains
out of reach, an autistic spirit. In English Romantic poetry, and in later
nineteenth-century prose romance, there is the parallel being that Shelley
called "the Spirit of Solitude," the daemon or shadow of the self-destructive
young poet who is the hero of Shelley's *Alastor*. But Whitman's very
American "real Me" is quite unlike the Shelleyan or Blakean Spectre. It does
not quest or desire, and it does not want to be wanted.

Though Zweig hints that Whitman has been a bad influence on
other writers, I suspect that a larger view of influence would reverse this
implicit judgment. Whitman has been an inescapable influence not only
for most significant American poets after him (Frost, indebted directly to
Emerson, is the largest exception) but also for the most gifted writers of
narrative fiction. This influence transcends matters of form, and has
everything to do with the Whitmanian split between the persona of the
rough Walt and the ontological truth of the real Me. Poets as diverse as
Wallace Stevens and T.S. Eliot have in common perhaps only their
hidden, partly unconscious reliance upon Whitman as their main
precursor. Hemingway's acknowledged debt to *Huckleberry Finn* is real
enough, but the deeper legacy came from Whitman. The Hemingway

protagonist, split between an empirical self of stoic courage and a real Me endlessly evasive of others while finding its freedom only in an inner perfection of loneliness, is directly descended from the dual Whitman of "Song of Myself." American elegiac writing since Whitman (and how surprisingly much of it *is* covertly elegiac) generally revises Whitman's elegies for the self. *The Waste Land* is "When Lilacs Last in the Dooryard Bloom'd" rewritten, and Stevens's "The Rock" is not less Whitmanian than Hart Crane's *The Bridge*.

Zweig's book joins itself to the biographical criticism of Whitman: Bliss Perry, Gay Wilson Allen, Joseph Jay Rubin, Justin Kaplan, and others, a useful tradition that illuminates the Americanism of Whitman and yet cannot do enough with Whitman's many paradoxes. Of these, I judge the most crucial to be expressed by this question: How did someone of Whitman's extraordinarily idiosyncratic nature become so absolutely central to nearly all subsequent American literary high culture? This centrality evidently cannot ebb among us, as can be seen in the most recent poems of John Ashbery, in his forthcoming book, *The Wave*, or in the stories of Harold Brodkey, excerpted from his vast work-in-progress. Whitman's powerful yet unstable identities were his own inheritance from the Orphic Emerson, who proclaimed the central man or poet to come as necessarily metamorphic, Bacchic, and yet original, and above all American and not British or European in his cultural vistas. This prescription was and is dangerous, because it asks for pragmatism, and yet affirms impossible hopes. The rough Whitman is democratic, the real Me an elitist, but both selves are equally Emersonian.

Politically, Whitman was a Free-Soil Democrat, who rebelled against the betrayal by the New York Democratic party of its Jacksonian tradition, but Zweig rightly emphasizes the survival of Emersonian "Prudence" in Whitman, which caused him to oppose labor unions. I suspect that Whitman's politics paralleled his sexual morality: the rough Walt homoerotic and radical, the real Me autoerotic and individualistically elitist. The true importance of this split emerges neither in Whitman's sexuality nor in his politics, but in the delicacy and beauty of his strongest poems. Under the cover of an apparent rebellion against traditional literary form, they extend the poetic tradition without violating it. Whitman's elegies for the self have much in common with Tennyson's, but are even subtler, more difficult triumphs of High Romanticism.

Here I dissent wholly from Zweig, who ends his book with a judgment I find both wrong and puzzling:

...Leaves of Grass was launched on a collision course with its age. Whitman's work assaulted the institution of literature and language itself and, in so doing, laid the groundwork for the anti-cultural ambition of much modernist writing. He is the ancestor not only of Henry Miller and Allen Ginsberg but of Kafka, Beckett, André Breton, Borges—of all who have made of their writing an attack on the act of writing and on culture itself.

To associate the subtle artistry, delicate and evasive, of Whitman's greatest poems with Miller and Ginsberg, rather than with Hemingway and Stevens and Eliot, is already an error. To say that Kafka, Beckett, Borges attack, by their writing, the act of writing and culture is to mistake their assault upon certain interpretative conventions for a war against literary culture. But the gravest misdirection here is to inform readers that Whitman truly attacked the institutions of language and literature. Whitman's real Me has more to do with the composition of the great poems than the rough Walt ever did. "Lilacs," which Zweig does not discuss, is as profoundly traditional an elegy as *In Memoriam* or *Adonais*. Indeed, "Lilacs" echoes Tennyson, while "As I Ebb'd" echoes Shelley and "Crossing Brooklyn Ferry" invokes *King Lear*. Zweig is taken in by the prose Whitman, who insists he will not employ allusiveness, but the poet Whitman knew better, and is brilliantly allusive, as every strong poet is compelled to be, echoing his precursors and rivals but so stationing the echoes as to triumph with and in some sense even over them.

Zweig's study is an honorable and useful account of Whitman's poetic emergence, but it shares in some of the severe limitations of nearly all Whitman criticism so far published. More than most of the biographical critics, Zweig keeps alert to Whitman's duality, and I am grateful to him for his eloquent representations of the poet's war years. Yet Whitman's subtle greatness as a poet seems to me not fully confronted, here or elsewhere. The poetry of the real Me, intricate and forlorn, is addressed to the real Me of the American reader. That it reached what was best and most deeply rooted in tradition in Eliot and Stevens is attested to by their finest poetry, in contradistinction to their prose remarks on Whitman.

Paradoxically, Whitman's best critic remains, not an American, but D.H. Lawrence, who lamented: "The Americans are not worthy of their Whitman." Lawrence believed that Whitman had gone further, in actual living expression, than any other poet. The belief was extravagant, certainly, but again the Whitmanian poems of Lawrence's superb final phase show us what Lawrence meant. I give the last word here though, not to Lawrence, but to Emerson, who wrote the first words about Whitman in his celebrated

1855 letter to the poet, words that remain true nearly a hundred and thirty years further on in our literary culture:

> I am not blind to the worth of the wonderful gift of LEAVES OF GRASS. I find it the most extraordinary piece of wit and wisdom that America has yet contributed.

D.H. LAWRENCE

Whitman

P OST MORTEM, effects?

But what of Walt Whitman?

The "good grey poet."

Was he a ghost, with all his physicality?

The good grey poet.

Post mortem effects. Ghosts.

A certain ghoulish insistency. A certain horrible pottage of human parts. A certain stridency and portentousness. A luridness about his beatitudes.

DEMOCRACY! THESE STATES! EIDOLONS! LOVERS, ENDLESS LOVERS! ONE IDENTITY!

ONE IDENTITY!

I AM HE THAT ACHES WITH AMOROUS LOVE.

Do you believe me, when I say post mortem effects?

When the *Pequod* went down, she left many a rank and dirty steamboat still fussing in the seas. The *Pequod* sinks with all her souls, but their bodies rise again to man innumerable tramp steamers, and ocean-crossing liners. Corpses.

What we mean is that people may go on, keep on, and rush on, without souls. They have their ego and their will, that is enough to keep them going.

From *Studies in Classic American Literature.* © 1961 by The Estate of the late Mrs. Frieda Lawrence.

So that you see, the sinking of the *Pequod* was only a metaphysical tragedy after all. The world goes on just the same. The ship of the *soul* is sunk. But the machine-manipulating body works just the same: digests, chews gum, admires Botticelli and aches with amorous love.

I AM HE THAT ACHES WITH AMOROUS LOVE.

What do you make of that? I AM HE THAT ACHES. First generalization. First uncomfortable universalization. WITH AMOROUS LOVE! Oh, God! Better a bellyache. A bellyache is at least specific. But the ACHE OF AMOROUS LOVE!

Think of having that under your skin. All that!

I AM HE THAT ACHES WITH AMOROUS LOVE.

Walter, leave off. You are not HE. You are just a limited Walter. And your ache doesn't include all Amorous Love, by any means. If you ache you only ache with a small bit of amorous love, and there's so much more stays outside the cover of your ache, that you might be a bit milder about it.

I AM HE THAT ACHES WITH AMOROUS LOVE.

CHUFF! CHUFF! CHUFF!

CHU-CHU-CHU-CHU-CHUFF!

Reminds one of a steam-engine. A locomotive. They're the only things that seem to me to ache with amorous love. All that steam inside them. Forty million foot-pounds pressure. The ache of AMOROUS LOVE. Steam-pressure. CHUFF!

An ordinary man aches with love for Belinda, or his Native Land, or the Ocean, or the Stars, or the Oversoul: if he feels that an ache is in the fashion.

It takes a steam-engine to ache with AMOROUS LOVE. All of it.

Walt was really too superhuman. The danger of the superman is that, he is mechanical.

They talk of his "splendid animality." Well, he'd got it on the brain, if that's the place for animality.

"I am he that aches with amorous love:
Does the earth gravitate, does not all matter, aching,
     attract all matter?
So the body of me to all I meet or know."

What can be more mechanical? The difference between life and matter is that life, living things, living creatures, have the instinct of turning right away from *some* matter, and of blissfully ignoring the bulk of most matter, and of turning towards only some certain bits of specially selected matter. As for living creatures all helplessly hurtling together into one great snowball, why, most very living creatures spend the greater part of their time getting out of the sight, smell or sound of the rest of living creatures. Even bees only cluster on their own queen. And that is sickening enough. Fancy all white humanity clustering on one another like a lump of bees.

No, Walt, you give yourself away. Matter *does* gravitate, helplessly. But men are tricky-tricksy, and they shy all sorts of ways.

Matter gravitates because it *is* helpless and mechanical.

And if you gravitate the same, if the body of you gravitates to all you meet or know, why, something must have gone seriously wrong with you. You must have broken your mainspring.

You must have fallen also into mechanization.

Your Moby Dick must be really dead. That lonely phallic monster of the individual you. Dead mentalized.

I only know that my body doesn't by any means gravitate to all I meet or know. I find I can shake hands with a few people. But most I wouldn't touch with a long prop.

Your mainspring is broken, Walt Whitman. The mainspring of your own individuality. And so you run down with a great whirr, merging with everything.

You have killed your isolate Moby Dick. You have mentalized your deep sensual body, and that's the death of it.

I am everything and everything is me and so we're all One in One Identity, like the Mundane Egg, which has been addled quite a while.

"Whoever you are, to endless announcements—"
"And of these one and all I weave the song of myself."

Do you? Well, then, it just shows you haven't *got* any self. It's a mush, not a woven thing. A hotch-potch, not a tissue. Your self.

Oh, Walter, Walter, what have you done with it? What have you done with yourself? With your own individual self? For it sounds as if it had all leaked out of you, leaked into the universe.

Post mortem effects. The individuality had leaked out of him.

No, no, don't lay this down to poetry. These are post mortem effects. And Walt's great poems are really huge fat tomb-plants, great rank graveyard growths.

All that false exuberance. All those lists of things boiled in one pudding-cloth! No, no!

I don't want all those things inside me, thank you.

"I reject nothing," says Walt.

If that is so, one must be a pipe open at both ends, so everything runs through.

Post mortem effects.

"I embrace ALL," says Whitman. "I weave all things into myself."

Do you really! There can't be much left of *you* when you've done. When you've cooked the awful pudding of One Identity.

"And whoever walks a furlong without sympathy walks to his own funeral dressed in his own shroud."

Take off your hat then, my funeral procession of one is passing.

This awful Whitman. This post mortem poet. This poet with the private soul leaking out of him all the time. All his privacy leaking out in a sort of dribble, oozing into the universe.

Walt becomes in his own person the whole world, the whole universe, the whole eternity of time. As far as his rather sketchy knowledge of history will carry him, that is. Because to be a thing he had to know it. In order to assume the identity of a thing, he had to know that thing. He was not able to assume one identity with Charlie Chaplin, for example, because Walt didn't know Charlie. What a pity! He'd have done poems, paeans and what not, Chants, Songs of Cinematernity.

Oh, Charlie, my Charlie, another film is done—"

As soon as Walt *knew* a thing, he assumed a One Identity with it. If he knew that an Eskimo sat in a kyak, immediately there was Walt being little and yellow and greasy, sitting in a kyak.

Now will you tell me exactly what a kyak is?

Who is he that demands petty definition? Let him behold me *sitting in a kyak*.

I behold no such thing. I behold a rather fat old man full of a rather senile, self-conscious sensuosity.

DEMOCRACY. EN MASSE. ONE IDENTITY.

The universe, in short, adds up, to ONE.

ONE.

1.

Which is Walt.

His poems, *Democracy, En Masse, One Identity*, they are long sums in addition and multiplication, of which the answer is invariably MYSELF.

He reaches the state of ALLNESS.

And what then? It's all empty. Just an empty Allness. An addled egg.

Walt wasn't an Eskimo. A little, yellow, sly, cunning, greasy little Eskimo. And when Walt blandly assumed Allness, including Eskimoness, unto himself, he was just sucking the wind out of a blown egg-shell, no more. Eskimos are not minor little Walts. They are something that I am not, I know that. Outside the egg of my Allness chuckles the greasy little Eskimo. Outside the egg of Whitman's Allness too.

But Walt wouldn't have it. He was everything and everything was in him. He drove an automobile with a very fierce headlight, along the track of a fixed idea, through the darkness of this world. And he saw Everything that way. Just as a motorist does in the night.

I, who happen to be asleep under the bushes in the dark, hoping a snake won't crawl into my neck, I, seeing Walt go by in his great fierce poetic machine, think to myself: What a funny world that fellow sees!

ONE DIRECTION! toots Walt in the car, whizzing along it.

Whereas there are myriads of ways in the dark, not to mention trackless wildernesses. As anyone will know who cares to come off the road, even the Open Road.

ONE DIRECTION! whoops America, and sets off also in an automobile.

ALLNESS! shrieks Walt at a cross-road, going whizz over an unwary Red Indian.

ONE IDENTITY! chants democratic En Masse, pelting behind in motor-cars, oblivious of the corpses under the wheels.

God save me, I feel like creeping down a rabbithole, to get away from all these automobiles rushing down the ONE IDENTITY track to the goal of ALLNESS.

"A woman waits for me—"

He might as well have said: "The femaleness waits for my maleness." Oh, beautiful generalization and abstraction! Oh, biological function.

"Athletic mothers of these States—" Muscles and wombs. They needn't have had faces at all.

"As I see myself reflected in Nature,
As I see through a mist, One with inexpressible com-
    pleteness, sanity, beauty,
See the bent head, and arms folded over the breast,
    the Female I see."

Everything was female to him: even himself. Nature just one great function.

"This is the nucleus—after the child is born of woman,
    man is born of woman,
This is the bath of birth, the merge of small and
    large, and the outlet again—"

"The Female I see—"
If I'd been one of his women, I'd have given him Female. With a flea
in his ear.
    Always wanting to merge himself into the womb of something or other.
    "The Female I see—"
Anything, so long as he could merge himself.
Just a horror. A sort of white flux.
Post mortem effects.
    He found, like all men find, that you can't really merge in a woman,
though you may go a long way. You can't manage the last bit. So you have to
give it up, and try elsewhere. If you *insist* on merging.
    In *Calamus* he changes his tune. He doesn't shout and thump and exult
any more. He begins to hesitate, reluctant, wistful.
    The strange calamus has its pink-tinged root by the pond, and it sends
up its leaves of comradeship, comrades from one root, without the
intervention of woman, the female.
    So he sings of the mystery of manly love, the love of comrades. Over
and over he says the same thing: the new world will be built on the love of
comrades, the new great dynamic of life will be manly love. Out of this manly
love will come the inspiration for the future.
    Will it though? Will it?
    Comradeship! Comrades! This is to be the new Democracy: of
Comrades. This is the new cohering principle in the world: Comradeship.
    Is it? Are you sure?
    It is the cohering principle of true soldiery, we are told in *Drum Taps*.
It is the cohering principle in the new unison for creative activity. And it is
extreme and alone, touching the confines of death. Something terrible to
bear, terrible to be responsible for. Even Walt Whitman felt it. The soul's last
and most poignant responsibility, the responsibility of comradeship, of manly
love.

"Yet you are beautiful to me, you faint-tinged roots,
    you make me think of death.
Death is beautiful from you (what indeed is finally beau-
    tiful except death and love?)

I think it is not for life I am chanting here my chant of
    lovers, I think it must be for death,
For how calm, how solemn it grows to ascend to the
    atmosphere of lovers,
Death or life, I am then indifferent, my soul declines to
    prefer
(I am not sure but the high soul of lovers welcomes
    death most)
Indeed, O death, I think now these leaves mean precisely
    the same as you mean—"

This is strange, from the exultant Walt.
Death!
Death is now his chant! Death!
Merging! And Death! Which is the final merge.
The great merge into the womb. Woman.
And after that, the merge of comrades: man-for-man love.
And almost immediately with this, death, the final merge of death.
There you have the progression of merging. For the great mergers,
woman at last becomes inadequate. For those who love to extremes. Woman
is inadequate for the last merging. So the next step is the merging of man-
for-man love. And this is on the brink of death. It slides over into death.
David and Jonathan. And the death of Jonathan.
It always slides into death.
The love of comrades.
Merging.
So that if the new Democracy is to be based on the love of comrades,
it will be based on death too. It will slip so soon into death.
The last merging. The last Democracy. The last love. The love of
comrades.
Fatality. And fatality.
Whitman would not have been the great poet he is if he had not taken
the last steps and looked over into death. Death, the last merging, that was
the goal of his manhood.
To the mergers, there remains the brief love of comrades, and then Death.

"Whereto, answering, the sea
Delaying not, hurrying not
Whispered me through the night, very plainly before
    daybreak,

Lisp'd to me the low and delicious word death,
And again death, death, death, death.
Hissing melodions, neither like the bird nor like my
    arous'd child's heart,
But edging near as privately for me rustling at my feet,
    Creeping thence steadily up to my ears and laying me
    softly all over,
Death, death, death, death, death—"

Whitman is a very great poet, of the end of life. A very great post mortem poet, of the transitions of the soul as it loses its integrity. The poet of the soul's last shout and shriek, on the confines of death. *Après moi de déluge*.

But we have all got to die, and disintegrate.
We have got to die in life, too, and disintegrate while we live.
But even then the goal is not death.
Something else will come.

"Out of the cradle endlessly rocking."

We've got to die first, anyhow. And disintegrate while we still live.
Only we know this much. Death is not the *goal*. And Love, and merging, are now only part of the death-process. Comradeship—part of the death-process. Democracy—part of the death-process. The new Democracy—the brink of death. One Identity—death itself.
We have died, and we are still disintegrating.
But IT IS FINISHED.
Consummatum est.

Whitman, the great poet, has meant so much to me. Whitman, the one man breaking a way ahead. Whitman, the one pioneer. And only Whitman. No English pioneers, no French. No European pioneer-poets. In Europe the would-be pioneers are mere innovators. The same in America. Ahead of Whitman, nothing. Ahead of all poets, pioneering into the wilderness of unopened life, Whitman. Beyond him, none. His wide, strange camp at the end of the great high-road. And lots of new little poets camping on Whitman's camping ground now. But none going really beyond. Because Whitman's camp is at the end of the road, and on the edge of a great precipice. Over the precipice, blue distances, and the blue hollow of the future. But there is no way down. It is a dead end.

Pisgah. Pisgah sights. And Death. Whitman like a strange, modern, American Moses. Fearfully mistaken. And yet the great leader.

The essential function of art is moral. Not aesthetic, not decorative, not pastime and recreation. But moral. The essential function of art is moral.

But a passionate, implicit morality, not didactic. A morality which changes the blood, rather than the mind. Changes the blood first. The mind follows later, in the wake.

Now Whitman was a great moralist. He was a great leader. He was a great changer of the blood in the veins of men.

Surely it is especially true of American art, that it is all essentially moral. Hawthorne, Poe, Longfellow, Emerson, Melville: it is the moral issue which engages them. They all feel uneasy about the old morality. Sensuously, passionally, they all attack the old morality. But they know nothing better, mentally. Therefore they give tight mental allegiance to a morality which all their passion goes to destroy. Hence the duplicity which is the fatal flaw in them: most fatal in the most perfect American work of art, *The Scarlet Letter*. Tight mental allegiance given to a morality which the passional self repudiates.

Whitman was the first to break the mental allegiance. He was the first to smash the old moral conception, that the soul of man is something "superior" and "above" the flesh. Even Emerson still maintained this tiresome "superiority" of the soul. Even Melville could not get over it. Whitman was the first heroic seer to seize the soul by the scruff of her neck and plant her down among the potsherds.

"There!" he said to the soul. "Stay there!"

Stay there. Stay in the flesh. Stay in the limbs and lips and in the belly. Stay in the breast and womb. Stay there, Oh Soul, where you belong.

Stay in the dark limbs of negroes. Stay in the body of the prostitute. Stay in the sick flesh of the syphilitic. Stay in the marsh where the calamus grows. Stay there, Soul, where you belong.

The Open Road. The great home of the Soul is the open road. Not heaven, not paradise. Not "above." Not even "within." The soul is neither "above" nor "within." It is a wayfarer down the open road.

Not by meditating. Not by fasting. Not by exploring heaven after heaven, inwardly, in the manner of the great mystics. Not by exaltation. Not by ecstasy. Not by any of these ways does the soul come into her own.

Only by taking the open road.

Not through charity. Not through sacrifice. Not even through love. Not through good works.

Not through these does the soul accomplish herself.

Only through the journey down the open road.

The journey itself, down the open road. Exposed to full contact. On two slow feet. Meeting whatever comes down the open road. In company with those that drift in the same measure along the same way. Towards no goal. Always the open road.

Having no known direction, even. Only the soul remaining true to herself in her going.

Meeting all the other wayfarers along the road. And how? How meet them, and how pass? With sympathy, says Whitman. Sympathy. He does not say love. He says sympathy. Feeling with. Feel with them as they feel with themselves. Catching the vibration of their soul and flesh as we pass.

It is a new great doctrine. A doctrine of life. A new great morality. A morality of actual living, not of salvation. Europe has never got beyond the morality of salvation. America to this day is deathly sick with saviourism. But Whitman, the greatest and the first and the only American teacher, was no Saviour. His morality was no morality of salvation. His was a morality of the soul living her life, not saving herself. Accepting the contact with other souls along the open way, as they lived their lives. Never trying to save them. As leave try to arrest them and throw them in gaol. The soul living her life along the incarnate mystery of the open road.

This was Whitman. And the true rhythm of the American continent speaking out in him. He is the first white aboriginal.

"In my Father's house are many mansions."

"No," said Whitman. "Keep out of mansions. A mansion may be heaven on earth, but you might as well be dead. Strictly avoid mansions. The soul is herself when she is going on foot down the open road."

It is the American heroic message. The soul is not to pile up defences round herself. She is not to withdraw and seek her heavens inwardly, in mystical ecstasies. She is not to cry to some God beyond, for salvation. She is to go down the open road, as the road opens, into the unknown, keeping company with those whose soul draws them near to her, accomplishing nothing save the journey, and the works incident to the journey, in the long life-travel into the unknown, the soul in her subtle sympathies accomplishing herself by the way.

This is Whitman's essential message. The heroic message of the American future. It is the inspiration of thousands of Americans today, the best souls of today, men and women. And it is a message that only in America can be fully understood, finally accepted.

Then Whitman's mistake. The mistake of his interpretation of his watchword: Sympathy. The mystery of SYMPATHY. He still confounded it with Jesus' LOVE, and with paul's CHARITY. Whitman, like all the rest of us, was at the end of the great emotional highway of Love. And because he couldn't help himself, he carried on his Open Road as a prolongation of the emotional highway of Love, beyond Calvary. The highway of Love ends at the foot of the Cross. There is no beyond. It was a hopeless attempt, to prolong the highway of love.

He didn't follow his Sympathy. Try as he might, he kept on automatically interpreting it as Love, as Charity. Merging!

This merging, *en masse*, One Identity, Myself monomania was a carry-over from the old Love idea. It was carrying the idea of Love to its logical physical conclusion. Like Flaubert and the leper. The decree of unqualified Charity, as the soul's one means of salvation, still in force.

Now Whitman wanted his soul to save itself, he didn't want to save it. Therefore he did not need the great Christian receipt for saving the soul. He needed to supersede the Christian Charity, the Christian Love, within himself, in order to give his Soul her last freedom. The high-road of Love is no Open Road. It is a narrow, tight way, where the soul walks hemmed in between compulsions.

Whitman wanted to take his Soul down the open road. And he failed in so far as he failed to get out of the old rut of Salvation. He forced his Soul to the edge of a cliff, and he looked down into death. And there he camped, powerless. He had carried out his Sympathy as an extension of Love and Charity. And it had brought him almost to madness and soul-death. It gave him his forced, unhealthy, post-mortem quality.

His message was really the opposite of Henley's rant:

> "I am the master of my fate.
> I am the captain of my soul."

Whitman's essential message was the Open Road. The leaving of the soul free unto herself, the leaving of his fate to her and to the loom of the open road. Which is the bravest doctrine man has ever proposed to himself.

Alas, he didn't quite carry it out. He couldn't quite break the old maddening bond of the love-compulsion, he couldn't quite get out of the rut of the charity habit. For Love and Charity have degenerated now into habit: a bad habit.

Whitman said Sympathy. If only he had stuck to it! Because Sympathy means feeling with, not feeling for. He kept on having a passionate feeling *for* the negro slave, or the prostitute, or the syphilitic—which is merging. A sinking of Walt Whitman's soul in the souls of these others.

He wasn't keeping to his open road. He was forcing his soul down an old rut. He wasn't leaving her free. He was forcing her into other peoples' circumstances.

Supposing he had felt true sympathy with the negro slave? He would have felt *with* the negro slave. Sympathy—compassion—which is partaking of the passion which was in the soul of the negro slave.

What was the feeling in the negro's soul?

"Ah, I am a slave! Ah, it is bad to be a slave! I must free myself. My soul will die unless she frees herself. My soul says I must free myself."

Whitman came along, and saw the slave, and said to himself: "That negro slave is a man like myself. We share the same identity. And he is bleeding with wounds. Oh, oh, is it not myself who am also bleeding with wounds?"

This was not *sympathy*. It was merging and self-sacrifice. "Bear ye one another's burdens." "Love thy neighbour as thyself": "Whatsoever ye do unto him, ye do unto me."

If Whitman had truly *sympathised*, he would have said: "That negro slave suffers from slavery. He wants to free himself. His soul wants to free him. He has wounds, but they are the price of freedom. The soul has a long journey from slavery to freedom. If I can help him I will: I will not take over his wounds and his slavery to myself. But I will help him fight the power that enslaves him when he wants to be free, if he wants my help. Since I see in his face that be needs to be free. But even when he is free, his soul has many journeys down the open road, before it is a free soul."

And of the prostitute Whitman would have said:

Look at that prostitute! Her nature has turned evil under her mental lust for prostitution. She has lost her soul. She knows it herself. She likes to make men lose their souls. If she tried to make me lose my soul, I would kill her. I wish she may die."

But of another prostitute he would have said:

"Look! She is fascinated by the Priapic mysteries. Look, she will soon be worn to death by the Priapic usage. It is the way of her soul. She wishes it so."

Of the syphilitic he would say:

"Look! She wants to infect all men with syphilis. We ought to kill her."

And of still another syphilitic:

"Look! She has a horror of her syphilis. If she looks my way I will help her to get cured."

This is sympathy. The soul judging for herself, and preserving her own integrity.

But when, in Flaubert, the man takes the leper to his naked body; when Bubi de Montparnasse takes the girl because he knows she's got syphilis; when Whitman embraces an evil prostitute: that is not sympathy. The evil prostitute has no desire to be embraced with love; so if you sympathise with her, you won't try to embrace her with love. The leper loathes his leprosy, so if you sympathise with him, you'll loathe it too. The evil woman who wishes to infect all men with her syphilis hates you if you haven't got syphilis. If you sympathise, you'll feel her hatred, and you'll hate too, you'll hate her. Her feeling is hate, and you'll share it. Only your soul will choose the direction of its own hatred.

The soul is a very perfect judge of her own motions, if your mind doesn't dictate to her. Because the mind says Charity! Charity! you don't have to force your soul into kissing lepers or embracing syphilitics. Your lips are the lips of your soul, your body is the body of your soul; your own single, individual soul. That is Whitman's message. And your soul hates syphilis and leprosy. Because it is a soul, it hates these things, which are against the soul. And therefore to force the body of your soul into contact with uncleanness is a great violation of your soul. The soul wishes to keep clean and whole. The soul's deepest will is to preserve its own integrity, against the mind and the whole mass of disintegrating forces.

Soul sympathises with soul. And that which tries to kill my soul, my soul hates. My soul and my body are one. Soul and body wish to keep clean and whole. Only the mind is capable of great perversion. Only the mind tries to drive my soul and body into uncleanness and unwholesomeness.

What my soul loves, I love.

What my soul hates, I hate.

When my soul is stirred with compassion, I am compassionate.

What my soul turns away from, I turn away from.

That is the *true* interpretation of Whitman's creed: the true revelation of his Sympathy.

And my soul takes the open road. She meets the souls that are passing, she goes along with the souls that are going her way. And for one and all, she has sympathy. The sympathy of love, the sympathy of hate, the sympathy of simple proximity: all the subtle sympathisings of the incalculable soul, from the bitterest hate to passionate love.

It is not I who guide my soul to heaven. It is I who am guided by my own soul along the open road, where all men tread. Therefore, I must accept her deep motions of love, or hate, or compassion, or dislike, or indifference. And I must go where she takes me. For my feet and my lips and my body are my soul. It is I who must submit to her.

This is Whitman's message of American democracy.

The true democracy, where soul meets soul, in the open road. Democracy. American democracy where all journey down the open road. And where a soul is known at once in its going. Not by its clothes or appearance. Whitman did away with that. Not by its family name. Not even by its reputation. Whitman and Melville both discounted that. Not by a progression of piety, or by works of Charity. Not by works at all. Not by anything but just itself. The soul passing unenhanced, passing on foot and being no more than itself. And recognized, and passed by or greeted according to the soul's dictate. If it be a great soul, it will be worshipped in the road.

The love of man and woman: a recognition of souls, and a communion of worship. The love of comrades: a recognition of souls, and a communion of worship. Democracy: a recognition of souls, all down the open road, and a great soul seen in its greatness, as it travels on foot among the rest, down the common way of the living. A glad recognition of souls, and a gladder worship of great and greater souls, because they are the only riches.

Love, and Merging, brought Whitman to the Edge of Death! Death! Death!

But the exultance of his message still remains. Purified of MERGING, purified of MYSELF, the exultant message of American Democracy, of souls in the Open Road, full of glad recognition, full of fierce readiness, full of the joy of worship, when one soul sees a greater soul.

The only riches, the great souls.

KENNETH BURKE

Policy Made Personal:
Whitman's Verse and Prose-Salient Traits

The plan here is to consider first Whitman's statement of policy in *Democratic Vistas*. Even there his views of history, society, and nature are personalized somewhat. But the full job of personalization is done in his *Leaves of Grass*, which is to be considered in a second section. And finally, since both of these sections are general in their approach, a third section will put the main stress upon one poem, "When Lilacs Last in the Dooryard Bloom'd." Throughout, however, we shall proceed as much as practicable by the inspection and comparison of contexts. Unless otherwise specified, all words or expressions in quotation marks are Whitman's. (Perhaps a better subtitle would be: On Interrelations Among Key Terms in Whitman's Language.)

I. VISTAS

The design of Whitman's essentially idealistic thought is neatly indicated in the three stages of historical unfolding he assigns to "America, type of progress." This alignment seems a handy place to spin from.

The first stage was embodied in the Declaration of Independence, the Constitution, and its Amendments. It "was the planning and putting on record the political foundation rights of immense masses of people ... not for classes, but for universal man."

From *Leaves of Grass One Hundred Years After*, ed. Milton Hindus. © 1955 by the Board of Trustees of the Leland Stanford Junior University.

The second stage is in the "material prosperity" that resulted after the democratic foundations had been laid: "wealth, labor-saving machines ... a currency," etc.

A third stage, still to come but "arising out of the previous ones," would bring about the corresponding "spiritualization" of the nation's sheerly material development.

The first and third stages are in the realm of idea, or spirit. The second stage is in the realm of matter. Writing his essay a few years after the close of the Civil War, he placed himself and his times in stage two, a time marked by "hollowness at heart," lack of honest belief in "the underlying principles of the States," "depravity of the business classes," while all politics were "saturated in corruption" except the judiciary ("and the judiciary is tainted"). "A mob of fashionably dressed speculators and vulgarians ... crude defective streaks in all the strata of the common people ... the alarming spectacle of parties usurping the government ... these savage, wolfish parties[1] ... delicatesse ... polite conformity ... exterior appearance and show, mental and other, built entirely on the idea of caste" ... in sum "Pride, competition, segregation, vicious wilfulness, and license beyond example, brood already upon us."

One could cite many other statements of like attitude. But the idealistic design of his thinking permitted him without discouragement to take full note of such contemporary ills, and perhaps even to intensify them as one step in his essay. For against the dissatisfactions of the present, he could set his "planned Idea," a promise for the future. Since "the fruition of democracy, on aught like a grand scale, resides altogether in the future," he would "presume to write, as it were, upon things that exist not, and travel by maps yet unmade, and a blank." Thus, the technically negative nature of the "fervid and tremendous Idea" is made in effect positive, so far as *personal* considerations go. By seeing contemporary conditions in terms of future possibilities, in "vistas" that stressed "results to come," he could treat "America and democracy as convertible terms," while having high hopes for both. He says, "It is useless to deny" that "Democracy grows rankly up the thickest, noxious, deadliest plants and fruits of all—brings worse and worse invaders—needs newer, larger, stronger, keener compensations and compellers"; but, in line with post-Hegelian promises, he saw in any greater challenge the possibility of a correspondingly greater response.

In sum, then, as regards the basic design of his thinking, the *Vistas* found elation in a project for the "spiritualization of our nation's wealth." (He likes words like "richness" and "luxuriance," words that readily suggest both material and spiritual connotations, gaining resonance and persuasiveness from this ambiguity.) "The extreme business energy, and this almost maniacal appetite for wealth prevalent in the United States, are parts of amelioration and progress," he says (in terms that, of all things, suggest Marxist patterns of thought with regard to material development under capitalism); but a different order of motives is manifest in the statement (he would probably have said "promulgation") of his ideal: "Offsetting the material civilization of our race ... must be its moral civilization."

If, by very definition, one can view all materially acquisitive behavior in terms of ideal future fulfillment, it follows that the poet could contemplate with "joy" the industrious industrial conquest of the continent. Not until late in life (after his paralytic stroke) does this "ecstatic" champion of the "athletic" and "electric" body turn from identification with the feller of trees (as in *Song of the Broad-Axe*) to identification with the fallen tree itself (as in *Song of the Redwood-Tree*), though he always had fervid ways of being sympathetic to child, adult, and the elderly. Our point is simply that the zestfulness of the typical Whitman survey could follow logically from his promissory principle, his idealization of the present in terms of the future.

Halfway between the realm of materials amassed by his countrymen's "oceanic, variegated, intense, practical energy" and the realm of spirit, or idea, we might place his cult of the sturdy human body, its "spinal," "athletic," "magnetic" qualities and the "appetites" that make for "sensuous luxuriance." (As the recipe also called for a male type "somewhat flushed," we dare wonder ironically whether his notion of the perfect "manly" temperament also concealed a syndrome of symptoms, an idealistic recognition, without realistic diagnosis, of the hypertension that must have preceded his paralysis. Surely, prophesying after the event, we might propose that Whitman's headlong style should involve high blood pressure as its nosological counterpart.)

For an "over-arching" term here, Whitman could speak of "nature" in ways that, while clearly referring to the materialistic on one side, also have pontificating aspects leading into a Beyond, along Emersonian lines. (In fact, toward the close of the *Vistas*, one is often strongly reminded of Emerson's earlier and longer transcendentalist essay, *Nature*, first published in 1836.) Democracy was Nature's "younger brother," and Science was "twin, in its field, of Democracy in its." But such equations were idealistically weighted to one side: for while "Dominion strong is the body's; dominion stronger is the mind's."

Somewhere between the grounding of his position in time, and its grounding in eternity, there is its grounding in terms of personality (two of his special words to this end being "identity" and "nativity").

For grounding in time, one obvious resource is a contrast with some previous time (antithesis being one of the three major stylistic resources, as we are informed in Aristotle's *Rhetoric*). But though "democracy" is thus pitted against "feudalism," Whitman admonishes that "feudalism, caste, ecclesiastical traditions ... still hold essentially, by their spirit, even in this country, entire possession of the more important fields." For "All smells of princes' favors." And "The United States are destined either to surmount the gorgeous history of feudalism, or else prove the most tremendous failure of time." Whereas now we tend to think of Shakespeare as poignantly at the crossing between the feudal and the modern, the antithetical genius of Whitman's scheme led him to say: "The great poems, Shakespeare included, are poisonous to the idea of the pride and dignity of the common people." For though Shakespeare was conceded to be "rich," and "luxuriant as the sun," he was the "artist and singer of feudalism in its sunset." In contrast, Whitman called: "Come forth, sweet democratic despots of the west." And being against "parlors, parasols, piano-songs," he matched his praise of the "divine average" by words against "the mean flat average." Declaring, "We stand, live, move, in the huge flow of our age's materialism," he quickly added, "in its spirituality." And "to offset chivalry," he would seek "a knightlier and more sacred cause today." In so far as the claims of traditional culture were effete and pretentious (and "for a single class alone"), he admonished against "Culture"—and later, apologists of Nazism could take over the tenor of his slogans by the simple device of but half-hearing him.

As for eternity: His attacks upon traditional ecclesiastical forms were stated in terms of an "all penetrating Religiousness" that vigorously proclaimed its scorn of "infidels." He always identified democracy with what he called "the religious element," however that might differ from the norms of conventional churchgoing (and it differed greatly, as regards its relation to his cult of the "body electric").

His notion of "succession" (a eulogistic word that sounds nearly like his very dyslogistic one, "secession") we have already touched upon. It is in line with the typical nineteenth-century doctrine of permanent evolution, into ever higher forms, a design that falls in the realm of time, so far as the manifestations of history are concerned, but that would be above time, in so far as its operation were constant. "The law over all, the law of laws, is the law of successions; that of the superior law, in time, gradually supplanting and overwhelming the inferior one." Fittingly, the essay reverts to this "law" in the paragraph-long closing sentence, where America, "illumined and illuming," is saluted in terms of the ideal future, when she will have "become a full-formed world, and divine Mother, not only of material but spiritual worlds, in ceaseless succession, through time—the main thing being the average, the bodily, the concrete, the democratic, the popular, on which all the superstructures of the future are to permanently rest."

The lines succinctly assemble the main components of his Ideal Matrix, or "divine Mother." (And what better words for an *ending* than "permanently rest"?) But the personalizing of this "Mother" (the democratic creed) will take on attributes not strictly germane to either the politics of democracy or the personality of motherhood.

The logic of his terminology centers in his emphasis upon the individual person ("rich, luxuriant, varied personalism"). In proclaiming that "the ripeness of religion" is to be sought in the "field of individuality," and is "a result that no organization or church can ever achieve," he automatically sets up the dialectical conditions for a principle of division matched by a principle of merger. While his brand of "personalism" will "promulge" the "precious idiocrasy and special nativity and intention that he is, the man's self," all such individual. selves are to be joined in democratic union, or "cohesion"; and the result is "ensemble-Individuality," an "idiocrasy of universalism," since the "liberalist of today" seeks "not only to individualize, but to universalize." And while the aim is to formulate "one broad, primary, universal, common platform," he says, "even for the treatment of the universal" it is good "to reduce the whole matter to the consideration of a single self, a man, a woman, on permanent grounds."

In sum: There is "the All, and the idea of All, with the accompanying idea of eternity" (the poems will speak of "the all-mother," and the "Mother of All"). And in silence, in the "solitariness of individuality," one can "enter the pure ether of veneration," to "commune" with the "mysteries" and the "unutterable." Or (as regards the timely), "individuality" and its "unimpeded branchings" will "flourish best under imperial republican forms" (for the grandeur of spiritualized democratic "expansion" will make for an "empire of empires").[2]

So we have the "idea of perfect individualism," of "completeness in separation," with its dialectical counterpart: "the identity of the Union at all hazards." Not only must man become "a law, a series of laws, unto himself"; also "the great word Solidarity has arisen." The "individualism, which isolates" is but "half only," and has for its other half the "adhesiveness or love, that fuses." Thus, both of these trends (contradictory or complementary?) are "vitalized by religion," for you in your solitude can "merge yourself" in the "divine." (A sheerly politico-economic variant of this dialectic for fitting the one and the many together is in his statement: "The true gravitation-hold of liberalism in the United States will be a more universal ownership of property, general homesteads, general comfort—a vast, inter-twining reticulation of wealth.")

But if the three stages are handiest as a way into the underlying idealistic *design* of Whitman's thinking, perhaps the most succinct *doctrinal* passage is this:

"Long ere the second centennial arrives, there will be some forty to fifty States, among them Canada and Cuba. When the present century closes, our population will be sixty or seventy millions. The Pacific will be ours, and the Atlantic mainly ours. There will be daily electric communication with every part of the globe. What an age! What a land! Where, elsewhere, one so great? The individuality of one nation must then, as always, lead the world. Can there be any doubt who the leader ought to be? Bear in mind, though, that nothing less than the mightiest original non-subordinated Soul, has ever really, gloriously led, or ever can lead."

Then comes the very important addition, in parentheses: "This SOUL—its other name, in these Vistas, is LITERATURE." Then follows typical talk of "ideals," and of a "richness" and "vigor" that will be in letters "luxuriantly."

The essay's opening reference to "lessons" attains its fulfillment in these views of Whitman on the didactic or moralizing element in his ideal literature, its social service in the training of personalities. By the "mind," which builds "haughtily," the national literature shall be endowed "with grand and archetypal models," as we confront the "momentous spaces" with a "new and greater personalism," aided by the "image-making faculty."

Here, then, is the grand melange: "Arrived now, definitely, at an apex for these Vistas," Whitman sees in dream "a new and greater literatus order," its members "always one, compact in soul," though "separated ... by different dates or States." This band would welcome materialistic trends both "for their oceanic practical grandeur" and "for purposes of spiritualization." And by "serving art in its highest," such a "band of brave and true" would also be "serving God, and serving humanity."

Such a literature would affirm the "fervid comradeship," "adhesive love," between man and man that Whitman so strongly associated with his evangel of democracy. And as for woman, the "prophetic literature of these States," inspired by "Idealism," will train toward "the active redemption of woman," and "a race of perfect Mothers."

He offers four portraits of ideal female types: a servant, a businesswoman, a housewife, and a fourth that we might call a grand old lady ("a resplendent person ... known by the name of the Peacemaker"). It is particularly relevant to look more closely at this fourth figure.

Whitman has just been referring to "that indescribable perfume of genuine womanhood ... which belongs of right to all the sex, and is, or ought to be, the invariable atmosphere and common aureola of old as well as young." The next paragraph begins: "My dear mother once described to me ...," etc. Eighty years old, this fourth type of personality that his mother is said to have described was a kind of grandmotherly Whitman. She had lived "down on Long Island " She was called the "Peacemaker" because of her role as "the reconciler in the land." She was "of happy and sunny temperament," was "very neighborly"; and she "possessed a native dignity." "She was a sight to look upon, with her large figure, her profuse snow-white hair (uncoifed by any head-dress or cap) ... and peculiar personal magnetism"—and when reading the word on which the recital of his four "portraits" ends, might we not fittingly recall that Whitman's poems are dotted with references to the "electric" and "magnetic"?

We consider this all of a piece: the steps from "the indescribable perfume of genuine womanhood," to "My dear mother," to the grandmotherly figure in which this entire set of portraits culminates (and thus toward which the series might be said to have tended from the start). Frankly, we stress the point for use later, when we shall be considering the scent of lilacs; "the perfume strong I love," mentioned in commemoration of the poet's great dead democratic hero. Meanwhile, a few more considerations should be noted, before we turn from his prose statement of policy to its personalizing in his verse.

We should recall his principle of cultural *ascesis* (the notion that "political democracy" is "life's gymnasium ... fit for freedom's athletes," and that books are "in highest sense, an exercise, a gymnast's struggle"). It is easy to see how thought thus of a *studious athleticism* might, on the one hand, proclaim "health, pride, acuteness, noble aspirations" as the "motive-elements of the grandest style"; on the other hand, given the "appetites" that go with such exercisings and exertions, the poet might find no embarrassments in equating democracy with the grandeur of ever expanding empire.

But there is one mild puzzler to be noted with regard to the Whitman cult of democratic expansionism. When saying that the "spine-character of the States will probably run along the Ohio, Missouri and Mississippi rivers, and west and north of them, including Canada," he describes the "giant growth" thus: "From the north, intellect, the sun of things, also the idea of unswayable justice, anchor amid the last, the wildest tempests. From the south the living soul, the animus of good and bad, haughtily admitting no demonstration but its own. While from the west itself comes solid personality, with blood and brawn, and the deep quality of all-accepting fusion."

One automatically waits for some mention of the east here—but there is none. Interestingly enough, one of the poems ("To the Leaven'd Soil They Trod") discusses "vistas" and *ends* on a similar design

> The prairie draws me close, as the father to bosom broad the son,
> The Northern ice and rain that began me nourish me to the end,
> But the hot sun of the South is to fully ripen my songs.

Presumably, the poet mentions only three points of the compass, since he was born in the *East*, and was so *tendency-minded*. And perhaps, since the *Vistas* contain the equation, "the democratic, the west," the East is, by the dialectical or rhetorical pressures of antithesis, the vestigially and effetely "feudal," except in so far as it is inspirited by the other three sources of motivation. (South, by the way, is in Whitman's idiom the place from which "perfume" comes. As regards North, we must admit to not having fully done our lessons at this time.)

A few further points, before turning from the *Vistas* to the *Leaves*:

In connection with the notion of guidance through literature, Whitman writes: "A strong mastership of the general inferior self by the superior self, is to be aided, secured, indirectly, but surely, by the literatus." And we might remember this word "mastership," to puzzle over it, when in the poem of the "Lilacs" he says: "Yet the lilac with mastering odor holds me," even though we may not quite succeed in fitting the passages to each other.

And we should note Whitman's words in praise of a strong political digestion, since they bear so directly upon the relation between his design and his doctrine: "And as, by virtue of its cosmical, antiseptic power, Nature's stomach is fully strong enough not only to digest the morbific matter always presented ... but even to change such contributions into nutriment for highest use and life—so American democracy's."

Such faith in the virtues of a healthy appetite is doubtless implied when, on the subject of political corruption, Whitman assures us that "the average man ... remains immortal owner and boss, deriving good uses, somehow, out of any sort of servant in office." (Or, more generally, here is the encouragement of the sprout-out-of-rot principle.) At every step along the way, whatever tax is levied by their Lordships, Favoritism and Dishonesty, it remains a fact that Democracy does build, its roads and schools and courthouses—and the catalogue of its accumulations, when listed under one national head, becomes truly "oceanic" and "over-arching." But at the mention of catalogues, we might well turn to a survey of the verse.

II. LEAVES

No two opening lines of a poet's work ever indicated more clearly the sheer dialectics of a position than in the Inscription" with which *Leaves of Grass* begins

> One's-Self I sing, a simple separate person,
> Yet utter the word Democratic, the word En-Masse.

For a poet generally so voluble, this entire poem of eight lines is astoundingly efficient. Note how the second stanza (proclaiming that "physiology" is equally important with "physiognomy" and "brain," and that he sings "The Female equally with the Male") ambiguously translates his code into its corresponding *sexual* terms. Then, in the third stanza, he merges life, work, God's laws, song, and his futuristic cult of the present, all, under the sign of strong motives and hopeful attitudes

> Of Life immense in passion, pulse, and power,
> Cheerful, for freest action form'd under the laws divine,
> The Modern Man I sing.

The main themes that are lacking are: (1) his merging of birth and death in the allness of the mother, and (2) his stress upon perpetual passage (what would Whitman do without the word "pass" or its components: "I come and I depart"?). And, of course, the notable equating of democracy with the love of male for male is manifest here only if we read as a *double-entendre* his words about Male and Female (though most likely they were not so intended).

In his "oceanic" accumulation of details, the catalogues that characterize most of his longer poems (such as *Salut au Monde!*), there is obviously the "spiritualization" of matter. Here is his primary resource for those loosely yet thematically guided associations of ideas which enable him to "chant the chant of dilation or pride." Of such spiritual possessions, he has "stores and plenty to spare." Who was more qualified than Whitman to write a *Song of the Exposition* with its closing apostrophe to the "universal Muse" and maternal Union: "While we rehearse our measureless wealth, it is for thee, dear Mother"? In effect, the Whitman catalogue locates the rhetorical device of amplification in the very nature of things.

It is possible that, after long inspection, we might find some "overarching" principle of development that "underlies" his typical lists. Always, of course, they can be found to embody some principle of repetitive form, some principle of classification whereby the various items fall under the same head (as with the third stanza of the *Salut*, for instance, which races through a scattering of nationalities, with a scattering of details hastily allotted to each: the Australians "pursuing the wild horse," the Spanish semipleonastically dancing "with castanets in the chestnut shade," "echoes from the Thames," "fierce French liberty songs," and so on, ending with the Hindoo "teaching his favorite pupil the loves, wars, adages, transmitted safely from poets who wrote three thousand years ago"). Some critic might also discern a regular canon of *development* in such "turbulent" heapings. Meanwhile, in any case, there are the many variations by internal contrast (as with varying rhythm and length of line, or as the variations on "out of" that mark the opening lines of "Out of the Cradle Endlessly Rocking" out of, over, down from, up from, out from, from the, from your, from under, from those, from such, borne hither). And even where epanaphora is extreme, there are large tidal changes from stanza to stanza, or rhetorical forms that suggest the shifting of troops in military maneuvers.

"Melange mine own ... Omnes! Omnes! ... the word En-Masse ... the One formed out of all ... toward all ... made ONE IDENTITY ... they shall flow and unite ... merge and unite ... to merge all in the travel they tend to ... All, all, toward the mystic Ocean tending ... Song of the Universal ... O public road ... to know the universe itself as a road ... along the grand roads of the universe ... All, all, for immortality ... it makes the whole coincide ... I become part of that, whatever it is ..."—such lines state the "omnific" principle behind the aggregates of the catalogues.

To such a cult of the "divine average," good will and good cheer sometimes come easy: "I love him, though I do not know him ... I know not where they go; / But I know they go toward the best ... surely the drift of them is something grand ... illustrious every one ... Great is Wealth—great is Poverty ... Flaunt away, flags of all nations! ... I believe materialism is true, and spiritualism is true—I reject no part ... I do not see one imperfection in the universe ... the venerealee is invited."[3] He thinks happily of "easily written, loose-fingered chords," and "the loose drift of character, the inkling through random types." He assures us, in hale and hearty camaraderie: "I turn the bridegroom out of bed, and stay with the bride myself"—nay more:

"My voice is the wife's voice." His gusto suggests something like a cheerleader's at a chess tournament when he proclaims: "Hurrah for positive science! long live exact demonstration!" But the tactics are much subtler when, addressing a locomotive, he says: "Law of thyself complete, thine own track firmly holding."

In a poet capable of maintaining "this is Ocean's poem," a poet "aware of the mighty Niagara," the principle of joyously infused oneness can be centered in various terms of high generalization: the "greatness of Religion ... the real and permanent grandeur of These States ... efflux of the Soul ... great City ... transcendental Union ... teeming Nation of nations ... the immortal Idea ... Sex" (which "contains all" ... "every hour the semen of centuries")—all such subjects serve as variants on his theme of unified diversity. "Underneath all, Nativity" ("I swear I am charmed with nothing except nativity, / Men, women, cities, nations, are only beautiful from nativity"), by which he meant the individual being's uniqueness of identity ("singleness and normal simplicity and separation"). When he thinks of "Death, merged in the thought of materials," he swears "there is nothing but immortality!" When he "wander'd, searching among burial places," he "found that every place was a burial place." All "to the Ideal tendest"; "Only the good is universal"; "All swings around us. / I have the idea of all, and am all and believe in all"; "He resolves all tongues into his own."

In his prophetic role as "Chanter of Personality," he can use the Idea of Allness as justification for his claim to act as the spokesman for all: "I act as the tongue of you; / Tied in your mouth, in mine it begins to be loosened." Corresponding to "the great Idea, the idea of perfect and free individuals," an idea for which "the bard walks in advance," there are the many forms of idealized "appetite." These range from thoughts of a gallant and adventurous launching of "all men and women forward with me into the Unknown," to the notion of normal physical sensations programmatically made excessive, an abnormality of super-health: "Urge, and urge, and urge ... complete abandonment ... scattering it freely ... athletic Democracy ... ecstatic songs ... the smoke of my own breath ... the boundless impatience of restraint ... unmitigated adoration ... I inhale great draughts of space ... tumbling on steadily, nothing dreading ... give me the coarse and rank ... fond of his sweetheart, relishing well his steak ... aplomb in the midst of irrational things ... turbulent, fleshy, sensual, eating, drinking, and breeding." In earlier versions of this last set honorifically describing himself, "turbulent" had been "disorderly." And we glimpse something of his rhetorical tactics when we recall that "I am he who goes through the streets" later became "I am he who walks the States." He gains concreteness in such inventions as "love-juice," "limitless limpid jets of love," and "life-lumps." Or analogies between the physical body and what J.C. Ransom has called the world's body are exploited in such statements as "Through you I drain the pent-up rivers of myself" (elsewhere he similarly speaks of "pent-up, aching rivers").

When we turn from the physical body and the world's body to the body politic, we note how such concretizing of the "democratic" code almost automatically vows the poet to imagery of a homosexual cast. For if Democracy is to be equated with "the manly love of comrades," and if such love is to be conceived *concretely*, in terms of bodily intimacy, such social "adhesiveness" ("the great rondure, the cohesion of all") that he advocates is almost necessarily matched by many expressions of "robust love" that would be alien to the typical heterosexual poet, as conditioned by our mores. And though the sex of his lover is not specified in the startling section 5 of *Song of Myself*, the many similarly motivated poems in *Calamus* give reason enough to assume that he is here writing of a male attachment, as with the "hugging and loving bed-fellow" of section 3 (though this passage may also be complicated by infantile memories of the mother). In any case, we should note, for what little it may be worth, that in *The Sleepers* Whitman associates the "onanist" with the color "gray," the same color with which he associates himself ("gray eyes" and "gray-necked"), while the "hermit thrush" singing in the "swamps" of the "Lilacs" poem is "gray-brown" (though "smoke" and "debris" here are also gray; and there are other grays that are still further afield). The directest association of himself with an onanistic motive is in the last two lines of "Spontaneous Me." Also, he uses a spiritual analogue (frequently encountered in devotional verse) when, concerning his literary motive, he apostrophizes his tongue: "Still uttering—still ejaculating—canst never cease this babble?"

As regards the poetic I, who would "promote brave soldiers," has "voyagers' thoughts," would "strike up for a New World," is "he that aches with amorous love," would "dilate you with tremendous breath," or "buoy you up": here his motives and motifs get their summarization in his title of titles, *Leaves of Grass*. Accordingly, one direct way into his verse is to ask what associations clearly cluster about these two nouns, "leaves" and "grass" (which are related to each other as individuals are to the group, thus being in design like his term in the *Vistas*, "ensemble-Individuality," though in that formula the order is reversed). Here we are at the core of his personalizing tactics. And, typically, it is in his *Song of Myself* that he specifically offers answers to the question, "What is the grass?" (As indication that he would here be the Answerer to a fundamental question, he tells us that it has been asked by a child.) In section 6 of this poem, he offers several definitions

First, he says of grass: "I guess it must be the flag of my disposition, out of hopeful green stuff woven." Other references to "stuff" in this poem are: "voices ... of wombs and of the father-stuff"; "This day I am jetting the stuff of far more arrogant republics": "I am ... / Maternal as well as paternal, a child as well as a man, / Stuff'd with the stuff that is coarse and stuff'd with the stuff that is fine." Elsewhere we have noted "I pour the stuff to start sons and daughters fit for these States," and "these States with veins full of poetical stuff." Interestingly enough, all other three references to "flag" in this poem are in contrast with "hopeful green." There are "flag-tops ... draped with black muslin" to "guard some corpse"—and twice the word is used as a verb, in the sense of "droop": "Did you fear some scrofula out of the unflagging pregnancy?" and "The hounded slave that flags in the race." (Note that "draped" is an ablaut form of "drooped" and "dropt.")

Second: "Or I guess it is the handkerchief of the Lord, / A scented gift and remembrancer designedly dropt, / Bearing the owner's name ..." We have noted no other references to handkerchiefs in Whitman, though there is always *Othello* in the offing! But the verb "dropt" recalls the "drooped" and "dropt" of the "Lilacs" poem (which also refers to "inlooped flags with the cities draped in black") and since the matter of *scent* also links these two contexts, we shall wait for further leads here when we specifically deal with this theme. So far as the internal organization is concerned, by the way, we might note that the reference to the "owner's name" attains an enigmatic fulfillment near the end of the poem, when the poet decides that his motive is "without name ... a word unsaid," though "To it the creation is the friend whose embracing awakes me."

Other meanings he offers are:

"I guess the grass is itself a child"; ... "Or I guess it is a uniform hieroglyphic, / ... Growing among black folks as among white." Again, it seems like "the beautiful uncut hair of graves"—and as Whitman frequently shuttles back and forth along the channel of affinity that links love and death or womb and tomb, his next stanza, beginning "Tenderly will I use you curling grass," contrives by quick transitions to go from "the breasts of young men" to "mothers' laps." In the following stanza, grass is related to both "the white heads of old mothers". and "the colorless beards of old men," while a reference to "the faint red roofs of mouths" leads to the specifically poetic motive, in the mention of "uttering tongues."

Near the close of the poem (section 49) the theme of grass as the "hair of graves" is developed further ("O grass of graves"), while the connotations are generally of a maternal, or even obstetrical sort, in the references to the "bitter hug of mortality," the "elder-hand pressing," and the "accoucheur" who helps bring about "the relief and escape" through Death.

The scent theme figures here likewise, thanks to a bit of rhetorical alchemy. For after apostrophizing the "Corpse" as "good manure," the poet assures us: "but that does not offend me, / I smell the white roses sweet-scented and growing," whereat the associations, taking their lead from the vital connotations of the participle "growing," shift into quite a different order: "I reach to the leafy lips, I reach to the polish'd breasts of melons." And do we not find tonal vestiges of "leafy" in the two similar-sounding words of the next line: "And as to you Life I reckon you are the leavings of many deaths"?

To trail down the various uses of the verb "leave," in the light of the possibility that it may secondarily involve motives intrinsic to the noun "leaves," would take us on a longer journey than we could manage now. But let us look at a few. Consider, for instance, in *Song of Myself*, section 3: "As the hugging and loving bed-fellow sleeps at my side through the night ... / Leaving me baskets cover'd with white towels swelling the house with their plenty." In this context for "leaving," the hug is not overtly maternal, though the food connotations suggest that it may be secondarily so, quite as the "baskets" in this passage might correspond food-wise to the "polish'd breasts of melons" in the other. And similarly, in *Song of Myself*, section 6, an implicit food motive seems to guide the steps from "curling grass" to "the breasts of young men," and thence finally via "mothers" to "mouths," with a final turn from the nutriently oral to the poetically eloquent, in "uttering tongues." Yet, as regards "swelling the house with their plenty": we might recall that in "I Sing the Body Electric" we find the step from "love-flesh swelling and deliciously aching" to "jets of love hot and enormous," and two pages later: "There swells and jets a heart" (after talk of "blood" that might well bear study in connection with the talk of blood in the poem beginning "Trickle drops! my blue veins leaving! / O drops of me! trickle, slow drops, / Candid from me falling, drip, bleeding drops"). So the "hug" of Death or bed-fellows seems sometimes maternal, sometimes "democratic," or indeterminately something of both.

But our main intention at this point was to consider some more obvious cases where we might seem justified in adding the verb forms to our inquiry into the various major meanings of "leaves." Perhaps the perfect *pontificating* case is in *Starting from Paumanok*, where the line, "Take my leaves America" suggests something midway between "receive my offerings" and "put up with my constant departures." Or in so far as Whitman sometimes uses "blade" as a synonym for "leaf," there is another kind of bridge between noun and verb when, in "Scented Herbage of My Breast," in connection with male love, he says: "Emblematic and capricious blades I leave you." And before moving on, we'd like to consider one more context where the verb form seems quite relevant to our concerns. We have in mind the passage on Death, the "hug of mortality," the "sweet-scented," and Life as "the leavings of many deaths," a development that is immediately preceded by the lines (except for fifteen words):

> I find letters from God dropt in the street, and every one is sign'd
>   by God's name,
> And I leave them where they are ...

This is in section 48 of *Song of Myself*. Though this longest poem is sometimes entitled "Walt Whitman," we have said that there is in it a *problem of name* (that is, a problem of *essence*, of *fundamental motivation*; and we would base our position, naturally, upon the fact that, as the poet nears his windup, he centers upon the problem of locating a substance "without name"). But, relevantly reverting to the context where the word "name" first appears, we find it precisely in that passage (of section 6) where he speaks of the Lord's "scented" handkerchief, "bearing the owner's name," and "designedly dropt."

There are the many obvious places where the leaves are the leaves of books (a usage that fits well with a pun on utterance, in the notion of a tree's "uttering" leaves). A three-line poem in *Calamus* embodies this usage incidentally, in the course of a somewhat secretive confession:

> Here the frailest leaves of me and yet my strongest lasting,
> Here I shade and hide my thoughts, I myself do not expose them,
> And yet they expose me more than all my other poems.

The word "calamus" itself is apparently within the same orbit, and even allows us to watch "flag" for signs of similar meaning, since calamus is "sweet flag," of which our dictionary says: "The root has a pungent, aromatic taste, and is used in medicine as a stomachic; the leaves have an aromatic odor, and were formerly used instead of rushes to strew on floors." Thus, we might assume that "calamus" is one of his "scent" words, though our incomplete reading has not as yet given us a clear title to this assumption. However, we can cite a one-page poem ("These I Singing in Spring") in which the mention of "calamus-root" accompanies such clearly scent-conscious references as "smelling the earthy smell," "lilac, with a branch of pine," and "aromatic cedar" (calamus-root here being specified as "the token of comrades"). Since "calamus" is the Latin word for "reed," we also dare note inklings of grassiness in the "reedy voice" of the hermit thrush that warbles through the "Lilacs" poem.

"Herbage" clearly belongs here—as in "Scented Herbage of My Breast" (though the subsequent references to "tomb-leaves," "body-leaves," "tall leaves," and "slender leaves ... blossoms of my blood," while they are clear as radiations from the leaf motif, are somewhat vague in themselves). Herbage for grass is matched by feuillage for leaves; and as judged by the assemblage of details in *Our Old Feuillage*, leaves can be any item that he includes in his surveys and poetic catalogues, here called "bouquets" ("Always ... All sights ... All characters ..."; "Always the free range and diversity—always the continent of Democracy"; and "Encircling all, vast-darting up and wide, the American Soul, with equal hemispheres, one Love, one Dilation or Pride").

Leaves are sometimes called "blades"; and the blade of the broad-axe is called a "gray-blue leaf" (thereby adding the *gray* strand—and since the axe was "to be leaned and to lean on," we recall: "I lean and loafe at my ease observing a spear of summer grass"). Besides adding "spear" to our radiations, we note that "lean and loafe" are here attitudinally identical. But further, lo! not only is "loafe" tonally an ablaut form of "leaf"—change the unvoiced "f" to its voiced cognate, "v," and you have the close tonal proximity between "loafe" and "love."

"Leaves" and "grass" cross over into the scent category, in the reference to roots and leaves as "perfume," or in lines such as "The prairie-grass dividing, its special odor breathing," and "The sniff of green leaves and dry leaves ... and of hay in the barn"—or the reference to "words simple as grass" that are "wafted with the odor of his body or breath."

Nowhere do we recall encountering such connotations as in the 129th Psalm, "Let them be as the grass upon the housetops, which withereth afore it groweth up"; or in Isaiah 40: "The grass withereth, the flower fadeth: because the spirit of the Lord bloweth upon it: surely the people is grass."

We should note two other major principles of unity:

First, there are the references to the "first," a common poetic and narrative device for the *defining of essence*. Perhaps the central example is his line: "I speak the password primeval, I give the sign of democracy." The more familiar we become with Whitman's vocabulary, the more condensed this line is felt to be. Identity is proclaimed quasi-temporally, in the word "primeval." Such firstness is further established in terms of the poetic I as spokesman for a public cause. But the more closely one examines the word "sign" in Whitman, the more one comes to realize that it has a special significance for him ranging from signs of God ("and every one is sign'd by God's name, / And I leave them where they are") to such signs as figure in a flirtation. (In "Among the Multitude," for instance: "I perceive one picking me out by secret and divine signs / ... that one knows me. / Ah lover and perfect equal," as per the ambiguously "democratic" kind of equality especially celebrated in the *Calamus* poems.) "Password" is notable for merging one of his major verbs with the term that sums up his own specialty (elsewhere he has "passkey").

When proclaiming "a world primal again," he characteristically identifies it with the "new," the "expanding and swift," and the "turbulent." Another variant of such quasi-temporal firstness is in his term "nativity," as with "Underneath all, Nativity." And often references to the "child" serve the same reductive function (as with "Years looking backward resuming in answer to children").

Lines such as "Unfolded out of the folds of the woman, man comes unfolded," and "Out of the cradle endlessly rocking" reveal how readily such essentializing in terms of the "primal" can lead into the realm of the maternal (which may range from the sheer abstract principle of Union to the personally "electric," "magnetic," or "athletic"). And we might discern a "democratic" variant of the attitude implicit in the German epithet *wohlgeboren*, when he temporally defines his personal essence thus: "Starting from fish-shape Paumanok where I was born, / Well-begotten, and rais'd by a perfect mother."

There is a notable variant of the temporal idiom in "Crossing Brooklyn Ferry." For as the literal crossing of the river becomes symbolically a vision of crossing into the future, so the poet becomes a kind of essentializing past, defining the nature of his future readers. In "With Antecedents," we see how this temporal or narrative mode of defining essence can fit into the dialectics of *logical* priority (priority in the sense that the first premise of a syllogism can be considered prior to the second premise). For while, as his very title indicates, he is concerned with the temporally prior, he reduces his temporal sequence in turn to terms of "all" when he says: "We stand amid time beginningless and endless, we stand amid evil and good, / All swings around us."

In his *Song of the Open Road*, which calls upon us continually to "reach" and "pass," and "to merge all in the travel they tend to," he uses a reverse kind of temporal priority; namely: seniority. "Old age, calm, expanded, broad with the haughty breadth of the universe, / Old age, flowing free with the delicious near-by freedom of death." (The broad–breadth pair here could lead us into his notable breast–breath set.) But with the subject of Death, we come upon another kind of summing up, since it names the direction in which the "ever-tending" is headed. ("Tend" is as typical a Whitman word as "pass," though it occurs much less frequently.) So, let us consider Whitman's poetizing of Death. But since Death is the Great Positive-Seeming Negative, perhaps we might best consider it with relation to the poet's use of the negative in general.

The incidence of negatives is probably highest in the poems of the *Calamus* period; at least, in many places here they come thick and fast. There is almost an orgy of not's and nor's in "Not Heaving from My Ribb'd Breast Only," as sixteen of the poem's seventeen lines so begin, while one line contains a second. Since the poem is composed of a single periodic sentence about "adhesiveness" (the "pulse of my life"), we should certainly be justified in asking whether there may be a substantive relation in these poems between the negative and the resolve to celebrate democracy with songs of "manly attachment." (See also particularly in this same series: "Not Heat Flames Up and Consumes" "City of Orgies"; "No Labor-Saving Machine"; or the way in which a flat "no" serves as fulcrum in "What Think You I Take My Pen in Hand?")

It might also be worth noting that the *Calamus* theme of the "subtle electric fire that for your sake is playing within me" produces two significant and quite appealing instances of anacoluthon: "City whom that I have lived and sung in your midst will one day make you illustrious," and "O you whom I often and silently come where you are that I may be with you." (We mention anacoluthon here because, tentatively, though not for certain, we incline to believe that the figure indicates a certain deviousness in thinking, hence may remotely indicate a "problematical" motive.)

A more orthodox strategy of deflection (almost a diplomacy) is to be seen in another poem of the *Calamus* series, "Earth, My Likeness." Beginning on the theme of the analogy between the poet's body and the earth as a body, the poet then avows a questionable motive in himself, after figuratively attributing a like motive to the earth

> I now suspect there is something fierce in you eligible to burst
>   forth,
> For an athlete is enamour'd of me, and I of him,
> But toward him there is something fierce and terrible in me
>   eligible to burst forth,
> I dare not tell it in words, not even in these songs.[4]

In *Song of Myself* (section 44) there is an absolute negative, identified with a "first":

Afar down I see the huge first Nothing, I know I was even there,
I waited unseen and always, and slept through the lethargic mist,
And took my time, and took no hurt from the fetid carbon.

Long I was hugg'd close—long and long.

Immediately after, the thought is developed in terms of the maternal. For instance: "Cycles ferried my cradle," and "Before I was born out of my mother generations guided me," lines that overlap upon even the sheer titles of *Crossing Brooklyn Ferry* and "Out of the Cradle Endlessly Rocking." The word "hugg'd" might remind us of the previously quoted reference to "the hugging and loving bed-fellow ... / Leaving me baskets," etc. (section 3). Or there was the "hug of mortality" in section 49, and the death-smell that "does not offend me" and was quickly replaced by talk of the "sweet-scented."

Section 12 in *Starting from Paumanok* has some interesting involvements with the negative. First the poet addresses his femme, Democracy. In her name he will make both the "songs of passion" and the "true poem of riches." He will "effuse egotism," and will show that male and female are equal.

We might note that such equality of sex could mean one thing as applied to the body politic, but something quite different if applied to the individual personality. For within the individual personality, an "equality" of "male" and "female" motives could add up to an ambivalence of the *androgynous* sort, as it would not, strictly in the realm of politics. Yet we must also bear in mind the fact that, however close language may be to the persuasions and poetics of sexual courtship, language as such is nonsexual; and in so far as motivational perturbations arising from purely *linguistic* sources become personalized in terms of any real or imagined distinctions between "male" and "female," such sexual-seeming differentiations should be inadequate to the case; hence, any purely linguistic situations that happened to be stated in sexual terms (involving either sexual differentiations or sexual mergers) should have elements that could be but *prophetically glimpsed* beyond a terminology formed by sexual analogies.

For instance, though language necessarily has a realm of dialectical resources wholly extrinsic to sexuality, there is the ironic linguistic fact that concrete bisexual imagery may be inevitable, if a poet, let us say, would give us not at one time the image of *mother* and at another the image of *father*, but would rather seek to localize in concrete imagery the idea of *parent*. At the very least, thinking of such a linguistic embarrassment along psychoanalytic lines, we might expect some kind of merger or amalgam like that in Whitman's exclamation: "Mother! with subtle sense severe, with the naked sword in your hand." (And after the analogy of "spears" of grass, we might well have swords of grass, too, not forgetting the naked broad-axe. Further, a poet given to homosexual imagery might well, when writing of his verbal art, glimpse the wholly nonsexual quandaries that lie in the bed of language, far beyond any and all sociopolitical relations.)[5]

But we were on the subject of the negatives in section 12 of *Starting from Paumanok*. Immediately after the poet has proclaimed the equality of male and female, and has vowed that he will prove "sexual organs and acts" to be "illustrious," the negatives come piling in. He will show that "there is no imperfection in the present, and can be none in the future," and that "nothing can happen more beautiful than death." The next stanza has a negative in four of its five verses, and the positive line is introduced by a disjunctive conjunction:

> I will not make poems with reference to parts,
> But I will make poems, songs, thoughts, with reference to
>   ensemble,
> And I will not sing with reference to a day, but with reference
>   to all days,
> And I will not make a poem nor the least part of a poem but
>   has reference to the soul,
> Because having look'd at the objects of the universe, I find there
>   is no one nor any particle of one but has reference to the soul.

Whereas the Whitman negative, at one extreme, seems to involve the notions of No-No that trouble the scruples of "manly love" (scruples that somehow connect with thoughts of the maternal and, of course, with the problem of his identity, or "nativity," as a poet), in the above quotation we see how such matters fade into purely technical considerations. For if the *particulars* of life are positive, then the "ensemble" or "soul" would be correspondingly negative; or if you considered the "ensemble" positive, then the "parts" would be negative (as with Spinoza's principle: *omnis determinatio est negatio*). Or in a fluctuant medium such as Whitman's, where the issues need not be strictly drawn, the talk of parts and wholes may merely call forth a general aura of negativity. However, once we consider this problem from the standpoint of the distinction between positive and negative, we should note the dialectical resources whereby, above the catalogues of positive details that characteristically make up so many of his poems, there should hover some summarizing principle—and this principle would be "negative," at least in the sense that no single detail could be it, though each such positive detail might partitively stand for it, or be infused with its spirit. (The problem is analogous to that of negative theology.)

When the technical principles of positive and negative are projected into their moralistic counterparts (as good and evil), the poet can assert by the doubling of negatives, as in "I will show that there is no imperfection." And if you will agree that death is negative (in so far as it is the privation of life), then you will note double negativity lurking in the statements that "nothing can happen more beautiful than death," or "Copulation is no more rank to me than death is."

Sometimes the *principle* of negativity is present, but in a positive-seeming statement that is really a denial of a social negative, as with "the bowels sweet and clean," or "perfect and clean the genitals previously jetting." Or here is a line that runs heretically counter to vast sums expended in the advertising of deodorants for people who think that their vague sense of personal guilt is to be eliminated by purely material means: "the scent of these armpits aroma finer than "prayer." In keeping with this pattern, he can also celebrate the "joy of death," likening it to the discharging of excrement ("My voided body nothing more to me, returning to the purifications"). Similarly, farther afield, as though boasting of virtues, he can tell of the vices that were "not wanting" in him ("the wolf, the snake, the hog," among others). For he "will make the poem of evil also," for "I am myself just as much evil as good, and my nation is"—whereat, expanding further, "and I say there is in fact no evil." Accordingly, "none can be interdicted, None but are accepted."

At one point in *Song of the Open Road* he formulates the principle in general terms, in ways suggesting Hegel: "It is provided in the essence of things that from any fruition of success, no matter what, shall come forth something to make a greater struggle necessary," a principle that could provide good grounds for feeling downcast, if one were so inclined. Elsewhere, "after reading Hegel," he avows: "the vast all that is called Evil I saw hastening to merge itself and become lost and dead." And in keeping with the same design, he could praise the earth because "It grows such sweet things out of such corruptions."

In sum, Whitman would programmatically make all days into a kind of permanent Saturnalian revel, though celebrating not a golden age of the past, but rather the present in terms of an ideal future. And, in poetically personalizing his program, he "promulges" democracy in terms of a maternal allness or firstness and fraternal universality ambiguously intermingling in a death hug that presents many central problems for the patient pedestrian analyzer of The Good Gray Poet's terminology.

But when we remind ourselves that the Roman Saturnalia traditionally involved a ritualistic reversal of roles, with the slaves and servants playing as masters for a day while the masters playfully took orders, we wonder whether the ironic bitterness of Whitman's poem, "Respondez! Respondez!" (first published in 1856 as "Poem of the Proposition of Nakedness") might be studied as a kind of Saturnalian-in-reverse.

"Let the slaves be masters! let the masters become slaves!" he exhorts— but this call to the answerer is phrased rather in the accents of outrage. "Let the cow, the horse, the camel, the garden-bee—let the mudfish, the lobster, the mussel, eel, the sting-ray, and the grunting pig-fish—let these, and the like of these, be put on a perfect equality with man and woman!"

In this almost splutteringly ferocious poem, the nation is surveyed wholly without benefit of his normal "spiritualization"

> Stifled, O days, O lands! in every public and private corruption
> Smothered in thievery, impotence, shamelessness, mountain-
>   high;
> Brazen effrontery, scheming, rolling like ocean's waves around
>   and upon you, O my days! my lands! ...
> —Let the theory of America still be management, caste, com-
>   parison! (Say! what other theory would you?)

And so on, and so on. "Let there be money, business, imports, exports, custom, authority, precedents, pallor, dyspepsia, smut, ignorance, unbelief!"

As for this sullen poem in which he stylistically turns his usual promulgations upside down, we perhaps have here the equivalent of such reversal as marks the mystic state of "accidie." In any case, of all his negatives, this poem would seem to have been one that carried him quite outside his characteristic literary role. It shows how very harsh things could seem to him, in those days, when for a moment he let himself look upon the conditions of his day without the good aid of his futuristic IDEA.

III. LILACS

Having considered Whitman's political philosophy in general, and the general way in which he personalized his outlook by translation into the rapt editorializing of his verse, we would here narrow our concerns to a close look at one poem, his very moving dirge, "When Lilacs Last in the Dooryard Bloom'd," perhaps poem of his in which policies and personalizations came most nearly perfectly together.

The programmatic zestfulness that marks Whitman's verse as strongly as Emerson's essays encountered two challenges for which it had not been originally "promulged": the Civil War, and the valetudinarianism forced upon him by his partial paralytic stroke in 1873.

Before these developments, his stylistics of "spiritualization" had provided him with a categorical solution for the problem of evil as he saw it. Except for the outlaw moment of "Respondez! Respondez!" (or its much briefer form, "Reversals") his futuristic idealizing could readily transform all apprehensions into promises, and could discern a unitary democratic spirit behind any aggregate of natural or manmade places or things that added up to national power and prowess. This same principle was embodied in the random samplings that made up his poetic surveys and catalogues (which do impart a note of exhilaration to his text, even though one inclines to skim through them somewhat as when running the eye down the column of a telephone directory). And whatever guilt was left unresolved by his code could be canceled by the accents of perfervid evangelism (notably in his celebrating of "adhesiveness").

But since the entire scheme was based upon an ideal of all-pervasive and almost promiscuous Union, the motives of secession that culminated in the Civil War necessarily filled him with anguish. And even many of the inferior poems in *Drum-Taps* become urgent and poignant, if read as the diary of a man whose views necessarily made him most sensitive to the dread of national dismemberment. Here, above all, was the development in history itself which ran harshly counter to the basic promises in which his poetry had invested. He reproaches not himself but "America": "Long, too long ... / you learned from joys and prosperity only." And, in slightly wavering syntax, he says the need is henceforth "to learn from crises of anguish."

Yet in one notable respect, his doctrines had prepared him for this trial. In contrast with the crudity of mutual revilement and incrimination that marks so many contemporary battles between the advocates of Rightist and Leftist politics, Whitman retained some of the spontaneous gallantry toward the enemy that sometimes (as in *Chevy-Chase*) gives the old English-Scottish border ballads their enlightening moral nobility. And whatever problematical ingredients there may have been in his code of love as celebrated in the *Calamus* poems, these motives were sacrificially transformed in his work and thoughts as wound-dresser ("I have nourished the wounded and soothed many a dying soldier" ... "Upon this breast has many a dying soldier leaned to breathe his last" ... "Many a soldier's loving arms about this neck have cross'd and rested, / Many a soldier's kiss dwells on these bearded lips").

Similarly, when ill health beset him, though it went badly with one who had made a particular point of celebrating the body at the height of its physical powers, here too he had a reserve to draw upon. For his cult of death as a kind of all-mother (like the sea) did allow him a place in his system for infirmities. Further, since death was that condition toward which all life *tends*, he could write of old age, "I see in you the estuary that enlarges and spreads itself grandly as it pours in the great sea"—and though this is nearly his briefest poem, it is surely as *expansionist* a view as he ever proclaimed in his times of broad-axe vigor. We have already mentioned his new-found sympathy with the fallen redwood tree. Other identifications of this sort are imagined in his lines about an ox tamer, and about a locomotive in winter (he now wrote "recitatives").

As for the lament on the death of Lincoln: here surely was a kind of Grand Resolution, done at the height of his powers. Embodied in it, there is a notable trinity of sensory images, since the three major interwoven symbolic elements—evening star, singing bird, and lilac—compose a threeness of sight, sound, and scent respectively. Also, perhaps they make a threeness of paternal, filial, and maternal respectively. Clearly, the star stands for the dead hero; and the "hermit" bird, "warbling a song," just as clearly stands for the author's poetizing self. But whereas vicarious aspects of star and bird are thus defined within the poem itself, we believe that the role of the lilac is better understood if approached through an inquiry into the subject of scent in general, as it figures in Whitman's idiom.

In the section on *Vistas*, we put much store by the passage where, after referring to "that indescribable perfume of genuine womanhood," Whitman next speaks of his mother, then proceeds to describe an elderly lady, a "resplendent person, down on Long Island." We consider this set of steps strongly indicative, particularly in so far as many other passages can be assembled which point in the same direction. And though Whitman's associations with scent radiate beyond the orbit of the feminine, maternal, and grandmotherly, we believe that his terms for scent have their strongest motivational jurisdiction in this area, with the *Calamus* motive next.

In this Lincoln poem, the lilac is explicitly called "the perfume strong I love." The sprigs from the lilac bushes ("to perfume the grave of him I love") are not just for this one coffin, but for "coffins all." And the Death figured in such lilac-covered coffins is called a "Dark Mother." In "Out of the

Cradle Endlessly Rocking," where there is the same identification of the maternal and the deathy, the development is built about the account of a solitary "he-bird ... warbling" for his lost mate, quite as with the mournful warbling of the hermit thrush—and the incident is said to have taken place "When the lilac-scent was in the air and Fifth-month grass was growing."

The cedars and pines in the "recesses" of the swamp where the hermit thrush is singing are also explicitly included in the realm of scent, as evidenced by the lines: "From the fragrant cedars and the ghostly pines"; "Clear in the freshness moist and the swamp-perfume"; "There in the fragrant pines and the cedars dusk and dim." See also, in *Starting from Paumanok*, that poem of his origins and of his femme Democracy: having heard "the hermit thrush from the swamp-cedars, / Solitary, singing in the West, I strike up for a New World." But it is the lilac that holds the poet "with mastering odor," as he says in the Lincoln poem.

In another poem, *A Broadway Pageant* (and one should think also of broad-axe and broad breast), there is a passage that clearly brings out the identification between scent and the maternal, though in this case the usage is somewhat ambiguous in attitude, whereas by far the great majority of references to scent in Whitman are decidedly on the favorable side: "The Originatress comes, / The nest of languages, the bequeather of poems, the race of eld, / Florid with blood, pensive, rapt with musings, hot with passion, / Sultry with perfume." (His word "florid" here could be correlated with a reference to "Florida perfumes," in a poem on Columbia, "the Mother of All.") In this same poem, near the end, there is a passage about "the all-mother" and "the long-off mother" which develops from the line: "The box-lid is but perceptibly open'd, nevertheless the perfume pours copiously out of the whole box." Psychoanalytically, the point about identification here could be buttressed by the standard psychoanalytic interpretation of "box," and thus perhaps by extending the same idea to the coffin—but we would prefer to stress merely the sequence of steps in this passage itself, while noting that the terms for derivation ("out of") take us once again back to the "Cradle" poem. Consider also this passage, near the windup of *Song of Myself*:

The past and present wilt—I have fill'd them, emptied them,
And proceed to fill my next fold of the future.

Listen up there! what have you to confide to me?
Look in my face while I snuff the sidle of evening ...

Does not "snuff the sidle" here suggest the picture of a youngster nosing against the side of the evening, as were the evening an adult, with a child pressing his face against its breast? In any case, "fold" is a notable word in Whitman, with its maternal connotations obvious in the line where the syllable is repeated almost like an *idée fixe*: "Unfolded out of the folds of the woman, man comes unfolded," an expression that also has the "out of" construction. Another reference, "Endless unfolding of words of ages," leads into talk of acceptance ("I accept Reality and dare not question it, / Materialism first and last imbuing")—and two lines later he speaks of "cedar and branches of lilac." Recall also the traditional association of the feminine with matter (as in Aristotle). In the "Lilacs" poem, immediately before the words "dark mother," death is called "cool-enfolding."

In one of the *Calamus* poems, a reference to "perfume" follows immediately after the line, "Buds to be unfolded on the old terms," and there are other lines that extend the area of the perfume beyond the feminine and maternal to the realm of manly adhesiveness, and to his poetic development in general, as in "In Cabin'd Ships at Sea": "Bear forth to them folded my love, (dear mariners, for you I fold it here in every leaf)."

There are many other references, direct and indirect, which we could offer to establish the maternal as a major element in the lilac theme. But we believe that these should be enough to prove the point.

Imagine, then, a situation of this sort:

A poet has worked out a scheme for identifying his art with the ideal of a democratic "empire" that he thinks of as a matrix, an All-Mother, a principle of unity bestowing its sanctions upon a strong love of man for man, an "adhesiveness" generally "spiritual," but also made concrete in imagery of "athletic" physical attachment. Quite as God is conceived as both efficient cause and final cause, so this poet's unitary principle is identified with both a source from which he was "unfolded" (the maternal origins "out of" which his art derived) and an end toward which he "ever-tended" (death, that will receive him by "enfolding" him, thus completing the state of "manifold ensemble" through which he had continually "passed," by repeatedly "coming" and "departing"). A beloved democratic hero has died—and the lyric commemoration of this tragic death will be the occasion of the poem.

How then would he proceed, within the regular bounds of his methods and terminology, to endow this occasion with the personal and impersonal *dimensions* that give it scope and resonance? (For a good poem will be not just one strand, but the interweaving of strands.)

Note, first, that the poem involves several situations. There is the commemorated situation, the death of the hero, as made specific in the journey of the coffin on its last journey. There is the immediate situation of the commemorating poet, among a set of sensory perceptions that he associates, for us, with the hero's death. There is the national scene that he can review, after the fashion of his catalogues, when charting the journey of the coffin (and when radiating into other details loosely connected with this). Near the end, a national scene that had *preceded* the hero's death will be recalled (the time of civil war, or intestine strife, that had accounted historically for the tragic sacrifice). And in the offing, "over-arching" all, there is the notion of an ultimate scene (life, death, eternity, and a possibility of interrelationships in terms of which immediate sensory images can seem to take on an element of the marvelous, or transcendent, through standing for correspondences beyond their nature as sheerly physical objects). The reader shifts back and forth spontaneously, almost unawares, among these different scenes, with their different orders of motivation, the interpenetration of which adds subtlety and variety to the poem's easy simplicity.

The three major *sensory* images are star, bird, and bush (each with its own special surroundings: the darkening Western sky for the "drooping" star, the "recesses" of the swamp for the "hermit" bird, the dooryard for the lilac, with its loved strong perfume—and for all three, the evening in "ever-returning spring"). As regards their correspondences with things beyond their nature as sheerly sensory images: the star stands for the dead loved hero (in a scheme that, as with so much of the Wagnerian nineteenth century, readily equates love and death). The bird crosses over, to a realm beyond its sheerly sensuous self, by standing for the poet who mourns, or celebrates, the dead hero (while also ambiguously mourning or celebrating himself).

And what of the third image, the scent of lilac? It fits the occasion in the obvious sense that it blooms in the springtime and is a proper offering for coffins. And though it is from a realm more material, more earthy, than sight or sound, it has a strong claim to "spirit" as well, since scent is *breathed*. (Passages elsewhere in Whitman, such as "sweet-breathed," "inhaling the ripe breath of autumn," and "the shelves are crowded with perfumes, / I breathe the fragrance," remind us that references to breathing can be secondarily in the scent orbit, and often are in Whitman's idiom.)

Though, in the lore of the Trinity, the Father is equated with power, the Son with wisdom, and the Holy Spirit with love, it is also said that these marks of the three persons overlap. And similarly, in this trinity (of star, bird, and bush) there are confusions atop the distinctions. In so far as the bird stands for the poet whose art (according to the *Vistas*) was to teach us lessons, the bird would correspond to the son, and wisdom. The star, in standing for the dead Lincoln, would surely be an equivalent of the father, implying power in so far as Lincoln had been a national democratic leader. Yet the nearest explicit attribution of power, the adjective "strong," is applied only in connection with the lilac, which would be analogous to the third person of the trinity, the holy spirit (with the notable exception that we would treat it as *maternal*, whereas the Sanctus Spiritus is, *grammatically* at least, imagined after the analogy of the masculine, though often surrounded by imagery that suggests maternal, quasi-Mariolatrous connotations).

The relation of lilac to love is in the reference to "heart-shaped leaves." Since the evening star is unquestionably Venus, the love theme is implicitly figured, though ambiguously, in so far as Venus is feminine, but is here the sign of a dead man. As for the "solitary" thrush, who sings "death's outlet song of life," his "carol of death" is a love song at least secondarily, in so far as love and death are convertible terms. Also, in so far as the bird song is explicitly said to be a "tallying chant" that matches the poet's own "thought of him I love," the love motif is connected with it by this route.

But the words, "song of the bleeding throat," remind us of another motive here, more autistic, intrinsic to the self, as might be expected of a "hermit" singer. Implicit in the singing of the thrush, there is the theme most clearly expressed perhaps in these earlier lines, from *Calamus*:

> Trickle drops! my blue veins leaving!
> O drops of me I trickle, slow drops,
> Candid from me falling, drip, bleeding drops,
> From wounds made to free you whence you were prison'd,
> From my face, from my forehead and lips,
> From my breast, from within where I was conceal'd, press forth
>   red drops, confession drops,
> Stain every page, stain every song I sing, every word I say,
>   bloody drops,
> Let them know your scarlet heat, let them glisten,
> Saturate them with yourself all ashamed and wet,
> Glow upon all I have written or shall write, bleeding drops,
> Let it all be seen in your light, blushing drops.

Do we not here find the theme of utterance proclaimed in and for itself, yet after the analogy of violence done upon the self?

Regrettably, we cannot pause to appreciate the "Lilacs" poem in detail. But a few terministic considerations might be mentioned. There is the interesting set of modulations, for instance, in the series: night, black murk, gray debris, dark-brown fields, great cloud darkening the land, draped in black, crepe-veiled, dim-lit, netherward black of the night, gray smoke, gray-brown bird out of the dusk, long black trail, swamp in the dimness, shadowy cedars, dark mother, dusk and dim—all in contrast with the "lustrous" star. (If you will turn to *Song of Myself*, section 6, you will find the "dark mother" theme interestingly foreshadowed in the "dark ... darker ... dark" stanza that serves as a transition from "mothers' laps" to "uttering tongues.") And noting the absence of Whitman's distance-blue, we find that he has moved into the more solemn area of lilac, purple, and violet. Note also the spring–sprig modulation.

There are many devices for merging the components. At times, for instance, the swampy "recesses" where the bird is singing are described in terms of scent. Or sight and scent are intermingled when "fragrant cedars" are matched with "ghostly pines" at one point, and "fragrant pines" are matched with "cedars dusk and dim" at another. And of course, there is the notable closing merger, "Lilac and star and bird twined with the chant of my soul," a revision of his "trinity" in the opening stanzas, where the bird does not figure at all, the third of the three being the poet's "thought of him I love."

Prophesying after the event, of course, we could say that the bird had figured implicitly from the very first, since the bird duplicates the poet, though this duplex element will not begin to emerge until section 4, where the bird is first mentioned. But once the bird has been introduced, much effectiveness derives from the poem's return, at intervals, to this theme, which is thus astutely released and developed. One gets the feel of an almost frenzied or orgiastic outpouring, that has never stopped for one moment, and somehow even now goes unendingly on.

One gets no such clear sense of progression in the poem as when, say, reading *Lycidas*. But if pressed, we could offer grounds for contending that section 13 (the mathematical center of the poem) is the point of maximum internality. For instance, whereas in sections 4 and 9, the thrush is "warbling" in the swamp, here the song is said to come *from* the swamps, *from* the bushes, *out of* the dusk, *out of* the cedars and pines (a prepositional form which we, of course, associate with the maternal connotations it has in the opening stanzas of "Out of the Cradle Endlessly Rocking"). Thus, one might argue that there is a crucial change of direction shaping up here. Also, whereas section 4 had featured the sound of the bird's song, and section 9 had added the star along with talk of the bird's song, in section 13 we have bird, star, and lilac, all three (plus a paradox which we may ascribe at least in part to the accidental limitations of English—for whereas we feel positive in associating lilac with the feminine or maternal, the poet writes of the "mastering" odor with which the lilac holds him).

We could say that the theme of the cradle song, or "Death Carol" (that follows, after a brief catalogue passage) had been implicitly introduced in the "from's" and "out of's" that characterize the first stanza of section 13. But in any case, a clear change of direction follows this movement, with its theme of death as "dark mother." And since we would make much of this point, let us pause to get the steps clear:

As regards the purely sensory imagination, the theme (of the "Death Carol" as cradle song) is developed in the spirit of such words as soothe, serenely, undulate, delicate, soft, floating; loved, laved. And whereas there is no sensory experience suggested in the words "praise! praise! praise!" surely they belong here wholly because of the poet's desire to use whatever associations suggest total relaxation, and because of the perfect freedom that goes with the act of genuine, unstinted praise, when given without ulterior purpose, from sheer spontaneous delight.

What next, then, after this moment of farthest yielding? Either the poem must end there (as it doesn't), or it must find some proper aftermath. The remaining stanzas, as we interpret them, have it in their favor that they offer a solution of this problem.

As we see it, a notable duality of adjustment takes place here (along lines somewhat analogous to the biologists' notion of the correspondence between ontogenetic and phylogenetic evolution, with regard to the stages that the individual foetus passes through, in the course of its development).

In brief, there are certain matters of recapitulation to be treated, purely within the conditions of the poem; but if these are to be wholly vital, there must be a kind of *new act* here, even thus late in the poem, so far as the momentum of the poet is concerned. And we believe that something of the following sort takes place:

In imagining death as maternal, the poet has imagined a state of ideal infantile or intra-uterine bliss. Hence, anything experienced *after* that stage will be like the emergence of the child from its state of Eden into the world of conflict. Accordingly, after the "Death Carol," the poet works up, to a recital in terms of armies, battle flags, the "torn and bloody," "debris," etc. Strictly within the conditions of the poem, all these details figure as recollections of the Civil War, with its conditions of strife which accounted historically for the hero's death. But from the standpoint of this section's place *after* the imagining of infantile contentment, all such imagery of discord is, in effect, the recapitulation of a human being's emergence into the intestine turmoils of childhood and adolescence.

After this review of discord, there is a recapitulation designed to bring about the final mergings, fittingly introduced by the repetition of Whitman's password, "passing." There had been much merging already. Now, in the gathering of the clan, there is a final assertion of merger, made as strong and comprehensive as possible. The "hermit song" is explicitly related to the "tallying song" of the poet's "own soul." The "gray-brown bird" is subtly matched by the "silver face" of the star. Our previous notion about the possible pun in "leaves" (as noun and verb) comes as near to substantiation as could be, in the line "Passing, I leave thee lilac with heart-shaped leaves." There is a comradely holding of hands.

So, with the thought of the hero's death, all is joined: "the holders holding my hand"; "lilac and star and bird twined with the chant of my soul"; "and this for his dear sake," a sacrifice that ends on the line, "The fragrant pines and cedars dusk and dim"—nor should we forget that the sounds issuing from there came from the "recesses" of the "swamp-perfume."[6]

The first line of a Whitman poem is usually quite different rhythmically from the lines that follow. The first line generally has the formal rhythm of strict verse, while even as early as the second line he usually turns to his typical free-verse style. (*Song of the Broad-Axe* is an exception to the rule, as it opens with no less than six lines that do not depart far from the pattern: long-short/long-short/long-short/long, as set by the verse: "Weapon, shapely, naked, wan.") We copied out a batch of first lines, just to see how they would look if assembled all in one place, without reference to the kind of line that characterizes most notably the poet's catalogues. When reading them over, we noted that they are so much of a piece, and gravitate so constantly about a few themes, one might make up a kind of Whitman Medley, composed of nothing but first lines, without a single alteration in their wording. Here is one version of such an arrangement. It is offered as a kind of critical satyr-play, to lighten things after the tragic burden of our long analysis

First O Songs for a Prelude

Lo, the unbounded sea!.
Flood-tide below me! I see you face to face
In cabined ships at sea,
Out of the cradle endlessly rocking,
Over the Western sea hither from Niphon come
As I ebb'd with the ocean of life,

Facing west from California's shore,
Give me the splendid silent sun with all his beams full-dazzling.

O to make the most jubilant song!
A song for occupations
A song of the rolling earth, and of words according,
I hear America singing, the varied carols I hear.
These I singing in spring collect for lovers,
Trickle drops! my blue veins leaving!
America always! Always our old feuillage!
Come, said the Muse,
Come my tan-faced children.

(Now list to my morning's romanza, I tell the signs of the
    Answerer.
An old man bending I come upon new faces,
Spirit whose work is done—spirit of dreadful hours!
Rise, O days, from your fathomless deeps, till you loftier, fiercer
    sweep.)

As I pondered in silence,
Starting from fish-shape Paumanok where I was born,
From pent-up aching rivers;
As I lay with my head in your lap camerado,
Thou who has slept all night upon the storm;
Vigil strange I kept on the field one night,
On the beach at night
By blue Ontario's shore.

I sing the body electric,
Weapon shapely, naked, wan,
Scented herbage of my breast,
Myself and mine gymnastic ever,
Full of life now, compact visible,
I celebrate myself and sing myself;
Me imperturbe, standing at ease in Nature.

On journeys through the States we start,
Among the men and women, the multitude,
In paths untrodden,

The prairie grass dividing, its special odor breathing—
Not heaving from my ribbed breast only,
Afoot and light-hearted I take to the open road.

You who celebrate bygones,
Are you the new person drawn toward me?
Whoever you are, I fear you are walking the walks of dreams.
Behold this swarthy face, these gray eyes;
Passing stranger! you do not know how longingly I look upon
   you.
Respondez! Respondez!
Here, take this gift—
Come, I will make the continent indissoluble.
O take my hand, Walt Whitman!
As Adam early in the morning
To the garden anew ascending.

NOTES

1. Since political parties are themselves a point at which present organization and future promises meet, we might expect him to waver here, and he does. Thus "I advise you to enter more strongly yet into politics"—but also "Disengage yourself from parties." The wavering even invades his syntax, when he says that he knows "nothing grander, better exercise, better digestion, more positive proof of the past, the triumphant result of faith in human kind, than a well-contested American national election."

2. "It seems as if the Almighty had spread before this nation charts of imperial destinies, dazzling as the sun yet with many a deep intestine difficulty, and human aggregate of cantankerous imperfection—saying, lo! the roads, the only plans of development, long and varied with all terrible balks and ebullitions." Might not these lines serve well as motto for his *Song of the Open Road*, and as indicating a notable ingredient in his cult of the roadway generally?

3. But not always. In *Song of the Open Road* we are told: "No diseas'd person, no rum-drinker or venereal taint is permitted here."

4. The lines contain many notable terms. First, since they twice say "eligible," we might remember the connotations here when we come upon the word elsewhere. Thus, when winding up *Our Old Feuillage*, Whitman writes: "Whoever you are I how can I but offer you divine leaves, that you also be eligible as I am?" Or in *By Blue Ontario's Shore*, see "All is eligible to all." And recalling the "lessons" on which *Democratic Vistas* began, note in *Starting from Paumanok*: "I sat studying at the feet of the great masters, / Now if eligible O that the great masters might return and study me." The repetition of "fierce" might recall the "fierce old mother" and "savage old mother" of "Out of the Cradle Endlessly Rocking." Also "liberty songs" were fierce. The poem gives us some specific meanings for "athlete," to be remembered even though the word can be extended to an "athletic matron." And the movement ends in the negative, with relation to his own verse.

5. See *Der Monat*, Juni 1954, Heft 69: *Die Alten Ägypter*, by J. A. Wilson, page 277: *Ein anderer, irdischerer Text macht aus der Erschafung von Schu und Tefnut einen Akt der Selbstbefleckung Atums—ein deutlicher Versuch, mit dem Problem fertig zu werden, wie ein Gott allein, ohne dazugehörige Göttin, etwas zeugen soll.* And on page 280, returning to the theme of a creation *aus einer Selbstbefleckung des Schöpfergottes*, a creation made "*aus seinem Samen und seinen Fingern,*" the author next says (and we consider this a thoroughly substantial association): *Wir sahen ja schon, urie das Aussprechen eines Namens an sich ein Schöpfungsakt ist.* We have many times been struck by the fact that the creative word could be called parthenogenesis or *Selbstbefleckung*, depending on whichever sexual analogies the analogizer preferred; but this is the first time we ever encountered so heroic a version of such thinking. And we are particularly struck by the writer's turn from the subject of this self-involved physical act on the part of a wholly independent god to the subject of creation by verbal fiat.

6. Five lines from the end, the expression "Comrades mine and I in the midst," restating in slight variation the words of section 14, "I in the middle with companions," might be used as an indication of the way in which the poet's terms radiate. In *Calamus* there is a poem that also has the expression, "I in the middle." One will also find there "lilac with a branch of pine," "aromatic cedar," the themes of singing and plucking (to match "A sprig with its flower I break"), and a reference to "the spirits of friends dead or alive." In *A Broadway Pageant*, there also appears the expression "in the middle." But just as the other usage had been a bridge into the theme of comradely attachment, here the context is definitely in the maternal orbit. This same stanza contains the reference to the perfume that "pours copiously out of the whole box," and "venerable Asia, the all-mother." In the "Lilacs" poem, the theme of copious pouring is distributed differently. In section 13, the bird is told to "pour" its song; in section 7, the idea is transferred to the breaking of the lilac: "Copious I break, I break the sprigs from the bushes, / With loaded arms I come pouring for you"—whereat again we would recall that the first reference to the "shy and hidden bird," with its "song of the bleeding throat," followed the line, "A sprig with its flower I break."

R . W . B . L E W I S

Walt Whitman:
Always Going Out and Coming In

Walt Whitman is the most blurred, even contradictory figure in the classical or mid-nineteenth-century period of American Literature. Recent scholarship and criticism have been clearing things up a good deal; but both the poet and his work remain something of a jumble. For a number of decades, Whitman was the most misrepresented of our major poets; and the misrepresentation began with Whitman himself, in the last twenty-five years of his life. It was during those years, from 1867 onward, that Whitman—initially a very self-exposed and self-absorbed poet—became willfully self-concealing, while at the same time he asserted in various ways an entity, a being, a persona radically other than the being that lay at the heart of his best poetry.

The chief mode of such concealment and assertion was not creative; it was editorial. Whitman wrote little poetry of lasting value after "Passage to India" (1871); what he did do in those later years was constantly to reshuffle the contents of his expanding book: to disperse the poems out of their original and effective order, to arrange them in new and fundamentally misleading groups, to suppress some of the more telling and suggestive of the items, and to revise or delete a series of key passages. The result of this process was a serious shift of emphasis whereby the authentic Whitman was gradually dismembered and replaced by a synthetic entity that was more

From *Trials of the Word: Essays in American Literature and the Humanistic Tradition.* © 1965 by R.W.B. Lewis.

posture than poet, more mere representative than sovereign person. It, or he, was the representative—in nearly the conventional political sense—of a rather shallowly and narrowly conceived democratic culture: a hearty voice at the center of a bustling and progressive republic, a voice that saluted the pioneers, echoed the sound of America singing, itself sang songs of joy that foretold the future union of the nation and the world and the cosmos, chanted the square deific, and wept over the country's captain lying cold and dead on the deck of the ship of state. Other and truer aspects of Whitman continued to exert an appeal, especially in certain lively corners of Europe. But in the English-speaking world, it was primarily the bombastic, or, as his disciples sometimes said, the "cosmic" Whitman that was better known; and it was this Whitman that was either revered or—in most literary circles after the advent of T.S. Eliot—dismissed or simply disregarded.

So much needs to be said: for our first task is to disentangle Whitman, to separate the real from the unpersuasive, to separate the poet from the posture. To do that, we have, first of all, to put Whitman's poems back into their original and chronological order. It might be argued that we have no right to tamper with the poet's own editorial judgment; that *Leaves of Grass* is, after all, Whitman's book and that we are bound to take it in the order and the form he eventually decided on. The answer to this proposition is that there is no satisfactory way around the critical necessity of discriminating among Whitman's successive revisions of his own work, of appealing from the Whitman of 1867 and 1871 and later to the earlier Whitman of 1855 and 1856 and 1860. The dates just named are all dates of various editions of *Leaves of Grass*; and the latter three, the ones we appeal to, are those of the editions in which most (not all) of the real Whitman is to be found. This Whitman is a great and unique figure who is also the recognizable ancestor of many significant poetic developments since his creative prime—from *symboliste* poetry to imagism to more recent neoromantic and, less interestingly, "beat" writing; a chief, though by no means the only, American begetter of Wallace Stevens and Hart Crane, to some extent of Ezra Pound (as he once reluctantly confessed), and to an obscure but genuine degree of T.S. Eliot.

The importance of chronology, in Whitman's case, cannot be exaggerated. Without it, we can have no clear sense of Whitman's development as a consciousness and as a craftsman: an affair of far graver concern with Whitman than with many other poets of his stature. For, as I shall propose, the development of his consciousness and his craft, from moment to moment and year to year, is the very root of his poetic subject matter. It is what his best poems are mainly about, or what they re-enact: the thrust and withdrawal, the heightening and declining, the flowing and ebbing of his psychic and creative energy. Whitman's poetry has to do with the drama of the psyche or "self" in its mobile and complex relation *to* itself, to the world of nature and human objects, and to the creative act. What is attempted here, consequently, is a sort of chart of Whitman's development—in the belief that such a chart is not simply a required preliminary for getting at Whitman, but, rather, that it is the proper way to identify the poetic achievement, and to evaluate it. And in a case like Whitman's, the chart of the development is not finally separable from the graph of the life, or biography; the biographical material, therefore, has likewise been distributed among the successive commentaries on the editions of Whitman's single lifelong book.

I: 1855

When *Leaves of Grass* was published on July 4, 1855, Walt Whitman, now thirty-six years old, was living in Brooklyn, with his parents and brothers, earning an occasional dollar by carpentering. Both his family and his carpentry served as sources of allusion and metaphor in the poetry; but neither—that is, neither his heredity nor his temporary employment—help much to explain how a relatively indolent odd-jobber and sometime journalist named Walter Whitman developed into Walt Whitman the poet. His mother, whom he salutes in "There Was a Child Went Forth" for having "conceiv'd him in her womb and birth'd him" (the birthday being the last day in May 1819; the place, rural Long Island), was of Dutch and Quaker descent, not especially cultivated, and remembered by her son, in the same poem of 1855, as quiet and mild and clean. His father was a farmer of deteriorating fortunes, temper, and health: "manly, mean, anger'd, unjust" in his son's account; and it is a psychological curiosity that the father died within a week of the son's first public appearance, or birth, as a poet. Other members of the family were sources of that compassionate intimacy with the wretched and the depraved reflected, for example; in "Song of Myself":

> *The lunatic is carried at last to the asylum a confirm'd case ...*
> *The prostitute draggles her shawl, her bonnet bobs on her tipsy*
>   *and pimpled neck ...*
> *Voices of the diseas'd and despairing and of thieves and dwarfs.*

Two of Whitman's brothers were diseased, one of them dying eventually in an insane asylum and the other (who was also a drunkard) married to a woman who became a prostitute. Yet another brother was a congenital idiot; and one of Whitman's sisters suffered from severe nervous melancholy. From these surroundings emerged the figure who, in the carpentering imagery of "Song of Myself," felt "sure as the most certain sure, plumb in the uprights, well entretied, braced in the beams"; a figure who not only felt like that but could write like that.

So remarkable and indeed so sudden has the appearance of Whitman the poet seemed, and out of so unlikely and artistically inhospitable a background, that literary historians have been driven to making spectacular guesses about the miraculous cause of it: an intense love affair, for instance, with a Creole lady of high degree; an intense love affair with an unidentified young man; a mystical seizure; the explosive impact of Emerson or of Carlyle or of George Sand. The literary influences can be documented, though they can scarcely be measured; with the other guesses, evidence is inadequate either to support or altogether to discount them. But perhaps the problem itself has not been quite properly shaped. Whitman's poetic emergence was remarkable enough; but it was not in fact particularly sudden. Nor was the career, seen retrospectively, as haphazard and aimless as one might suppose. Looked at from a sufficient distance, Whitman's life shows the same pattern of thrust and withdrawal, advance and retreat, that pulsates so regularly in the very metrics as well as the emotional attitudes of his verses; and to much the same effect. Up to about 1850, when he was thirty-one, Whitman—like the child in the autobiographical poem already quoted—was always going forth, always brushing up against the numberless persons and things of his world, and always *becoming* the elements he touched, as they became part of him. After 1850, he withdrew for a while into the privacies not only of his family but, more importantly, of his own imagination, in touch now with what he called the "Me myself"—his genius, or muse. It was this latter union between man and muse that, by 1855, produced the most extraordinary first volume of poems this country has so far seen.

One of the things Whitman did not become was a scholar, or even a college graduate. His school days, all spent in the Brooklyn to which his family moved in 1823, ended when he was eleven. Thereafter he was apprenticed as a typesetter for a Long Island newspaper; and characteristically, the boy not only worked at the job, he *became* a typesetter, and typesetting became a part of his imagination. The look of a printed page and the rhetoric of punctuation were integral elements in his poetry—the printing of which he actually set with his own hands or carefully supervised. Between 1831 and 1836, Whitman occasionally wrote articles as well as set type for the paper; and he continued to compose fugitive little pieces from time to time during the five years following, from 1836 to 1841, while he was teaching in a variety of schools in a variety of Long Island villages. Writing, too, became part of him; and Whitman became a writer—at least by intention, announcing very firmly in a newspaper article of 1840, that he "would compose a wonderful and ponderous book ... [treating] the nature and peculiarities of men, the diversities of their characters.... Yes: I *would* write a book! And who shall say that it might not be a very pretty book?"

In 1841, Whitman moved into New York City, where he was absorbed especially by what he called "the fascinating chaos" of lower Broadway, and by the life of saloons and theaters, of operas and art museums.[1] Operatic techniques and museum lore went into his later verses; but what Whitman became at this stage was that elegant stroller, or *boulevardier*, known as a dandy. This role persisted during the five years passed as reporter for a number of New York newspapers; and even after he returned to Brooklyn in 1846 and became editor of the *Eagle*, he came back by ferry to stroll Manhattan on most afternoons. But he was a dandy much caught up in public and political affairs. Among the personae he took on was that of the political activist, an ardent Freesoiler in fact, arguing the exclusion of Negro slavery from the territories with such editorial vehemence that the newspaper's owner fired him in February 1848. Within a matter of days, however, Whitman left for what turned out to be a three-month stay in New Orleans, where he served its assistant editor to that city's *Crescent*. It was there that rumor once assigned him the affair with the Creole lady, that soul-turning initiation into love that is said to have made a poet of him. The legend is almost certainly baseless; but something did happen to Whitman nonetheless. During the long weeks of travel, passing over the vast stretches of land and along the great rivers and the lakes (all that "geography and natural life" he catalogues so lavishly in the 1855 Preface), Whitman had his first encounter with the national landscape, and became (it may be hazarded) another of the personalities announced in *Leaves of Grass*: an American.

Back in Brooklyn, Whitman accepted the post of editor-in-chief on the liberal *Freeman* and stayed with it till he resigned in political outrage the following year. He had clearly "become" a journalist, an uncommonly able and effective one; his best poetry sprang in good part from a journalistic imagination—"I witness the corpse with its dabbled hair, I note where the pistol has fallen." At the same time, the forthgoing impulse was nearly—for the moment—exhausted. After expressing his sense of both national and personal betrayal by the Fugitive Slave Law in 1850, Whitman withdrew from the political arena; withdrew from active or regular journalism, and from the life of the city. He moved back to his family and commenced a leisurely existence in which, according to his brother George, "he would lie abed late, and after getting up would write a few hours if he took the notion"—or work at "house-building" for a bit, with his father and brothers, if he took that notion. Now he became a workman; and it was in the role of working-class artisan that he presented himself both in the verses of the 1855 *Leaves of Grass* and in the portrait which appeared as substitute for the author's name in the front of the volume.

For Whitman, I am suggesting, the act of becoming a poet was not a sudden or an unpredictable one. He had always been in process of becoming a poet, and the figures he successively became, from his school days onward, were not false starts or diversions, but moments in the major process. Typesetter, reporter, dandy, stroller in the city, political activist, surveyor of the national scenery, skilled editor, representative American workman: none of these was ever fully replaced by any other, nor were all at last replaced by the poet. They were absorbed into the poet; and if they do not explain the appearance of genius (nothing can explain that), they explain to some real degree the kind of writing—observant, ambulatory, varied, politically aware, job-conscious—in which *this* particular genius expressed itself.

Signs and symptoms of the poet proper, however, can also be isolated over a good many years. The determination to write a "wonderful" book, in 1840, has already been mentioned; but that was presumably to be a philosophical disquisition in prose. In the early 1840s, the writer-in-general became a writer of fiction, and Whitman contributed a number of moralistic short stories to different New York periodicals, all signed by "Walter Whitman" and none worth remembering. Not much later than that, certainly not later than 1847, Whitman's aspiration turned toward poetry. He began to carry a pocket-size notebook about with him; in this he would jot down topics for poems as they occurred, experimental lines, and trial workings of new metrical techniques. The process was stepped up from 1850 onward. In June 1850, the New York *Tribune* published two free-verse poems by Whitman, the second—later called "Europe: The 72d and 73d Year of These States," on the uprisings of 1848—to be included as the eighth item in the 1855 *Leaves of Grass*. It was probably in 1852 that he composed, though he did not publish, a fairly long poem called "Pictures," which had everything characteristic of his genuine poetry except its maritime movement. And in 1854, the repeal of the Missouri Compromise, and the arrest in Boston of a runaway slave named Anthony Bums, drew from Whitman a forty-line satiric exclamation that would comprise the ninth poem in the first edition—later called "A Boston Ballad."

These creative forays were increasingly stimulated by Whitman's reading, which was not only wide but, as evidence shows, surprisingly careful. He had reviewed works by Carlyle, George Sand, Emerson, Goethe, and others for the Brooklyn *Eagle*. He had known Greek and Roman literature, in translation, for years. "I have wonder'd since," he remarked in *A Backward Glance* (1888), "why I was not overwhelm'd by these mighty masters. Likely because I read them ... in the full presence of Nature, under the sun ... [with] the sea rolling in." (The comment suggests much of the quality of Whitman's poetry, wherein a natural atmosphere and sea rhythms help provide fresh versions of ancient and traditional archetypes.) It should be stressed that Whitman's literary education at this time, though it was by no means skimpy, was fairly conventional. It included the major English poets, Shakespeare and Milton especially, but it did not include Oriental writing or the literature of the mystical tradition or that of German idealism—except as those sources reached him faintly through his occasional readings in the essays of Emerson. This is probably to be reckoned fortunate: Whitman's mystical instinct, during his best creative years, was held effectively in check by a passion for the concrete, a commitment to the actual; and discussion of his "mysticism" is well advised to follow his example. Whitman became acquainted, too, with such American writers as Longfellow and Bryant, both of whom he came later to know personally. In addition, he took to making extensive notes and summaries of a long list of periodical essays, mostly dealing with art and artists.

"Art and Artists," in fact, was the title of an essay which Whitman himself read to the Brooklyn Art Union in 1851. And it was here that he first developed his large notion of the artist as hero—of the artist, indeed, as savior or redeemer of the community to which he offers his whole being as champion (sacrificial, if necessary) of freedom and humanity and spiritual health. "Read well the death of Socrates," he said portentously, "and of greater than Socrates." The image of the modern poet as godlike—even Christlike ("greater than Socrates")—was to run through and beneath Whitman's poetry from "Song of Myself" to "Passage to India"; and often, as here, it drew added intensity from Whitman's disillusion with other possible sources for that miraculous national transformation scene he seems to have waited for during most of his life. It was an extravagant notion; but it was one that anticipated several not much less extravagant images, in the twentieth century, of the artist as hero. It was this image, anyhow, that Whitman sought to bring into play in the whole body of the 1855 *Leaves of Grass* and particularly in "Song of Myself."

The first edition contained a long Preface introducing the poet-hero, who is then imaginatively created in the poems that follow. There were twelve of the latter, unnumbered and untitled and of varying length, with unconventional but effective typography—for example:

> *The atmosphere is not a perfume .... it has no taste of the*
> *   distillation .... it is odorless,*
> *It is for my mouth forever.... I am in love with it.*

The first and by far the longest entry was, of course, the poem that in 1881 was labeled "Song of Myself." It is in part genuine though highly original autobiography; in part, it is a form of wish projection. We may think of it, among many other things, as a free-flowing recapitulation of the two processes I have been describing—the process by which a man of many roles becomes a poet, and the process by which the poet becomes a sort of god. There are as many significant aspects to "Song of Myself" as there are critical discussions and analyses of it; if the comment here is mainly limited to the enlargement of its central figure—that is, to the question of its structure—it is because the structure tends to confirm one's sense of Whitman's characteristic movement both in life and in poetry. For if, again, this strange, sometimes baffling, stream-of-consciousness poem does have a discernible structure, an "action" with a beginning, middle, and end, it is almost certainly one that involves the two events or processes just named.

More than one astute reader, while acknowledging a typical pulse or rhythm in the poem, a tidal ebb and flow, has nonetheless denied to it any sustained and completed design. But it may be ventured, perhaps, that "Song of Myself" has not so much a single structure as a number of provisional structures—partly because Whitman, like Melville, believed in a deliberate absence of finish in a work of art; more importantly because of what we may call Whitman's democratic aesthetic. Just as the political activist was absorbed into the poet at some time after 1850, so, and at the same moment, a practical concern with the workings of a democratic society was carried over into the aesthetic realm and applied to the workings of poetry, to the writing and the reading of it. The shape of "Song of Myself" depended, in Whitman's view, on the creative participation of each reader—"I round and finish little," he remarked in *A Backward Glance*, "the reader will always have his or her part to do, just as much as I have had mine." In a real sense, the poem was intended to have as many structures as there were readers; and the reason was that Whitman aimed not simply to create a poet and then a god, but to assist at the creation of the poetic and godlike in every reader.

Like Emerson, Whitman was here giving a democratic twist to the European Romantic notion of the poet as mankind's loftiest figure. For both Emerson and Whitman the poet's superiority lay exactly in his representativeness. "The poet is representative," Emerson had said, in his essay "The Poet." "He stands among partial men for the complete man, and apprises us not of his wealth, but of the common wealth." This is what Whitman meant when he spoke of "the great poet" as "the equable man"; and it is what he asserted in the opening lines of "Song of Myself":

> *I celebrate myself and sing myself*
> *And what I assume you shall assume.*

As one or two commentators—notably Roy Harvey Pearce[2]—have rightly suggested, "Song of Myself" is the first recognizable American epic; but, if so, it is an epic of this peculiar and modern sort. It does not celebrate a hero and an action of ancient days; it creates (and its action is creative) a hero of future days—trusting thereby to summon the heroism implicit in each individual.

Considered in these terms, as the epic consequence of a democratic aesthetic, "Song of Myself" shows a variable number of structural parts. This reader discovers but does not insist upon the following. The invocation leads, in Sections 1 and 2, into a transition from the artificial to the natural—from perfume in houses to the atmosphere of the woods; uncontaminated nature is the first scene of the drama. Next comes the recollection of the union—mystical in kind, sexual in idiom—between the two dimensions of the poet's being: the limited, conditioned Whitman and the "Me, myself," his creative genius, what Emerson might have called the Over-Soul. This was the union that was consummated somehow and sometime in the early 1850s, and out of which there issued the poem in which the union was itself reenacted.

There follows a long portion, continuing at least through Section 17, where—as a result of union—the *man* becomes a *poet*, and by the very act of creation. What is created is a world, an abundant world of persons and places and things—all sprung into existence by the action of seeing and naming:

> *The little one sleeps in its cradle,*
> *I lift the gauze and look a long time ...*
> *The suicide sprawls on the bloody floor of the bedroom,*
> *I witness the corpse with its dabbled hair ...*
> *Where are you off to, lady? for I see you.*

The democratic aesthetic is most palpably at work here. What we take at first to be sheer disorder, what some early reviewers regarded as simple slovenliness and lack of form, is in fact something rather different. It is the representation of moral and spiritual and aesthetic equality; of a world carefully devoid of rank or hierarchy. In "Song of Myself," this principle of moral equivalence is not so much stated as "suggested" (one of Whitman's favorite words), and suggested by "indirection" (another favorite word)—by the artfully casual juxtaposition of normally unrelated and unrelatable elements, a controlled flow of associations.[3] Thus:

> *The prostitute draggles her shawl, her bonnet bobs on her tipsy*
> *   and pimpled neck ...*
> *The President holding a cabinet council is surrounded by the*
> *   great Secretaries,*
> *On the piazza walk three matrons stately and friendly with*
> *   twined arms,*
> *The crew of the fish-smack pack repeated layers of halibut in*
> *   the hold,*
> *The Missourian crosses the plains toting his wares and his*
> *   cattle*

and so on. In the 1855 Preface, Whitman was willing to make the case explicit: "Each precise object or condition or combination or process exhibits a beauty." And he there illustrated the idea in a succession of still more surprising incongruities: "the multiplication table .... old age .... the carpenter's trade .... the grand-opera."

When, therefore, toward the end of this phase of the poem, the speaker begins to claim for himself the gradually achieved role of poet, it is as the poet of every mode of equality that he particularly wishes to be acknowledged. The announcement runs through Section 25:

> *I play not marches for accepted victors only, I play marches*
> *   for conquer'd and slain persons ...*
> *I am the poet of the Body, and I am the poet of the Soul....*
> *I am the poet of the woman the same as the man ...*
> *I am not the poet of goodness only, I do not decline to be the*
> *   poet of wickedness also.*

The *poet* now makes ready for the second great adventure, the long journey, as we may say, toward *godhood*. By way of preparation, he undergoes a second ecstatic experience in Sections 26 and following: an experience of an almost overpoweringly sensuous kind, with the sense of touch so keen as to endanger his health or his sanity: "You villain touch! .... you are too much for me." The poet survives, and in Section 33 he is "afoot with [his] vision." In the visionary flight across the universe that is then recounted, the poet enlarges into a divine being by *becoming* each and every element within the totality that he experiences; while the universe in turn is drawn together into a single and harmonious whole since each element in it is invested in common with a portion of the poet's emergent divinity. It is no longer the prostitute who draggles her shawl, the President who holds a cabinet council, the Missourian who crosses the plain: it is "I" who does all that:

> *I anchor my ship for a little while only ...*
> *I go hunting polar furs and the seal ...*
> *I am the man, I suffer'd, I was there ...*
> *I am the hounded slave, I wince at the bite of dogs.*

And the "I" is itself no longer the individual man-poet; it is the very force or *élan vital* of all humanity.

The journey lasts through Section 33; and in its later moments, as will be noticed, the traveler associates especially with the defeated, the wretched, the wicked, the slaughtered. Whitman's poetic pores were oddly open, as were Melville's, to the grand or archetypal patterns common to the human imagination—so psychologists such as Carl Jung tell us—in all times and places; and the journey of "Song of Myself" requires, at this point, the familiar descent into darkness and hell—until (Section 33) "corpses rise, gashes heal, fastenings roll from me," and an enormous resurrection is accomplished. But what gets reborn, what "troop[s] forth" from the grave is not the poet simply; it is the poet "replenish'd with supreme power," the poet become a divine figure. Just as, by the poetic act of creating a world, the man had previously grown into a poet; so now, by experiencing and, so to speak, melting into the world's totality to its furthest width and darkest depth, the poet expands into a divinity. He has approximated at last that "greater than Socrates" invoked by Whitman in 1851; he has become that saving force which Whitman had proposed was to be the true role of the American poet. It is the divinity who speaks through Sections 39 to 51, proclaiming his divine inheritance ("Taking to myself the exact dimensions of Jehovah," etc.), performing as healer and comforter ("Let the physician and the priest go home"), exhorting every man to his supreme and unique effort. For it is a divinity who insists at every turn that he speaks but for the divine potential of all men. And, having done so, in Section 52 he departs.

Wallace Stevens, the most sophisticated among Whitman's direct poetic descendants, once specified his ancestor's recurrent and dual subject matter in the course of a resonant salute to him in "Like Decorations in a Nigger Cemetery":

> *Walt Whitman walking along a ruddy shore*
> *... singing and chanting the things that are part of him*
> *The worlds that were and will be, death and day.*

"Death and day," with its corollary "life and night," is as apt a phrase as one can think of for the extremes between which Whitman's poetry habitually alternates. "Song of Myself" is Whitman's masterpiece, and perhaps America's, in the poetry of "day"—"the song of me rising from bed and meeting the sun"—while "To Think of Time" or "Burial Poem," as Whitman once called it, belongs initially to the poetry of "death," and "the Sleepers" to the poetry of "night." But although both the latter, in their very different ways, explore in depth the dark undergrounds of experience, both return—as "Song of Myself" does—with the conviction of a sort of absolute life. "I swear I think there is nothing but immortality": so ends the meditation in "To Think of Time." And such is the determining sense everywhere in the 1855 edition; we shall shortly have occasion to contrast it with the sense of things in the edition of 1860. It may be helpful, meanwhile, to glance at the 1855 poem "There Was a Child Went Forth," to see how Whitman's characteristic psychological movement was reflected in his poetic technique—how the shifting play of his consciousness was reflected in the shifting play of his craft.

"There Was a Child Went Forth" is Whitman's most unequivocal account of the thrust toward being. It is a poem about growth, about burgeoning and sprouting; and it grows itself, quite literally, in size and thickness. The difference in the sheer physical or typographical look of the first and last stanzas is an immediate clue to the poem's thematic development. Yet what the poet enacts, on the technical side, is not an altogether uninterrupted increase in substance and vitality. The process is rather one of alternation, of enlarging and retracting, of stretching and shrinking—in which, however, the impulse toward growth is *always* dominant. The quantitatively shrunken fourth stanza, for example, is flanked by the longer eight-line stanza that precedes it and the longest or eighteen-line stanza that follows it and completes the poem's swelling motion: giving us a process in fact of stretching-shrinking-stretching. The same process is present more artfully still within the first stanza, with its rhythmic shift from short line to longer line to still longer and back to shorter once again; but where the line that contains the quantitative shrink is nonetheless a line accentuated by the word "stretching"—"Or for many years or stretching cycles of years." The psychic stretching is thus quietly affirmed at the instant of technical shrinking; and it is the stretching impulse that triumphs and defines the poem.

The same effect is accomplished metrically. "There Was a Child Went Forth" is what is now called free verse; and no doubt the word "free" in this context would have had, had Whitman known the whole term, a political aura, and become a part of his democratic aesthetic. Whitman was the first American poet to break free from the convention of iambic pentameter as the principal and most decorous meter for poetry in English; in so doing he added to the declaration of literary independence—from England, chiefly—that had been triumphantly proclaimed for his generation in Emerson's "The American Scholar" and was the predictable artistic consequence of the political fact. Whitman's was a major gesture of technical liberation, for which every American poet after him has reason to be grateful; every such poet, as William Carlos Williams (a manifest heir of Whitman) has said, must show cause why iambic pentameter is proper for him. But it was not an act of purely negative liberation; it was emancipation with a purpose. It freed Whitman to attempt a closer approximation of metrics and the kind of experience he naturally aimed to express; and it made possible an eventual and occasional return to older and more orderly metrics—to possess them, to use them freshly, to turn them to the poet's established poetic intentions. The long uneven alternations I have been describing could hardly have been conveyed by recurring five- and four-stress lines. Whitman instinctively depended, not on the regular alternating current of the iambic, but on an irregular alternation of *rising* and of *falling* rhythms—which corresponded happily to the rise and fall of the felt life, to the flowing and ebbing—and the rising rhythm, once again, is always in command:

  $\overline{There}$ $\breve{was}$ $\breve{a}$ $\overline{child}$ $\breve{went}$ $\overline{forth}$.

And in the poem's conclusion—when a world and a child have been brought fully to interdependent life—the rhythm settles back in a line that neither rises nor falls; a line that rests in a sort of permanent stillness; a subdued iambic of almost perfectly even stress—a convention repossessed in the last long slow series of monosyllables broken only and rightly by the key words "became," "always," and "every":

> *These became part of that child who went forth every day, and*
> *who now goes, and will always go forth every day.*

It is not possible to invoke the imagery of stretching and shrinking without being reminded of sexual analogies, and thereby of the sexual element so prevalent in Whitman's poetry. That element was notably, even blatantly more central to the 1856 edition—it was about several poems in this edition that Thoreau, otherwise much taken with Whitman, said that "It is as if the beasts spoke"—and it operated most tellingly in 1860. Still, it was evident enough in 1855 to startle sensibilities. "Song of Myself" exhibits a degree of sexual bravado mixed with a trace of sexual nostalgia. But the sexual aspect is more apparent in the poem that inhabits the world where Freud and Jung would look for signs of the sexual impulse—the world of dreams. "The Sleepers"—or "Sleep-Chasings," according to its 1860 title—is not only a poem of night and death—"I wander all night in my visions ... the white features of corpses"—it is a poem of profound psychic disturbance, as the speaker makes clear at once in a superb line that gained force from the 1855 typography: "Wandering and confused .... lost to myself .... ill-assorted .... contradictory." A portion of sexual shame contributes to the uncertainty and deepens the sense of tenor—the terror, as Richard Chase has usefully hazarded, of the ego, or conscious self, confronting the id, or the unconscious, and being threatened by extinction.[4] But, in the manner typical of the first *Leaves of Grass*, the poem moves to the discovery of solace amid fear, of pattern amid the random. Descending through the planes of night, "The Sleepers" encounters in its own heart of darkness sources of maternal comfort and spiritual revelation. Guilt is transcended and harmony restored. The adjectives of the opening stanza—"wandering and confused, lost to myself, ill-assorted, contradictory"—are matched and overcome by the adjectives of the poem's close: "sane," "relieved," "resumed," "free," "supple," "awake." There has occurred what Jung would call the "reintegration of the personality"; the ill-assorted psyche has become whole again after passing through what Jung would also call the "night journey." In "The Sleepers," Whitman displayed once more his remarkable talent for arriving by intuition at the great archetypes. And the night journey concludes in that confident recovery of day, that perfect reconciliation with night, that is the distinctive mark of the edition of 1855.

II: 1856

The second edition of *Leaves of Grass* appeared in June 1856, less than a year after the first. There had been several more printings of the latter; and, indeed, during the intervening months Whitman was mainly occupied with the new printings and with reading—and writing—reviews of his work. He still lived with his family in Brooklyn, but he had virtually given up any practical employment. He had "no business," as his mother told Bronson Alcott, "but going out and coming in to eat, drink, write and sleep."[5] The same visitor from Concord quoted Whitman himself as saying that he only "lived to make pomes." Over the months he had made twenty new ones, and included them all in the considerably expanded second edition.

Conventional norms of printing crept back a little into this edition. All the poems, old and new, were now numbered and given titles, the new poems always including the word "poem"—a word that obviously had a magical power for Whitman at the time. Among the poems added were: "Poem of Wonder at the Resurrection of Wheat" to be known more tamely as "This Compost"; "Bunch poem"—later "Spontaneous Me"; and "Sundown Poem" later "Crossing Brooklyn Ferry." The physical appearance of the poems had also become a trifle more conventional, as the eccentric but effective use of multiple dots was abandoned in favor of semicolons and commas. The poetry lost thereby its vivid impression of sistole and diastole, of speech and silence, of utterance and pause, always so close to Whitman's psychic and artistic intention: for example, "I am the man .... I suffered .... I was there" gets crowded together by punctuation and contraction into "I am the man, I suffer'd, I was there." But the earlier mode of punctuation might well have become exceedingly tiresome; and Whitman, in any event, had arrived at that necessary combination of originality and convention by which the most vigorous of talents always perpetuates itself.

For the rest, the new poems dilate upon the determining theme and emotion of the first edition. There is still the awareness of evil, both general and personal: "I am he *who* knew what it was to be evil / ... Had guile, anger, lust, hot wishes I dared not speak / ... the wolf, the snake, the hog, not wanting in me" (an unmistakable and highly suggestive borrowing from *King Lear*, III.iv.87 ff.—Whitman drew more on literary sources than he or his critics have normally admitted). There is even a fleeting doubt of his own abilities—"The best I had done seem'd to me blank and suspicious"—a note that would become primary in the 1850 edition. But by and large the compelling emotion is one of unimpeded creative fertility, of irresistible forward-thrusting energy. It registers the enormous excitement of the discovered vocation and of its miracle-making nature: Whitman's response to the experience of having published his first volume and to the headiest of the reviews of the book. Contrary to some reports, including Whitman's forgetful old-age account, the first edition had a reasonably good sale; and among the many reviews in America and England, some were admiring, some were acutely perceptive, and one or two were downright reverential and spoke of Whitman as almost that "greater than Socrates" he had been hoping to become. Much the most stirring for Whitman, of course, was the famous letter from Emerson, which found *Leaves of Grass* "the most extraordinary piece of wit and wisdom that America has yet contributed," with "incomparable things said incomparably well in it." One sentence from this letter—and without Emerson's permission—adorned the back cover of the 1856 edition: "I greet you at the beginning of a great career."

The tone of the new poems, consequently, was one of achieved and boundless fertility. This is the poetry of day and the poetry of unending flow. The feeling, indeed, is so large and intense as to produce a sense of profound awe: a sense, almost, of terror. That sense arises from Whitman's convinced and total association of his own fecundity ("Spontaneous Me") with that of nature at large ("This Compost"), an association itself enough to intoxicate one. It arises, too, from Whitman's startling view that the creative accomplishment—of the man-poet and of nature—issues from something superficially ugly or shameful or diseased or dead. "Spontaneous Me" mingles two kinds of poems: those that result from the artistic act and those that are involved with the physical act. The act of love, the expression of sexual energy, whether metaphorical or physical, whether heterosexual or homosexual, carries with it a sweeping sensation of shame ("the young man all color'd, red, ashamed, angry"). But the experience fulfills itself in triumph and pride, just as Whitman had deliberately expanded the erotic dimension of the new volume in triumph and pride; it leads to a great "oath of procreation," procreation in every sort; it ends in a full consciousness of wholesome abundance. In much the same way, nature, in "This Compost," reproduces life each spring out of the rotting earth: "Every spear of grass rises out of what was once a catching disease." The conduct of nature—creating life out of death, health out of sickness, beauty out of foulness, "sweet things out of such corruption"—provided Whitman with an example, an analogy to his own creative experience, so immense as to terrify him.

The terror, needless to say, did not disempower but electrified him. The most far-ranging and beautiful of the new poems, "Crossing Brooklyn Ferry," shows Whitman writing under the full force of his assurance—of his assured identification with the *élan vital* of all things. The interplay of the self and the large world it thrusts forward into is on a scale not unlike that of "Song of Myself"; the flow of the consciousness merges with the flow of reality. Every item encountered is a "dumb beautiful minister" to Whitman's responsive spirit; all the items in the universe are "glories strung like beads on my smallest sights and hearings." The complex of natural and human and created objects now forms a sort of glowing totality that is always in movement, always frolicking on. "Crossing Brooklyn Ferry" presents a vision of an entirety moving forward: a vision that is mystical in its sense of oneness but that is rendered in the most palpable and concrete language— the actual picture of the harbor is astonishingly alive and visible. And the poem goes beyond its jubilant cry of the soul—"Flow on river!"—to reach a peace that really does surpass any normal understanding. Whitman was to write poetry no less consummate; but he was never again to attain so final a peak of creative and visionary intoxication.

III: 1860

Whitman, as we have heard his mother saying, was always "going out and coming in." She meant quite literally that her son would go out of the house in the morning, often to travel on the ferry to Manhattan and to absorb the spectacle of life, and would come back into the household to eat and sleep, perhaps to write. But she unwittingly gave a nice maternal formula to the larger, recurring pattern in Whitman's career—the foray into the world and the retreat back into himself and into a creative communion with his genius. The poetry he came in to write—through the 1856 edition just examined— reflected that pattern in content and rhythm, and in a way to celebrate the commanding power of the outward and forward movement. The early poetry bore witness as well, to be sure, of the darker mode of withdrawal, the descent into the abysses of doubt, self-distrust, and the death-consciousness; but it was invariably overcome in a burst of visionary renewal. The poetry of 1855 and 1856 is the poetry of day, of flood tide.

The 1860 *Leaves of Grass*, however, gives voice to genuine desolation. In it, betimes, the self appears as shrunken, indeed as fragmented; the psyche as dying; the creative vigor as dissipated. The most striking of the new poems belong to the poetry not of day but of death. A suggestive and immediate verbal sign of the new atmosphere may be found in the difference of title between so characteristic a poem of 1855 as "There Was a Child Went Forth" and perhaps the key 1860 poem, "As I Ebb'd with the Ocean of Life." Yet the case must be put delicately and by appeal to paradox. For, in a sense, the new death poetry represents in fact Whitman's most remarkable triumph over his strongest feelings of personal and artistic defeat. There has been a scholarly debate over the precise degree of melancholy in the 1860 edition, one scholar emphasizing the note of dejection and another the occasional note of cheerfulness; but that debate is really beside the point. What we have is poetry that expresses the sense of loss so sharply and vividly that substantive loss is converted into artistic gain.

During the almost four years since June 1856, Whitman had once again gone out and come back in; but this time the withdrawal was compelled by suffering and self-distrust. Whitman's foray into the open world, beginning in the fall of 1856, took the form, first, of a brief new interest in the political scene and, second, of a return to journalism, as editor-in-chief of the Brooklyn *Daily Times* from May 1857 until June 1859. In the morning, he busied himself writing editorials and articles for the newspaper; in the afternoon, he traveled into New York, to saunter along lower Broadway and to sit watchful and silent near or amid the literati who gathered in Pfaff's popular Swiss restaurant in the same neighborhood. In the evening, he continued to write—prolifically: seventy poems, more or less, in the first year after the 1856 edition and probably a few more in the months immediately following. Then there occurred a hiatus: a blank in our knowledge of Whitman's life, and apparently a blank in his creative activity. We cannot say just when the hiatus began—sometime in 1858, one judges. It ended, anyhow, at some time before the publication in the December 1859 issue of the New York *Saturday Press* of a poem called "A Child's Reminiscence," its familiar title being "Out of the Cradle Endlessly Rocking."

On the political side, Whitman's disenchantment was even swifter than usual. The choices offered the American public in the election of 1856—Buchanan, Frémont, and Fillmore—seemed to him false, debased, and meaningless; and he called—in an unpublished pamphlet—for a president who might play the part of "Redeemer." His disappointment with the actual, in short, led as before to an appeal for some "greater than Socrates" to arise in America; and, also as before, Whitman soon turned from the political figure to the *poet*, in fact to himself, to perform the sacred function, asserting in his journal that *Leaves of Grass* was to be "the New Bible." (Not until 1866 would the two aspirations fuse in a poem—"When Lilacs Last in the Dooryard Bloom'd"—that found a new idiom of almost biblical sonority to celebrate death in the person of a Redeemer President, Abraham Lincoln.) Meanwhile, however, Whitman's private and inner life was causing him far more grief and dismay than the public life he had been observing.

A chief cause for Whitman's season of despair, according to most Whitman biographers, was a homosexual love affair during the silent months: an affair that undoubtedly took place, that was the source at once of profound joy and profound guilt, and that, when it ended, left Whitman with a desolating sense of loss. Such poems as "A Hand-Mirror" and "Hours Continuing Long, Sore and Heavy-Hearted" testify with painful clarity both to the guilt and to the subsequent misery of loneliness. At the same time, poems such as "As I Ebb'd with the Ocean of Life" and "So Long!" strike a different and perhaps deeper note of loss: a note, that is, of poetic decline, of the loss not so much of a human loved one but of creative energy—accompanied by a loss of confidence in everything that energy had previously brought into being. There had been a hint of this in "Crossing Brooklyn Ferry" in 1856—"The best I had done seem'd to me blank and suspicious"—but there self-doubt had been washed away in a flood of assurance. Now it had become central and almost resistant to hope. It may be that the fear of artistic sterility was caused by the moral guilt; but it seems no less likely that the artistic apprehension was itself at the root of the despair variously echoed in 1860. If so, the apprehension was probably due to a certain climacteric in Whitman's psychic career—what is called *la crise de quarantaine*, the psychological crisis some men pass through when they reach the age of forty. Whitman was forty in May 1859; and it was in the month after his birthday that he wrote two aggressive and, one cannot but feel, disturbed articles for the Brooklyn *Daily Times*—on prostitution and the right to unmarried sexual love—that resulted in his dismissal from the paper. Characteristically dismissed, Whitman characteristically withdrew. But no doubt the safest guess is that a conjunction of these factors—*la quarantaine*, the temporary but fearful exhaustion of talent after so long a period of fertility, the unhappy love affair—begot the new poems that gave "death and night" their prominence in the 1860 edition.

The edition of 1860 contained 154 poems: which is to say that 122 had been composed since 1856, and of these, as has been said, seventy by the summer of 1857. Most of the other fifty, it can be hazarded, were written late in 1859 and in the first six months of 1860. It can also be hazarded that among those latter fifty poems were nearly all the best of the new ones—those grouped under the title "Calamus," the name Whitman gave to his poetry of masculine love. These include "Scented Herbage," "Hours Continuing," "Whoever You Are," "City of Orgies," "A Glimpse," "I Saw in Louisiana," "Out of the Cradle," "As I Ebb'd" (published in the April 1860 issue of the *Atlantic Monthly* as "Bardic Symbols"), and "So Long!"

"A Hand-Mirror" records a feeling of self-loathing almost unequaled in English or American poetry. And it is representative of the entire volume in its emphatic reversal of an earlier work and an earlier course of feeling. In

"This Compost," in 1856, Whitman was seized with a wonder verging on terror at the capacity of nature and of man to produce the beautiful out of the foul or shameful; here, in 1860, he is smitten with the dreadful conviction of having, in his own being, produced the foul and the shameful out of the potentially beautiful. "Hours Continuing Long, Sore and Heavy-Hearted" is a statement of pain so severe, so unmitigated, that Whitman deleted the poem from all subsequent editions of *Leaves of Grass*. These poems of pain are uncommonly painful to read; and yet, in the other major new poems of 1860, we find Whitman executing what might be called the grand Romantic strategy—the strategy of converting private devastation into artistic achievement; of composing poetry of high distinction out of a feeling of personal, spiritual, and almost metaphysical extinction. Keats's "Ode on a Grecian Urn" offers an example of the same, at one chronological extreme; as, at another, does Hart Crane's "The Broken Tower."

That strategy is, indeed, what the 1860 edition may be said to be about; for more than the other versions of *Leaves of Grass*, that of 1860 has a sort of plot buried in it.[6] The plot—in a very reduced summary—consists in the discovery that "death" is the source and beginning of "poetry"; with "death" here understood to involve several kinds and sensations of loss, of suffering, of disempowering guilt, of psychic fragmentation; and "poetry" as the awakening of the power to catch and to order reality in language. What had so fundamentally changed since 1855 and 1856 was Whitman's concept of reality. In 1855, as we have seen, the thought of death led to a flat denial of it: "I swear I think there is nothing but immortality." But in "Scented Herbage" of 1860 he arrives at an opposite conclusion: "For now," as he says, "it is convey'd to me that you [death] are ... the real reality." If Whitman's poetic faculty had formerly been quickened by his sense of the absolute life, it now finds its inspiration in the adventure of death. In "So Long!" Whitman confesses to the death of his talent: "It appears to me that I am dying.... My songs cease, I abandon them." Yet in "Scented Herbage" poetry is identified as the very herbage and flower of death, as Baudelaire had a few years earlier identified poetry as the flower of evil; his new poems, for Whitman, are "growing up above me above death." By 1860 Whitman had reached the perception of Wallace Stevens—in "Sunday Morning" (1923)—that "death is the mother of beauty."

Stevens' phrase might serve as motto for the 1860 edition; as it might also serve for another of the several titles for the poem that was first called "A Child's Reminiscence," then "A Word Out of the Sea," and finally (in 1871) "Out of the Cradle Endlessly Rocking." Whatever else occurs in this in every sense brilliant poem, there unmistakably occurs the discovery of poetic power, the magical power of the word, through the experience—here presented as vicarious—of the departure and loss, perhaps the death, of the loved one. It is one of the most handsomely made of Whitman's poems; the craft is relaxed, firm, and sure. Only an artist in virtuoso control of his technical resources would attempt a poem with such effortless alternation of narrative (or recitatif) and impassioned aria, such dazzling metrical shifts, such hypnotic exactitude of language, not to mention a narrative "point of view" of almost Jamesian complexity: the man of forty recalling the child of, say, twelve observing the calamitous love affair of two other beings, and the same man of forty projecting, one assumes, his own recent and adult bereavement into the experience of an empathic child. Whitman, by 1860, was very impressively the poet in that word's original meaning of "maker," in addition to being still the poet as inspired singer; and "Out of the Cradle Endlessly Rocking"—for all its supple play of shadows and glancing light— will bear the utmost weight of analysis. But it has perhaps been sufficiently probed elsewhere,[7] and I will instead take a longer look at "As I Ebb'd with the Ocean of Life."

We will not be far wrong, and in any case it will illuminate the pattern of Whitman's career, if we take this poem as an almost systematic inversion of the 1855 poem "There Was a Child Went Forth," as well as an inversion of a key moment—Sections 4 and 5—in the 1855 "Song of Myself." As against that younger Whitman of morning and of spring, of the early lilacs and the red morning-glories, here is the Whitman of the decline of the day and of the year—a poet now found "musing late in the autumn day" (the phrase should be read slowly, as though the chief words were, in the older fashion, divided by dots). All the sprouts and blossoms and fruit of "There Was a Child Went Forth" are here replaced, in the poetically stunning second stanza by:

> *Chaff, straw, splinters of wood, weeds, and the sea-gluten,*
> *Scum, scales from shining rocks, leaves of salt-lettuce, left*
>   *by the tide;*

to which are added, later, "A few sands and dead leaves," "a trail of drift and debris," and finally:

>   *loose windrows, little corpses,*
> *Froth, snowy white, and bubbles,*
> *(See, from my dead lips the ooze exuding at last ....)*

The poem's rhythm, instead of pulsating outward in constantly larger spirals (though it seems to try to do that occasionally), tends to fall back on itself, to fall away, almost to disintegrate; no poem of Whitman's shows a more cunning fusion of technique and content. It is here, quite properly, the falling rather than the rising rhythm that catches the ear. As against:

> *There was a child went forth,*

we now hear:

> *Where the fierce old mother endlessly cries for her castaways*

—a dying fall that conveys the shrinking away, the psychological slide toward death, the slope into oblivion that the poem is otherwise concerned with.

The major turn in the action appears in the grammatical shift from the past tense of Section 1 ("As I ebb'd," etc.) to the present tense of Section 2 ("As I wend," etc.). It is a shift from the known to the unknown, a shift indeed not so much from one moment of time to another as from the temporal to the timeless, and a shift not so much accomplished as desired. For what produces in the poet his feeling of near-death is just his conviction that neither he nor his poetry has ever known or ever touched upon the true and timeless realm of reality. The essential reality from which he now feels he has forever been cut off is rendered as "the real Me." To get the full force of the despondent confession of failure, one should place the lines about "the real Me" next to those in Sections 4 and 5 in "Song of Myself" where Whitman had exultantly recalled the exact opposite. There he had celebrated a perfect union between the actual Me and the real Me: between the here-and-now Whitman and that timeless being, that Over-Soul or genius that he addressed as the Me myself. *That*, I suggest, was Whitman's real love affair; that was the union that was consummated in 1855 and that ended—so Whitman temporarily felt—in disunion three or four years later; "the real Me" was the loved one that departed. And now, divorced and disjoined from the real Me, the actual Me threatens to come apart, to collapse into a trail of drift and debris, with ooze exuding from dead lips. (So, by analogy, a Puritan might have felt when cut off, through sin, from the God that created him.)

Still, as Richard Chase has insisted, this poem is saved from any suggestion of whimpering self-pity by the astonishing and courageous tone of self-mockery—in the image of the real Me ridiculing the collapsing Me:

*before all my arrogant poems the real Me stands yet
    untouch'd, untold, altogether unreach'd,*
*Withdrawn far, mocking me with mock-congratulatory signs
    and bows,*
*With peals of distant ironical laughter at every word I have
    written,*
Pointing in silence to these songs, and then to the sand beneath.

It is an image of immeasurable effect. And it is, so to speak, a triumph over its own content. Anyone who could construct an image of the higher power—the one he aspires toward—standing far off and mocking him with little satiric bows and gestures, comparing and consigning his verses to the sandy debris under his feet: such a person has already conquered his sense of sterility, mastered his fear of spiritual and artistic death, rediscovered his genius, and returned to the fullest poetic authority. Within the poem, Whitman identifies the land as his father and the fierce old sea as his mother; he sees himself as alienated no less from them than from the real Me, and he prays to both symbolic parents for a rejuvenation of his poetic force, a resumption of "the secret of the murmuring I envy." But the prayer is already answered in the very language in which it is uttered; Whitman never murmured more beautifully; and this is why, at the depth of his ebbing, Whitman can say, parenthetically, that the flow will return.

IV: 1867

If Whitman, by the spring of 1860, had not been "rescued" by his own internal capacity for resurgence, he would, more than likely, have been rescued anyhow by the enormous public event that began the following April with the outbreak of a national civil war. During the war years, Whitman "went forth" more strenuously than in any other period of his life, and he immersed himself more thoroughly in the activities and sufferings of his fellows. The immediate poetic fruit of the experience was a small, separately published volume of fifty-three new poems, in 1865, called *Drum-Taps*, with a *Sequel to Drum-Taps*—containing "When Lilacs Last in the Dooryard Bloom'd"—tacked on to the original in 1866. Both titles were added as an Appendix to the fourth edition of *Leaves of Grass* in 1867, which otherwise contained only a handful of new poems. Several of Whitman's war poems have a certain lyric strength, either of compassion or of sheer imagistic precision; and the meditation occasioned by the death of Lincoln is among his finest artistic achievements. Nonetheless—and however remarkable and admirable his human performance was during the war—it was in this same period that Whitman the poet began to yield to Whitman the prophet, and what had been most compelling in his poetry to give way to the misrepresentation and concealment that disfigured *Leaves of Grass* over the decades to follow.

Until the last days of 1862, Whitman remained in Brooklyn, formally unemployed, making what he could out of earnings from *Leaves of Grass*, and—once the fighting had started—following the course of the war with the liveliest concern. He was initially very much on the side of the North, which he regarded as the side of freedom, justice, and human dignity. But as time went on, he came to be increasingly on the side of the nation as a whole, more anxious to heal wounds than to inflict them—and this, of course, is what he literally turned to doing in 1863. In December of the previous year, he learned that his younger brother Jeff had been wounded. Whitman journeyed south at once, found his brother recuperating satisfactorily near Falmouth, Virginia, and stayed for eight memorable days among the forward troops in the battle area. It was only eight days, but the spectacle of horror and gallantry of which he was the closest eyewitness had an enduring, almost a conversionary effect upon him. He came back north only as far as Washington; and from that moment until 1867, he spent every free moment in the military hospitals, ministering to the needs of the wounded. He became, in fact, a "wound-dresser," though a dresser primarily of spiritual wounds, bearing gifts, writing letters, comforting, sustaining, exhorting; he became, indeed, the physician-priest with whom, in "Song of Myself," he had associated the figure of the poet.

He made a living in Washington through a series of governmental jobs: as assistant to the deputy paymaster for a while; as clerk in the Indian Bureau—a position from which he was summarily dismissed when the bureau chief read *Leaves of Grass* and pronounced it unpardonably obscene; finally in the office of the Department of Interior. Here he stayed, relatively prosperous and content, until he suffered a partly paralyzing stroke in 1873. It was in the same year that, traveling north, ill and exhausted, he settled almost by accident in Camden, New Jersey, where he lived until his death in 1892.

In short, when Whitman went forth this time, or was drawn forth, into the American world of war, he was drawn not merely into New York City but into the center of the country's national life; to the actual battlefields, to the seat of the nation's political power, to the offices of government, to the hospitals, and into the presence of the men who carried on their bodies the burden of the nation's tragedy. It is not surprising that the outer and public life of the country absorbed most of his energy; it is only regrettable that, as a result, and in the course of time, the solitary singer disappeared into the public bard, into the singer of democracy, of companionship, the singer not of "this compost" but of "these States." This was the figure celebrated by William Douglas O'Connor in a book written as an angry and rhapsodic defense of Whitman at the time of his dismissal from the Indian Bureau; a book which, in its title, provided the phrase which all but smothered the genuine Whitman for almost a century: *The Good Gray Poet* (1866).

There had been a faint but ominous foreshadowing of the good gray poet in the 1860 edition: in the frontispiece, where Whitman appeared for the first time as the brooding, far-gazing prophetic figure; in the first tinkerings with and slight revisions of the earlier poems; and in the group of poems called "Chants Democratic," the volume's major blemish. The 1867 edition had no frontispiece at all; but now the process of revising, deleting, and rearranging was fully at work. A number of the "Calamus" poems on manly love, for example, were removed from *Leaves of Grass* once and for all: those which acknowledged or deplored his erotic attraction to another man—including "Hours Continuing." The sexuality of "Song of Myself" and "The Sleepers" was toned down by deleting in particular the orgasmic imagery in both of them. Much of the bizarre and the frantic was taken out of the 1856 and 1860 poetry, in the interest, as Roger Asselineau has put it, of placing "the accent on the poet-prophet rather than on the lover."[8] In a general way, it was the intense and personal self of Whitman that got shaded over by the new editing that self, in its always rhythmic and sometimes wild oscillations, that was the true source and subject of the true poetry. The private self was reshaped into the public person, and the public stage on which this person chanted and intoned became the major subject of the would-be national bard. Whitman became less and less the original artist singing by indirection of his own psychic advances and retreats; he was becoming and wanted to become the Poet of Democracy. No longer the watchful solitary, he was changing into the Poet of Comradeship.

It should not be assumed that, because these were postures, they were necessarily false or worthless; they were simply uncongenial to Whitman's kind of poetry. In the same year, 1867, that *Leaves of Grass* unveiled the prophet of the democratic culture, Whitman also published in the New York *Galaxy* a prose essay called "Democracy," where he set forth much of the evidence that, a few years later, went into the longer essay "Democratic Vistas"—as cogent and searching an account of the conditions of democracy in America, and of their relation to the life of letters, as any

American has ever written. But what Whitman could do with this material in prose, he could not do effectively in verse. The democratic element in the early poems was, as has been suggested, an aesthetic element. It was part of the very stress and rhythm of the verse, implicit in the poet's way of looking at persons and things, in the principle of equality in his catalogues and the freedom of his meters, in the dynamic of his relation to his readers. Tackling democracy head on in poetry, Whitman became unpersuasive, even boring.

In the same way, Whitman's poems about the actual war were least striking when they were least personal. There is critical disagreement on this point, but in one reader's opinion, Melville wrote far more authentic war poetry because he had what Whitman did not—a powerful sense of history as allegory. In "The Conflict of Convictions," for example, Melville could suggest the thrust and scale of the struggle in a frame of grand tragedy and in a somberly prophetic mode that the aspiring prophet, Whitman, could never approach. Whitman, the man, had entered the public arena, but his muse did not follow him there; and the enduring poems culled from the war are rather of the intimate and lyrical variety—tender reminiscences or crisp little vignettes like "Cavalry Crossing a Ford," where the image is everything.

There appears among these poems, however, like an unexpected giant out of an earlier age, the work that is widely regarded as Whitman's supreme accomplishment: "When Lilacs Last in the Dooryard Bloom'd." This poem does not, in fact, have quite the artistic finality of "As I Ebb'd" or "Out of the Cradle"; or, rather, its finality is more on the surface, where it is asserted, than in the interior and self-completing pulse of the verses. But, like the other two poems just named, "When Lilacs Last in the Dooryard Bloom'd"—a string of words, D. H. Lawrence once said, that mysteriously makes the ear tingle—has to do with the relation between death and poetry. The death of Lincoln provided the occasion, and the emergent grief of an entire nation served as large but distant background. What is enacted in the foreground, however, is what so often summoned up Whitman's most genuine power: the effort to come to terms with profound sorrow by converting that sorrow into poetry. By finding the language of mourning, Whitman found the answer to the challenge of death. By focusing not on the public event but rather on the vibrations of that event vibrations converted into symbols within his private self, Whitman produced one of his masterpieces, and perhaps his last unmistakable one.

V: 1871 AND LATER

The transformation that both Whitman's figure and his work had slowly undergone was acknowledged by Whitman himself in his Preface to the fifth edition of *Leaves of Grass*, which had two identical printings in 1871 and 1872, while Whitman was still in Washington. The earlier editions, he said, had dealt with the "*Democratic Individual*" (the italics are his); in the new edition, he is concerned instead with the "Vast, composite, electric *Democratic Nationality*." It was never clear just what the latter entity amounted to; and in any case, Whitman was not able to make it susceptible to satisfactory poetic expression. It became the subject not of poetry but of oratory and rant—elements that had always been present in Whitman's work but that, for the most part, had hitherto been sweetened by music and, as it were, liquified by verbal sea-drift.

Oratory and rant were unhappily notable even in the most interesting of the new poems added to the 1871 edition, "Passage to India." But the case of "Passage to India" is peculiar. It was stimulated by several public events (including, for one, the opening of the Suez Canal), stimuli usually dangerous for Whitman unless he could instantly personalize them, as here he could not. The poem not only bespeaks the ultimate union of all times and places and peoples but finds in that condition a universal reality; and as Richard Chase has remarked, "Whenever [Whitman] headed for the universal he was headed for trouble." The poem moves swiftly away from the tough entanglements of the concrete that were the vital strength of works as different as "Song of Myself" or "Crossing Brooklyn Ferry" or "As I Ebb'd"; and, arriving at a realm of bodiless vapor, Whitman can only utter such bodiless lines as: "the past—the infinite greatness of the past!"—which is an exclamation without content. Yet "Passage to India" is interesting, because, while providing an example of Whitman's bombast, it is also technically most accomplished. It completes a kind of parabola of Whitman's craftsmanship: from 1855, where consciousness and craft were discovering each other; through 1856 and 1860, where power and technique were very closely fused; to the later sixties, where technique almost superseded content. The technique in question is primarily a manipulation of sound patterns, something too involved to be analyzed here in detail: an extremely skillful distribution of sheer sounds, without any regard for substance. "Passage to India" is interesting too, by way of historical footnote, for the obsessive effect it was to have more than fifty years later on Hart Crane. It virtually supplied the initiating force for *The Bridge*, especially for the "Atlantis" section, the first portion of his symbolist epic that Crane composed.

Whitman spent the last nineteen years of his life in Camden, New Jersey. He made a partial recovery from the stroke of 1873, but then suffered further seizures from time to time until the one that carried him off. In between these bouts, he continued to "go out" as much as he could: to nearby Philadelphia frequently, to Baltimore and Washington, to New York, and once—in 1879—to Kansas, Colorado, and Canada. Otherwise he remained in Camden, writing short and generally trivial poems, a great amount of prose, and countless letters to friends and admirers all over the world. His old age was punctuated by a series of controversies about him in the public press: in 1876, for example, when a clamor from England to raise a subscription for Whitman was countered by a verbal assault upon him in the New York *Tribune* by Bayard Taylor. The charge was almost always obscenity; in the instance mentioned, the charge only aroused the English to greater efforts, and Whitman was so encouraged as to feel, in his own word, "saved" by the contributions then and later—of Rossetti, Tennyson, Ruskin, Gosse, Saintsbury, and others. Longfellow and Oscar Wilde, old Dr. Holmes and Henry James, Sr., were among the visitors to his Camden home. He became the genius of the city; and his birthday became an annual celebration. It was amid such flurries of support and defamation, idolatry and contempt, that the old man—cheerful and garrulous to the end— succumbed at last to a horde of diseases that would have killed most men many years sooner.

Whitman *was*, as M. Asselineau says of him, a "heroic invalid." But it may be that his physical and psychological heroism as a man was what produced, by overcompensating for the terrible discomforts he felt, the relentless optimism of so much of his writing in the last two decades— optimism not only about himself and his condition, but about America and about history: for which and in which every disaster, every betrayal was seen by Whitman as a moment in the irresistible progress of things toward the better. The "word signs" of his poetry after 1867 became, as Whitman himself remarked in *A Backward Glance O'er Travel'd Roads* (1888), "Good Cheer, Content and Hope," along with "Comradeship for all lands." Those were also the words that fixed and froze the popular understanding of the poet.

Mention of *A Backward Glance*, however, reminds one that Whitman's most valuable work after 1867 tended to be in prose rather than in verse. The sixth edition of *Leaves of Grass*, printed in 1876 and called the "Centennial Edition" (America's centennial—America now being Whitman's subject), added almost no significant new poetry; but it did include the remarkable essay "Democratic Vistas." The latter poises a noble emphasis upon individual integrity against the moral squalor of a society that was already an impossible mixture of chaos and conformity; and in its plea for "national original archetypes in literature" that will truly "put the nation in form," it presents one of the great statements about the relation between art and culture. The next or seventh edition, that of 1881–82, contained the fine little image of the copulative collision of two eagles—an image based on a written description of such an event by Whitman's friend John Burroughs—and a poem that, with two others, gave cause for the suppression of the entire volume, following a complaint by the Society for the Prevention of Vice. But this edition was also characterized by endless revisions and expurgations and, now especially, regroupings of earlier poems: the process whereby the old man steadily buried his youth. In the same year, though, Whitman also published a separate volume of prose: *Specimen Days and Collect*. In it, along with *Specimen Days* and the several indispensable prefaces to *Leaves of Grass*, were "Democratic Vistas," Civil War reminiscences, and Whitman's annual lecture on Lincoln. *A Backward Glance* first appeared in 1888; the following year it served as the Preface to, and was the one memorable new piece of writing in, the *Leaves of Grass* of 1889.

Though it is indeed memorable and even beguiling, *A Backward Glance* is also somewhat misleading. The real motivations and the actual achievement of *Leaves of Grass* lie half-forgotten behind the comradeship, good cheer, and democratic enthusiasm of the ailing elderly bard. Like F. Scott Fitzgerald, Whitman could have said, though one cannot imagine him doing so, that he had found his proper form at a certain moment in his career, but that he had then been diverted into other forms, other endeavors less appropriate to his talent. The fact that it was in these other forms that Whitman's reputation got established make the development more lamentable. At his best, Whitman was not really the bard of the democratic society at all; nor was he the prophet of the country's and the world's glorious future. He was, perhaps, the poet of an aesthetic and moral democracy. But he was above all the poet of the self and of the self's swaying motion—outward into a teeming world where objects were "strung like beads of glory" on his sight; backward into private communion with the "real Me." He was the poet of the self's motion downward into the abysses of darkness and guilt and pain and isolation, and upward to the creative act in which darkness was transmuted into beauty. When the self became lost to the world, Whitman was lost for poetry. But before that happened, Whitman had, in his own example, made poetry possible in America.

NOTES

1. Of special importance to Whitman were the Brooklyn Art Union, established by a group of Brooklyn painters about 1850, and the Egyptian Museum at 629 Broadway, in Manhattan. Whitman wrote an article about the former for the *New York Evening Post* in February 1851; he was personally acquainted with several of the younger painters involved, and he was particularly observant of their techniques for handling light and color. Through visits to the Egyptian Museum, meanwhile, and through considerable study under the supervision of his friend, the Museum's proprietor, Dr. Abbot, Whitman became remarkably well versed in Egyptology—allusions drawn from which are frequent and suggestive in *Leaves of Grass*.

2. *The Continuity of American Poetry* (Princeton, N.J., 1961), especially pp. 59–82.

3. Cf. the essay on Whitman by David Daiches in *The Young Rebel in American Literature*, ed. Carl Bode (New York, 1960).

4. *Walt Whitman Reconsidered* (New York, 1955), pp. 54–57.

5. Roger Asselineau, *The Evolution of Walt Whitman* (New York, 1960), pp. 92–93.

6. See the Facsimile Edition of the 1860 text, edited with an introduction by Roy Harvey Pearce (Ithaca, N.Y., 1961).

7. For example, in the four essays by Stephen E. Whicher, Paul Fussell, Jr., Richard Chase, and Roy Harvey Pearce contained in *The Presence of Walt Whitman*, ed. R. W. B. Lewis (New York, 1962).

8. *The Evolution of Walt Whitman*, p. 196.

HAROLD BLOOM

Whitman's Image of Voice:
To the Tally of My Soul

W here does the individual accent of an American poetry begin? How, then and now, do we recognize the distinctive voice that we associate with an American Muse? Bryant, addressing some admonitory lines, in 1830, *To Cole, the Painter, Departing for Europe*, has no doubts as to what marks the American difference:

> Fair scenes shall greet thee where thou goest—fair,
>   But different—everywhere the trace of men,
> To where life shrinks from the fierce Alpine air.
>   Gaze on them, till the tears shall dim thy sight,
>   But keep that earlier, wilder image bright.

Only the Sublime, from which life shrinks, constitutes a European escape from the trace of men. Cole will be moved by that Sublime, yet he is to keep vivid the image of priority, an American image of freedom, for which Emerson and Thoreau, like Bryant before them, will prefer the trope of "wildness." The wildness triumphs throughout Bryant, a superb poet, always and still undervalued, and one of Hart Crane's and Wallace Stevens's legitimate ancestors. The voice of an American poetry goes back before Bryant, and can be heard in Bradstreet and Freneau (not so much, I think, in

From *Agon: Towards a Theory of Revisionism*. © 1982 by Oxford University Press, Inc.

Edward Taylor, who was a good English poet who happened to be living in America). Perhaps, as with all origins, the American poetic voice cannot be traced; and so I move from my first to my second opening question: how to recognize the Muse of America. Here is Bryant, in the strong opening of his poem *The Prairies*, in 1833:

> These are the gardens of the Desert, these
> The unshorn fields, boundless and beautiful,
> For which the speech of England has no name—
> The Prairies. I behold them for the first
> And my heart swells, while the dilated sight
> Takes in the encircling vastness....

Bryant's ecstatic beholding has little to do with what he sees. His speech swells most fully as he intones "The Prairies," following on the prideful reflection that no English poet could name these grasslands. The reflection itself is a touch awkward, since the word after all is French, and not Amerindian, as Bryant knew. No matter; the beholding is still there, and truly the name is little more important than the sight. What is vital is the dilation of the sight, an encircling vastness more comprehensive even than the immensity being taken in, for it is only a New England hop, skip and a jump from this dilation to the most American passage that will ever be written, more American even than Huck Finn telling Aunt Polly that he lies just to keep in practice, or Ahab proclaiming that he would strike the sun if it insulted him. Reverently I march back to where I and the rest of us have been before and always must be again, crossing a bare common, in snow puddles, at twilight, under a clouded sky, in the company of our benign father, the Sage of Concord, teacher of that perfect exhilaration, in which, with him, we are glad to the brink of fear:

> ... Standing on the bare ground,—my head bathed by the blithe
> air and uplifted into infinite space,—all mean egotism vanishes. I
> become a transparent eyeball; I am nothing; I see all; the currents
> of the Universal Being circulate through me; I am part or parcel
> of God....

Why is this, ecstasy followed directly by the assertion: "The name of the nearest friend sounds then foreign and accidental ..."? Why does the dilation of vision to the outrageous point of becoming a transparent eyeball provoke a denaturing of even the nearest name? I hasten to enforce the obvious, which nevertheless is crucial: the name is not forgotten, but loses the sound of immediacy; it becomes foreign or out-of-doors, rather than domestic; and accidental, rather than essential. A step beyond this into the American Sublime, and you do not even forget the name; you never hear it at all:

> And now at last the highest truth on this subject remains unsaid; probably cannot be said; for all that we say is the far-off remembering of the intuition. That thought by what I can now nearest approach to say it, is this. When good is near you, when you have life in, yourself, it is not by any known or accustomed way; you shall not discern the footprints of any other; you shall not see the face of man; you shall not hear any name;—the way, the thought, the good, shall be wholly strange and new...

"This subject" is self-reliance, and the highest truth on it would appear to be voiceless, except that Emerson's voice does speak out to tell us of the influx of the Newness, in which no footprints or faces are to be seen; and no name is to be heard. Unnaming always has been a major mode in poetry, far more than naming; perhaps there cannot be a poetic naming that is not founded upon an unnaming. I want to leap from these prose unnamings in Emerson, so problematic in their possibilities, to the poem in which, more than any other, I would seek to hear Emerson's proper voice for once in verse, a "voice present triumphantly in so many hundreds of passages throughout his prose:

> Pour, Bacchus! the remembering wine;
> Retrieve the loss of me and mine!
> Vine for vine be antidote,
> And the grape requite the love!
> Haste to cure the old despair,—
> Reason in Nature's lotus drenched,
> The memory of ages quenched;
> Give them again to shine;
> Let wine repair what this undid;
> And where the infection slid,
> A dazzling memory revive;
> Refresh the faded tints,
> Recut the aged prints,
> And write my old adventures with the pen
> Which on the first day drew,

Upon the tablets blue,
The dancing Pleiads and eternal men.

But why is Bacchus named here, if you shall not hear any name? My
question would be wholly hilarious if we were to literalize Emerson's splendid
chant. Visualize the Sage of Concord, gaunt and spare, uncorking a bottle in
Dionysiac abandon, before emulating the Pleiads by breaking into a
Nietzschean dance. No, the Bacchus of Ralph Waldo is rather clearly another
unnaming. As for voice, it is palpably absent from this grand passage, its place
taken up not even by writing, but by rewriting, by that revisionary pen which
has priority, and which drew before the tablets darkened and grew small.

I am going to suggest shortly that rewriting is an invariable trope for
voicing, within a poem, and that voicing and reseeing are much the same
poetic process, a process reliant upon unnaming, which rhetorically means
the undoing of a prior metonymy. But first I am going to leap ahead again,
from Emerson to Stevens, which is to pass over the great impasse of
Whitman, with whom I have identified always Hart Crane's great trope:
"Oval encyclicals in canyons heaping / The impasse high with choir." Soon
enough this discourse will center upon Whitman, since quite simply he is the
American Sublime, he is voice in our poetry, he is our answer to the
Continent now, precisely as he was a century ago. Yet I am sneaking up on
him, always the best way for any critic to skulk near the Sublime Walt. His
revisionism, of self as of others, is very subtle; his unnamings and his voices
come out of the Great Deep. Stevens's are more transparent:

Throw away the lights, the definitions,
And say of what you see in the dark
That it is this or that it is that,
But do not use the rotted names.

* * *

Phoebus is dead, ephebe. But Phoebus was
A name for something that never could be named.
There was a project for the sun and is,

There is a project for the sun. The sun
Must bear no name, gold flourisher, but be
In the difficulty of what it is to be.

This is nothing until in a single man contained,
Nothing until this named thing nameless is
And is destroyed. He opens the door of his house

On flames. The scholar of one candle sees
An Arctic effulgence flaring on the frame
Of everything he is. And he feels afraid.

What have these three unnaming passages most in common? Well, what are we doing when we give pet names to those we love, or give no names to anyone at all, as when we go apart in order to go deep into ourselves? Stevens's peculiar horror of the commonplace in names emerges in his litany of bizarre, fabulistic persons and places, but though that inventiveness works to break casual continuities, it has little in common with the true break with continuity in poets like Lewis Carroll and Edward Lear. Stevens, *pace* Hugh Kenner, is hardly the culmination of the poetics of Lear. He may not be the culmination of Whitman's poetics either, since that begins to seem the peculiar distinction of John Ashbery. But like Whitman, Stevens does have a link to the Lucretian Sublime, as Paten the Epicurean did, and such a Sublime demands a deeper break with commonplace continuities than is required by the evasions of nonsense and fantasy. The most authentic of literary Sublimes has the Epicurean purpose of rendering us discontented with easier pleasures in order to prepare us for the ordeal of more difficult pleasures, When Stevens unnames he follows, however unknowingly, the trinity of negative wisdom represented by Emerson, Pater and Nietzsche. Stevens himself acknowledged only Nietzsche; but the unfashionable Emerson and Pater were even stronger in him, with Emerson (and Whitman) repressedly the strongest of strains. Why not, after all, use the rotted names? If the things were things that never could be named, is not one name as bad anyway as another? Stevens's masterpiece is not named *The Somethings of Autumn*, and not only because the heroic desperation of the Emersonian scholar of one candle is not enough. Whether you call the auroras flames or an Arctic effulgence or call them by the trope now stuck into dictionaries, auroras, you are giving your momentary consent to one arbitrary substitution or another. Hence Emerson's more drastic and Bacchic ambition; write your *old* adventures, not just your new, with the Gnostic pen of our forefather and foremother, the Abyss. I circle again the problematic American desire to merge voicing and revisionism into a single entity, and turn to Whitman for a central text, which will be the supposed elegy for Lincoln, *When Lilacs Last in the Dooryard Bloom'd*. So drastic is the amalgam of voicing, unnaming and revisionism here that I take as prelude first Whitman's little motto poem, *As Adam Early in the Morning*, so as to set some of the ways for approaching what is most problematic in the great elegy, its images of voice and of voicing.

What can we mean when we speak of the *voice* of the poet, or the voice of the critic? is there a pragmatic sense of voice, in discussing poetry and criticism, that does not depend upon the illusions of metaphysics? When poetry and criticism speak of "images of voice," what is being imaged? I think I can answer these questions usefully in the context of my critical enterprise from *The Anxiety of influence* on, but my answers rely upon a post-philosophical pragmatism which grounds itself upon what has worked to make up an American tradition. Voice in American poetry always necessarily must include Whitman's oratory, and here I quote from it where it is most economical and persuasive, a five-line poem that centers the canon of our American verse:

> As Adam early in the morning,
> Walking forth from the bower refresh'd with sleep,
> Behold me where I pass, hear my voice, approach,
> Touch me, touch the palm of your hand to my body as I pass,
> Be not afraid of my body.

What shall we call this striding stance' of the perpetually passing Walt, prophetic of Stevens's singing girl at Key West, and of Stevens's own Whitman walking along a ruddy shore, singing of death and day? Rhetorically the stance is wholly transumptive, introjecting earliness, but this is very unlike the Miltonic transuming of tradition. Walt is indeed Emerson's new Adam, American and Nietzschean, who can live as if it were morning, but though he is *as* the Biblical and Miltonic Adam, that "as" is one of Stevens's "intricate evasions of as." The Old Adam was not a savior, except in certain Gnostic traditions of Primal Man; the new, Whitmanian Adam indeed is Whitman himself, more like Christ than like Adam, and more like the Whitmanian Christ of Lawrence's *The Man Who Died* than like the Jesus of the Gospels.

Reading Whitman's little poem is necessarily an exercise both in a kind of repression and in a kind of introjection. To read the poem strongly, to voice its stance, is to transgress the supposed boundary between reading or criticism, and writing or poetry. "As" governs the three words of origins—

"Adam," "early" and "morning"—and also the outgoing movement of Whitman, walking forth refreshed from a bower (that may be also a tomb), emerging from a sleep that may have been a kind of good death. Whitman placed this poem at the close of the *Children of Adam* division of *Leaves of Grass*, thus positioning it between the defeated American pathos of *Facing West from California's Shores* and the poignant *In Paths Untrodden* that begins the homoerotic *Calamus* section. There is a hint, in this contextualization, that the astonished reader needs to cross a threshold also. Behold Whitman as Adam; do not merely regard him when he is striding past. The injunctions build from that "behold" through "hear" and "approach" to "touch," a touch then particularized to the palm, as the resurrected Walt passes, no phantom, but a risen body. "Hear my voice" is the center. As Biblical trope, it invokes Jehovah walking in Eden in the cool of the day, but in Whitman's American context it acquires a local meaning also. Hear my voice, and not just my words; *hear me as voice*. Hear me, as in my elegy for President Lincoln, I hear the hermit thrush.

Though the great elegy finds its overt emblems in the lilac-bush and the evening star, its more, crucial tropes substitute for those emblems. These figures are the sprig of lilac. that Whitman places on the hearse and the song of the thrush that floods the western night. Ultimately these are one trope, one image of voice, which we can follow Whitman by calling the "tally," playing also on a secondary meaning of "tally," as double or agreement. "Tally" may be Whitman's most crucial trope or ultimate image of voice. As a word, it goes back to the Latin *talea* for twig or cutting, which appears in this poem as the sprig of lilac. The word meant originally a cutting or stick upon which notches are made so as to keep count or score, but first in the English and then in the American vernacular it inevitably took on the meaning of a sexual score. The slang words "tallywoman," meaning a lady in an illicit relationship, and "tallywhack" or "tallywags," for the male genitalia, are still in circulation. "Tally" had a peculiar, composite meaning for Whitman in his poetry, which has not been noted by his critics. In the odd, rather luridly impressive death-poem *Chanting the Square Deific*, an amazing blend of Emerson and an Americanized Hegel, Whitman identifies himself with Christ, Hermes and Hercules and then writes: "All sorrow, labor, suffering, I, tallying it, absorb it in myself." My comment would be: "Precisely *how* does he tally it?" and the answer to that question, grotesque as initially it must seem, would be: "Why, first by masturbating, and then by writing poems." I am being merely accurate, rather than outrageous, and so I turn to *Song of Myself*, section 25, as first proof-text:

Dazzling and tremendous how quick the sun-rise would kill me,
If I could not now and always send sun-rise out of me.

We also ascend dazzling and tremendous as the sun,
We found our own O my soul in the calm and cool of the
    daybreak.
My voice goes after what my eyes cannot reach,
With the twirl of my tongue I encompass worlds and volumes of
    worlds.

Speech is the twin of my vision, it is unequal to measure itself,
It provokes me forever, it says sarcastically,
Walt you contain enough, why don't you let it out then?

Come now I will not be tantalized, you conceive too much of
    articulation,
Do you not know O speech how the buds beneath you are folded?
Waiting in gloom, protected by frost,
The dirt receding before my prophetical screams,
I underlying causes to balance them at last,
My knowledge my live parts, it keeping tally with the meaning of
    all things,
Happiness, (which whoever hears me let him or her set out in search
    of this day.)

My final merit I refuse, you, I refuse putting from me what I really am,
Encompass worlds, but never try to encompass me;
I crowd your sleekest and best by simply looking toward you.

Writing and talk do not prove me,
I carry the plenum of proof and every thing else in my face,
With the hush of my lips I wholly confound the skeptic.

At this, almost the mid-point of his greatest poem, Whitman is sliding
knowingly near crisis, which will come upon him in the crossing between
sections 27 and 28. But here he is too strong, really too strong, and soon will
pay the price of that over-strength, according to the Emersonian iron Law of
Compensation, that nothing is got for nothing. Against the sun's mocking
taunt: "See then whether you shall be master!" Whitman sends forth his own
sunrise, which is a better, a more Emersonian answer than what Melville's

Ahab threatens when he cries out, with surpassing Promethean eloquence: "I'd strike the sun if it insulted me!" As an alternative dawn, Whitman crucially identifies himself as a voice, a voice overflowing with presence, a presence that is a sexual self-knowledge: "My knowledge my live parts, it keeping tally with the meaning of all things." His knowledge and sexuality are one, and we need to ask: how does that sexual self-knowing keep tally with the meaning of all things? The answer comes in the crisis sequence of sections 26–39, where Whitman starts with listening and then regresses to touch, until he achieves both orgasm and poetic release through a Sublime yet quite literal masturbation. The sequence begins conventionally enough with bird song and human voice, passes to music, and suddenly becomes very extraordinary, in a passage critics have admired greatly but have been unable to expound:

> The orchestra whirls me wider than Uranus flies,
> It wrenches such ardors from me I did not know I possess'd
> them,
> It sails me, I dab with bare feet, they are lick'd by the
> indolent waves,
> I am cut by bitter and angry hail, I lose my breath,
> Steep'd amid honey'd morphine, my windpipe throttled in
> fakes of death,
> At length let up again to feel the puzzle of puzzles,
> And that we call Being.

This Sublime antithetical flight (or repression) not only takes Whitman out of nature, but makes him a new kind of god, ever-dying and ever-living, a god whose touchstone is of course voice. The ardors wrenched from him are operatic, and the cosmos becomes stage machinery, a context in which the whirling bard first loses his breath to the envious hail, then sleeps a drugged illusory death in uncharacteristic silence, and at last is let up again to sustain the enigma of Being. For this hero of voice, we expect now a triumphant ordeal by voice, but surprisingly we get an equivocal ordeal by sexual self-touching. Yet the substitution is only rhetorical, and establishes the model for the tally in the Lincoln elegy, since the sprig of lilac will represent Whitman's live parts, and the voice of the bird will represent those ardors so intense, so wrenched from Whitman, that he did not know he possessed them.

After praising his own sensitivity of touch, Whitman concludes section 27 with the highly equivocal line: "To touch my person to some one else's is about as much as I can stand." The crisis section proper, 28, centers upon demonstrating that to touch his own person is also about as much as Whitman can stand. By the time he cries out: "I went myself first to the headland, my own hands carried me there," we can understand how the whole 1855 *Song of Myself* may have grown out of an early notebook jotting on the image of the headland, a threshold stage between self-excitation and orgasm. Section 28 ends with frankly portrayed release:

> You villain touch! what are you doing? my breath is tight
>   in its throat,
> Unclench your floodgates; you are too much for me.

The return of the image of breath and throat; of voice, is no surprise, nor will the attentive reader be startled when the lines starting section 29 take a rather more affectionate view of touch, now that the quondam villain has performed his labor:

> Blind loving wrestling touch, sheath'd hooded sharp-tooth'd
>   touch!
> Did it make you ache so, leaving me?

Since Whitman's "rich showering rain" fructifies into a golden, masculine landscape, we can call this sequence of *Song of Myself* the most productive masturbation since the ancient Egyptian myth of a god who masturbates the world into being. I suggest now (and no Whitman scholar will welcome it) that a failed masturbation is the concealed reference in section 2 of the *Lilacs* elegy:

> O powerful western fallen start
> O shades of night—O moody, tearful night!
> O great star disappear'd—O the black murk that hides the start
> O cruel hands that hold me powerless—O helpless soul of met
> O harsh surrounding cloud that will not free my soul.

The cruel hands are Whitman's own, as he vainly seeks relief from his repressed guilt, since the death of Father Abraham has rekindled the death, a decade before, of the drunken Quaker carpenter-father, Walter Whitman, Senior. Freud remarks, in *Mourning and Melancholia*, that

... there is more in the content of melancholia than in that of normal grief. In melancholia the relation to the object is no simple one; it is complicated by the conflict of ambivalence. This latter is either constitutional, i.e. it is an element of every love-relation formed by this particular ego, or else it proceeds from precisely those experiences that involved a threat of losing the object.... Constitutional ambivalence belongs by nature to what is repressed, while traumatic experiences with the object may have stirred to activity something else that has been repressed. Thus everything to do with these conflicts of ambivalence remains excluded from consciousness, until the outcome characteristic of melancholia sets in. This, as we know, consists in the libidinal cathexis that is being menaced at last abandoning the object, only, however, to resume its occupation of that place in the ego whence it came. So by taking flight into the ego love escapes annihilation....

Both conflicts of ambivalence are Whitman's in the *Lilacs* elegy, and we will see love fleeing into Whitman's image of voice, the bird's tallying chant, which is the last stance of his ego. Freud's ultimate vision of primal ambivalence emphasized its origin as being the dialectical fusion/defusion of the two drives, love and death. Whitman seems to me profounder even than Freud as a student of the interlocking of these antithetical drives that darkly combine into one. Eros and its shadow of ruin, to appropriate a phrase from Shelley. Whitman mourns Lincoln, yes, but pragmatically he mourns even more intensely for the tally, the image of voice he cannot as yet rekindle into being, concealed as it is by a "harsh surrounding cloud" of impotence. The miraculous juxtaposition of the two images of the tally, sprig of lilac and song of the hermit thrush, in sections 3 and 4 following, points the possible path out of Whitman's death-in-life:

3
In the dooryard fronting an old farm-house near the
    white-wash'd palings,
Stands the lilac-bush tall-growing with heart-shaped leaves
    of rich green,
With many a pointed blossom rising delicate, with the
    perfume strong I love,
With every leaf a miracle—and from this bush in the dooryard,

With delicate-color'd blossoms and heart-shaped leaves of
    rich green,
A sprig with its flower I break.

    4
In the swamp in secluded recesses,
A shy and hidden bird is warbling a song.

Solitary the thrush,
The hermit withdrawn to himself, avoiding the settlements,
Sings by himself a song.

Song of the bleeding throat,
Death's outlet song of life, (for well dear brother I know,
If thou wast not granted to sing thou would'st surely die.)

Whitman breaks the *talea*, in a context that initially suggests a ritual of castration, but the image offers more than a voluntary surrender of manhood. The broken lilac sprig is exactly analogous to the "song of the bleeding throat," and indeed the analogy explains the otherwise baffling "bleeding." For what has torn the thrush's throat? The solitary song itself, image of wounded voice, is the other *talea*, and has been broken so that the soul can take count of itself, Yet why must these images, of voice be broken? Whitman's answer, a little further on in the poem, evades the "why" much as he evades the child's "What is the grass?" in *Song of Myself* 6, or, the *why* like the *what* is unknowable in the context of the Epicurean-Lucretian metaphysics that Whitman accepted. Whitman's answer comes in the hyperbolic, daemonic, repressive force of his copious over-breaking of the tallies:

Here, coffin that slowly passes,
I give you my sprig of lilac.

    7
(Nor for you, for one alone,
Blossoms and branches green to coffins all I bring,
For fresh as the morning, thus would I chant a song for you
    O sane and sacred death.

All over bouquets of roses,

O death, I cover you over with roses and early lilies,
But mostly and now the lilac that blooms the first,
Copious I break, I break the sprigs from the bushes,
With loaded arms I come, pouring for you,
For you and the coffins all of you O death.)

Why should we be moved that Whitman intones: "O sane and sacred death," rather than: "O insane and obscene death," which might seem to be more humanly accurate? "Death" here is a trope for the sane and sacred Father Abraham, rather than for the actual father. Whitman's profuse breaking of the tallies attempts to extend this trope, *so* as to make of death itself an ultimate image of voice or tally of the soul. It is the tally and not literal death, our death, that is sane and sacred. But that returns us to the figuration of the tally, which first appears in the poem as a verb, just before the carol of death:

And the charm of the carol rapt me,
As I held as if by their hands my comrades in the night,
And the voice of my spirit tallied the song of the bird.

"My knowledge my live parts, it keeping tally with the meaning of all things" now transfers its knowledge from the vital order to the death-drive. I am reminded that I first became aware of Whitman's crucial trope by pondering its remarkable use by Hart Crane, when he invokes Whitman directly in the "Cape Hatteras" section of *The Bridge*:

O Walt!—Ascensions of thee hover in me now
As thou at junctions elegiac, there; of speed,
With vast eternity, dost wield the rebound seed!
The competent loam, the probable grass, travail
Of tides awash the pedestal of Everest, fail
Not less than thou in pure impulse inbred
To answer deepest soundings! O, upward from the dead
Thou bringest tally, and a pact, new bound
Of living brotherhood!

Crane's allusion is certainly to the *Lilacs* elegy, but his interpretation of what it means to bring tally "upward from the dead" may idealize rather too generously. That Walt's characteristic movement is ascension cannot be doubted, but the operative word in this elegy is "passing." The coffin of the martyred leader passes first, but in the sixteenth and final section it is the bard who passes, still tallying both the song of the bird and his own soul. That the tally is crucial, Crane was more than justified in emphasizing, but then Crane was a great reader as well as a great writer of poetry. Flanking the famous carol of death are two lines of the tally: "And the voice of my spirit tallied the song of the bird" preceding, and "To the tally of my soul" following. To tally the hermit thrush's carol of death is to tally the soul, for what is measured is the degree of sublimity, the agonistic answer to the triple question: more? less? equal? And the Sublime answer in death's carol is surely "more":

> *Come lovely and soothing death,*
> *Undulate round the world, serenely arriving, arriving,*
> *In the day, in the night, to all, to each,*
> *Sooner or later delicate death.*

> *Prais'd be the fathomless universe,*
> *For life and joy, and for objects and knowledge curious,*
> *And for love, sweet love—but praise! praise! praise!*
> *For the sure-enwinding arms of cool-enfolding death.*

> *Dark mother always gliding near with soft feet,*
> *Have none chanted for thee a chant of fullest welcome?*
> *Then I chant it for thee, I glorify thee above all, .*
> *I bring thee a song that when thou must indeed come,*
>   *come unfalteringly.*

> *Approach strong deliveress,*
> *When it is so, when thou hast taken them I joyously sing*
>   *the dead,*
> *Lost in the loving floating ocean of thee,*
> *Laved in the flood of thy bliss O death.*

If this grand carol, as magnificent as the Song of Songs which is Solomon's, constitutes the tally or image of voice of the soul, then we ought now to be able to describe that image. To tally, in Whitman's sense, is at once to measure the soul's actual and potential sublimity, to overcome object-loss and grief, to gratify one's self sexually by one's self, to compose the thousand songs at random of *Leaves of Grass*, but above all, as Crane said, to bring a new covenant of brotherhood, and here that pact is new bound with the voice of the hermit thrush. The bird's carol, which invokes the oceanic mother of Whitman's *Sea-Drift cosmos*, is clearly not its tally but Whitman's own, the transgressive verbal climax of his own family romance. When, in the elegy's final section, Whitman chants himself as "Passing the song of the hermit bird and the tallying song of my soul," he prepares himself and us for his abandonment of the image of the lilac. And, in doing so, he prepares us also for his overwhelming refusal or inability to yield up similarly the darker image of the tally:

> Yet each to keep and all, retrievements out of the night,
> The song, the wondrous chant of the gray-brown bird,
> And the tallying chant, the echo arous'd in my soul....

The tally is an echo, as an image of voice must be, yet truly it does not echo the carol of the hermit thrush. Rather, it echoes the earlier Whitman, of *Out of the Cradle Endlessly Rocking*, and his literary father, the Emerson of the great *Essays*. But here I require an *excursus* into poetic theory in order to explain image of voice and its relation to echo and allusion, and rather than rely upon as recondite a theorist as myself, I turn instead to a great explainer, John Hollander, who seems to me our outstanding authority upon all matters of lyrical form. Here is Hollander upon images of voice and their relation to the figurative interplay I have called "transumption," since that is what I take "tally" to be: Whitman's greatest transumption or introjection or Crossing of Identification, his magnificent overcoming both of his own earlier images of poetic origins and of Emerson's story of how poetry comes into being, particularly American poetry. First Hollander, from his forthcoming book, *The Figure of Echo*:

> ... we deal with diachronic trope all the time, and yet we have no name for it as a class.... the echoing itself makes a figure, and the interpretive or revisionary power which raises the echo even louder than the original voice is that of a trope of diachrony....
>
> I propose that we apply the name of the classical rhetoricians' trope of *transumption* (or *metalepsis* in its Greek form) to these diachronic, allusive figures....
>
> Proper reading of a metaphor demands a simultaneous appreciation of the beauty of a vehicle and the importance of its freight.... But the interpretation of a metalepsis entails the recovery of the transumed material. A transumptive style is to be distinguished radically from the kind of conceited one which we

usually associate with baroque poetic, and with English seventeenth-century verse in particular. It involves an ellipsis, rather than a relentless pursuit, of further figuration...

Hollander then names transumption as the proper figure for interpretive allusion, to which I would add only the description that I gave before in *A Map of Misreading*: this is the trope-undoing trope, which seeks to reverse imagistic priorities. Milton crowds all his poetic precursors together into the space that intervenes between *himself and the truth*. Whitman also crowds poetic anteriority—Emerson and the Whitman of 1855–1860—into a little space between the carol of death and the echo aroused in the soul of the elegist of *Lilacs*. Emerson had excluded the questions of sex and death from his own images-of-voice, whether in a verse chant *like Bacchus* or a prose rhapsody like *The Poet*. The earlier Whitman had made of the deathly ocean at night his maternal image of voice, and we have heard the hermit thrush in its culmination of that erotic cry. Whitman's tally transumes the ocean's image, of voice, by means of what Hollander calls an ellipsis of further figuration. The tally notches a restored Narcissism and the return to the mode of erotic self-sufficiency. The cost is high as it always is in transumption. What vanishes here in Whitman is the presence of others and of otherness, as object-libido is converted into ego-libido again. Father Abraham, the ocean as dark mother, the love of comrades, and even the daemonic *alter ego* of the hermit thrush all fade away together. But what is left is the authentic American image of voice, as the bard brings tally, alone there in the night among the fragrant pines except for his remaining comrades, the knowledge of death and the thought of death.

In 1934 Wallace Stevens, celebrating his emergence from a decade's poetic silence, boldly attempted a very different transumption of the Whitmanian images of voice:

> It was her voice that made
> The sky acutest at its vanishing.
> She measured to the hour its solitude.
> She was the single artificer of the world
> In which she sang....

The tally, in *The Idea of Order at Key West*, becomes the "ghostlier demarcations, keener sounds" ending the poem. A year later, Stevens granted himself a vision of Whitman as sunset in our evening-land:

In the far South the sun of autumn is passing
Like Walt Whitman walking along a ruddy shore.
He is singing and chanting the things that are part of him,
The worlds that were and will be, death and day.
Nothing is final, he chants. No man shall see the end.
His beard is of fire and his staff is a leaping flame.

It is certainly the passing bard of the end of *Lilacs*, but did he chant that nothing is final? Still, this is Walt as Moses and as Aaron, leading the poetic children of Emerson through the American wilderness, and surely Whitman was always proudly provisional. Yet, the tally of his soul had to present itself as a finality, as an image of voice that had achieved a fresh priority and a perpetually ongoing strength. Was that an American Sublime, or only another American irony? Later in 1935, Stevens wrote a grim little poem called *The American Sublime* that seems to qualify severely his intense images of voice, of the singing girl and of Whitman:

But how does one feel?
One grows used to the weather,
The landscape and that;
And the sublime comes down
To the spirit itself,

The spirit and space,
The empty spirit
In vacant space.
What wine does one drink?
What bread does one eat?

The questions return us full circle to Emerson's *Bacchus*, nearly a century before:

We buy ashes for bread;
We buy diluted wine....

This is not transumptive allusion, but a repetition of figurations, the American baroque defeat. But that is a secondary strain in Stevens, as it was in Emerson and in Whitman. I leap ahead, past Frost and Pound, Eliot and Williams, past even Hart Crane, to conclude with a contemporary image-of-voice that is another strong tally, however ruefully the strength regards itself.

Here is John Ashbery's *The Other Tradition*, the second poem in his 1977 volume, *Houseboat Days*:

> They all came, some wore sentiments
> Emblazoned on T-shirts, proclaiming the lateness
> Of the hour, and indeed the sun slanted its rays
> Through branches of Norfolk Island pine as though
> Politely clearing its throat, and all ideas settled
> In a fuzz of dust under trees when it's drizzling:
> The endless games of Scrabble, the boosters,
> The celebrated omelette au Cantal, and through it
> The roar of time plunging unchecked through the sluices
> Of the days, dragging every sexual moment of it
> Past the lenses: the end of something.
> Only then did you glance up from your book,
> Unable to comprehend what had been taking place, or
> Say what you had been reading. More chairs
> Were brought, and lamps were lit, but it tells
> Nothing of how all this proceeded to materialize
> Before you and the people waiting outside and in the next
> Street, repeating its name over and over, until silence
> Moved halfway up the darkened trunks,
> And the meeting was called to order.
>   I still remember
> How they found you, after a dream, in your thimble hat,
> Studious as a butterfly in a parking lot.
> The road home was nicer then. Dispersing, each of the
> Troubadours had something to say about how charity
> Had run its race and won, leaving you the ex-president
> Of the event, and how, though many of these present
> Had wished something to come of it, if only a distant
> Wisp of smoke, yet none was so deceived as to hanker
> After that cool non-being of just a few minutes before,
> Now that the idea of a forest had clamped itself
> Over the minutiae of the scene. You found this
> Charming, but turned your face fully toward night,
> Speaking into it like a megaphone, not hearing
> Or caring, although these still live and are generous
> And all ways contained, allowed to come and go
> Indefinitely in and out of the stockade

They have so much trouble remembering, when your forgetting
Rescues them at last, as a star absorbs the night.

I am aware that this charming poem urbanely confronts, absorbs and in
some sense seeks to overthrow a critical theory, almost a critical climate, that
has accorded it a canonical status. Stevens's Whitman proclaims that nothing
is final and that no man shall see the end. Ashbery, a Whitman somehow
more studiously casual even than Whitman, regards the prophets of
belatedness and cheerfully insists that his forgetting or repression will rescue
us at last, even as the Whitmanian or Stevensian evening star absorbs the
night. But the price paid for this metaleptic reversal of American belatedness
into a fresh earliness is the yielding up of Ashbery's tally or image of voice to
a deliberate grotesquerie. Sexuality is made totally subservient to time, which
is indeed "the end of something," and poetic tradition becomes an ill-
organized social meeting of troubadours, leaving the canonical Ashbery as
"ex-president / Of the event." As for the image of voice proper, the
Whitmanian confrontation of the night now declines into: "You found this /
Charming, but turned your face fully toward night, / Speaking into it like a
megaphone, not hearing / Or caring." Such a megaphone is an apt image for
Paul de Man's deconstructionist view of poetic tradition, which undoes
tradition by suggesting that every poem is as much a random and gratuitous
event as any human death is.

Ashbery's implicit interpretation of what he wants to call *The Other
Tradition* mediates between this vision of poems as being totally cut off from
one another and the antithetical darkness in which poems carry overdetermined relationships and progress towards a final entropy. Voice in our
poetry now tallies what Ashbery in his *Syringa*, a major Orphic elegy in
Houseboat Days, calls "a record of pebbles along the way." Let us grant that
the American Sublime is always also an American irony, and then turn back
to Emerson and hear the voice that is great within us somehow breaking
through again. This is Emerson in his journal for August 1859, on the eve of
being burned out, with all his true achievement well behind him; but he gives
us the true tally of his soul:

> *Beatitudes of Intellect.*—Am I not, one of these days, to write
> consecutively of the beatitude of intellect? It is too great for
> feeble souls, and they are over-excited. The wineglass shakes, and
> the wine is spilled. What then? The joy which will not let me sit
> in my chair, which brings me bolt upright to my feet, and sends
> me striding around my room, like a tiger in his cage, and I cannot

have composure and concentration enough even to set down in English words the thought which thrills me—is not that joy a certificate of the elevation? What if I never write a book or a line? for a moment, the eyes of my eyes, were opened, the affirmative experience remains, and consoles through all suffering.

KERRY C. LARSON

Native Models

"The newspaper is so fleeting," Whitman once commented while musing over his career in journalism, "is so like a thing gone as quick as come; has no life so to speak; its birth and death coterminous" (*WWC* 4:2). While comparisons between *Leaves of Grass* and journalism abound—Emerson's quip about the *Bhagavad Gita* and the *New York Tribune* comes to mind—we have found reason to extend Whitman's analogy along more precise lines by noting how this co-presence of birth and death haunts the language of "Song of Myself," with its "prophetical screams" working their way to the surface only to be choked off at the moment of emergence. In view of this threatened foreclosure of beginning and end we can better understand why Whitman should be so irresistibly drawn to the parthenogenesis of self-evolving "truths" and other variants on the myth of "free growth": it defines the successful elaboration of a rhetoric which, in securing immediate conviction through its display of "undeniable growth," stands outside the need of argument or persuasive demonstration. In this way authority for his songs of the earth is, to paraphrase Wallace Stevens, not to be imposed but only discovered. But inasmuch as this notion of a self-willed, uncoerced genesis that neither hastens nor resists its delivery specifies a dream that both demands and defies representation, the pursuit of "free growth" and its self-evident truths seek a context for what cannot be

---

From *Whitman's Drama of Consensus*. © 1988 by The University of Chicago.

contextualized, seek to affirm what can only be inferred. What results is a critical hiatus between the moment of conception and the moment of its accepted "proof," a hiatus which is in turn responsible for the nightmare of the prolifically barren or what section twenty-five reveals to be a condition of overcharged plenitude which, finding no outlet for its energies, threatens to degenerate into a poetic that "stagnates in its vitals, cowardly and rotten."[1]

It may be that the tensions that accrue from the hiatus between initial acts of founding and their fully verified legitimacy plague any form of representative speech seeking public acceptance. Certainly, this predicament applies to the state of the nation Whitman found himself addressing in 1855, for when the South did eventually withdraw from the Union, its gesture of defiance merely brought to a head a crisis in constitutional legitimacy which had been in evidence long before then. Although legislation from 1820 onward made it possible to sustain and patch together the Union on the basis of compromise over slavery, it also sustained and perpetuated a rupture in the social contract which only civil war, as it turned out, could remedy. Over the course of his presidency Lincoln came to interpret this crisis in legitimacy in terms of a moral hiatus between 1776 and 1789, between the Declaration of Independence with its guarantee of equality for "all men" and the Constitution with its notorious silence concerning this same stipulation. "Four score and seven years ago," the year of 1776, marked the true beginning of nationhood, one whose founding Lincoln likewise evoked as a virgin birth conceived in liberty and brought forth by the Founders, less the "fathers" of the new nation than its midwife. In this "recontracting of society on the basis of the Declaration as [the] fundamental charter,"[2] as one analyst describes this revisionary gesture, Lincoln anticipated the day when "this nation under God shall have a new birth of freedom"—a rebirth, in other words, which would at last close the gap between the original moment of the nation's founding and its final, incontestable legitimacy. Needless to say, executing this goal exacted a staggering price, as the thousands slain on the fields of Gettysburg attested.

Whitman's motive, as we have seen, was to settle the matter of legitimacy itself by cultivating a song where the impasse between creation and validation would be a nonexistent issue. As the better President, his would be the naturalized decree of the executive "who judges not as a judge judges but as the sun falling upon a helpless thing." From what we have seen so far of "Song of Myself," however, it would appear that it is Whitman himself who is the helpless thing the sun falls upon; and while he does not enlist the sacrifice of slain soldiers to defend his self-evident truths his own ordeal with proof does require throttled windpipes and suicidal ventures in frantic vindication of his calling. To this extent, both literary and political institutions share the common plight of devising a vocabulary of justification which is not revealed to be inadequate or self-incriminating the moment it is asserted.

While the specter of disunion obviously lent added urgency to Whitman's quest, the importance of literary institutions should not be overlooked, particularly because Whitman's chosen method for "recontracting" society relies so heavily on the belief that literature alone is best qualified to define and vindicate the essential worth of a people and its culture. As he writes in *Democratic Vistas*, "the central point in any nation, and that whence it is itself really sway'd the most, and whence it sways others, is its national literature, especially its archetypal poems. Above all previous lands, a great original literature is surely to become the justification and reliance, (in some respects the sole reliance) of American democracy" (*PW* 2:365–66). In truth, "two or three really original American poets ... would give more compaction and more moral identity, (the quality to-day most needed) to these States, than all its Constitutions, legislative and judicial ties" (*PW* 2:368). With this appeal for "national expressers" Whitman adds his voice to a long chorus of pleas for an indigenous literature "fit for native models" and beyond the reach of the courtly muses of Europe. As various voices grouped under the rubric of literary nationalism, that chorus reached its peak in the interval falling between the nation's founding and the advent of those writers said to constitute the American Renaissance. Because it forms something of a hiatus in its own right, this period is by all accounts held to be among the most dismal in American letters, a cultural wasteland barren of talent and devoid of genius. This is not only the twentieth-century view but a contemporaneous assessment, for, as the periodicals, pamphlets, and fugitive essays of the first half of the nineteenth-century overwhelmingly attest, glorious predictions on the destined accomplishments of a National American Literature routinely coincided with the pained recognition, by turns defiant and apologetic, that It had not yet arrived. As early as the turn of the century Fisher Ames could in characteristic fashion begin a meditation on the prospects for "American Literature" by questioning "whether we are equal to the Europeans or only a race of degenerate creoles," while one generation later visitor Harriet Martineau was moved to comment that "if the American mind be judged of by its literature, it may be pronounced to have no mind at all."[3]

Thus, over the same period that witnessed disputes concerning the constitutional legitimacy of the nation there also arose debate regarding its cultural legitimacy. Criticism today affirms that Whitman and a select handful of contemporaries were instrumental in laying this second controversy to rest; in the words of R. W. B. Lewis *Leaves of Grass* provided "full poetic realization" to "the stored-up abundance of hope"[4] that accumulated over the decades-long struggle for literary distinction. This of course is a retrospective judgment which draws implicit support from the still more widespread belief that *Leaves of Grass* did not supplement or revise an established tradition in American poetry so much as single-handedly invented one. To a large extent, that belief is indisputable: there is no need to repeat, once again, that Walt Whitman is not Joel Barlow. Even so, there is perhaps a certain irony in crediting a work like "Song of Myself" with finally settling the issue of artistic legitimacy in the New World when that is a question so much at stake within the poem itself. More particularly, the intrinsically paradoxical act of openly asserting what must by definition be only inferred ("only what proves itself is so, only what nobody denies is so") not only specifies a quandary for Whitman's text but defines a long-standing dilemma among the many advocates for an "American Genius" who preceded him. If they too believed that "democracy can never prove itself beyond cavil until it founds and luxuriantly grows its own forms of art" (*PW* 2:365), they were also bound, like the author of "Song of Myself," to come up against the contradictions involved in mounting an *argument* for the virtues of self-evidence. The difficulty we have seen Whitman encounter in integrating his self-evident truths into "Song of Myself" has, in other words, a literary history of its own, one that considerably problematizes his hopeful division between those flawed instruments of sociability ("Constitutions, legislative and judicial ties") and the universal politics of "archetypal poems."

A brief inquiry into the procedures of literary nationalism can usefully detain us, then, not so much for suggesting a preview of better things to come but for dramatizing in its own right and on a more extensive scale the whole awkward business of undertaking to justify "that which has not yet come into existence."[5] No doubt it is this paradoxical imperative that stands behind the often circular and seemingly interminable debates that grip what Edwin Fussell describes, mock-heroically, as "The Age of Growing Discomfort and Inadequate Remedy": whether, for example, "Americanness" is best displayed through the treatment of strictly national subjects or whether it is best evinced by a thoroughgoing internationalism; whether we cannot have a genuine American literature until we have a genuine literary criticism to appraise it or whether that criticism will falter so long as it lacks models worthy of appraisal; whether genius will not emigrate to the New World so long as the country's epoch-making achievements are too imposing for the imagination or whether genius must surely languish so long as it remains bereft of a heritage of tradition rich enough to sustain it. As with any caricature, this oversimplifies a good deal. Still, it seems safe to generalize that amid the proliferating assessments of and proposed solutions to the scandal of "our cultural inferiority" each would-be prophet of the American genius shared the common plight of "trying to be midwife to the unborn homunculus."[6] With the onset of the 1840s—coeval with the first stirrings of Whitman's literary apprenticeship—such frustrations were becoming increasingly apparent and the subject was fast acquiring all the hallmarks of a public cliché: trite but inescapable, something of a bad joke but irresistibly calling for comment. During the same period it is perhaps inevitable that we should find a substantial weariness with, if not outright revulsion toward, "our figure of anticipation," a backlash illustrated in such works as Hawthorne's "The Great Stone Face," Poe's "How To Write A Blackwood Article," and Longfellow's *Kavanagh*. No doubt the *locus classicus* of this antinationalist trend remains James Russell Lowell's attack on "Nationality in Literature." First appearing in the *North American Review* in 1849, Lowell's essay is predominately parodic in spirit, scrupulously taking up so as to lampoon nationalism's stock divisions (imitation versus originality; Anglophilia versus Anglophobia), its stock imagery (the "cultivation" of culture; the "gestation" of genius), and its stock anxieties (shame, embarrassment, betrayal). He is as much amused by the craven deference paid by his countrymen to European reviewers as he is scornful of mindless demands for instant recognition, "as if [literature] were some school exercise in composition to be handed in by a certain day." Observing that "our criticism has oscillated between the two extremes of depreciation and over-praise," Lowell argues that the forty-year campaign for literary independence has proven to be not only futile but in many respects pernicious. "Literature survives," he claims, "not because of its nationality, but despite it."[7]

Yet Lowell's polemic, while astute in perceiving an ironic complicity between the widespread belief in the poverty of American letters and the impoverishing effects of nationalistic discourse, is also naive in assuming that once this complicity is identified it can be somehow dispensed with. For an element of antinationalism had always inhered in the balked procedures of a discourse which, in Hamlet-like distress, could but "make mouths at the invisible event." Mounting a critique on literary nationalism, even by 1849, could only be an anachronistic enterprise, since that is a project carried out, with varying degrees of explicitness, in the pages of nationalism itself. Speaking on the "peculiar motives to intellectual exertion in America" twenty-five years before Lowell, Edward Everett catches himself up in the

midst of his Phi Beta Kappa address with the reminder that "it is impossible
to tell what garments our native muses will wear. To foretell our literature
would be to create it." With that concession in hand there is little left for the
orator to do but look back with fondness on the revolutionary exploits of the
past and dismiss with contempt those cynical enough to brand his own
prophecy "the chimerical imagination of a future indefinitely removed."[8] But
Everett's disclaimer serves to project the skeptic within himself. Justification
runs aground here not simply because there is no literature deemed worthy
enough to justify (despite the recent work of Bryant, Cooper, or Irving, no
American authors are cited by Everett); his speech also fights a rearguard
action, defending itself against its own premises. In more explicit fashion E.
T. Channing abjures readers of the *North American Review* in 1816 to "get out
of the bad habit of dictating to great minds.... Genius is not willing to be
interfered with and told how to work, where to travel and what to admire.
And yet there are men who go so far as to hold up models for imitation and
standards of taste." No less emphatically than Lowell, Channing suggests
that the greatest obstacle to literary development may be found in the
moment of its advocacy. Not foreign models alone are to be deplored, "we
must also be shy of ourselves."[9] Some, to be sure, would take solace in
affirming the modest proposal that "a national literature uniting all the
requisites of excellence ... has as yet perhaps not existed [and] it may be
impossible to create such a one, but it is not therefore idle to aim at it."[10]
Among the more prescient spokesmen, however, the gap between prophecy
and accomplishment was too imposing to ignore. As often as not their
writing stops short at the divide signaled in Nietzsche's uncompromising
distinction: "of what is great one must either be silent or speak with
greatness."[11] Enjoying neither luxury, they alternately longed for one or the
other. Even so tireless a standard-bearer as William Cullen Bryant is moved
to confess that "were our rewards to be bestowed only on what is intrinsically
meritorious, merit alone would have any apology for appearing before the
public."[12] To the degree that the only possible proof for the cultural
legitimacy of the nation lay in the undeniable evidence of its results,
nationalism confronts a double scandal: not only the mortifying
"delinquency" of American letters but the corollary recognition that to
defend imminence of genius was thereby to register the fact of its absence.
Prophecy, too, required an apology for appearing before the public, since
merely to issue yet another call for a "Majestic Literature, self-reared, self-
sustaining, self-vindicated"[13] was from the outset to betray the cause. Or, as
Fisher Ames expresses this predicament with disarming candor in the first
paragraph of his early essay (1802), "it might, indeed, occur to our discretion

that, as the only admissible proof of literary excellence is the measure of its effects, our national claims ought to be abandoned as worthless the moment they are found to need asserting."[14]

Against this background there is ushered in the figure of Emerson, expounding the private infinitude of the Central Man. Coming in the wake of a generation given to lamenting the folly of holding Homer up against Joel Barlow or Plato against Thomas Paine, it was of course Emerson's vocation to insist that our genius is more native than we think. To the chronic rejoinder that "a right perception of the genius of others is not genius," Emerson would simply strike out the negative, recovering the usurped "majesty of [his] own rejected thoughts" in "every work of genius." This does not mean that Emerson thereby proposes, in one stroke, to overthrow or transcend the massive inferiority complex known as literary nationalism. He insists on this impasse with a candor that allows him to economize on its grievances more effectively. "Self-Reliance" he succinctly defines as "precisely that secret to make your supposed deficiency redundancy. If I am true, the theory is, the very want of action, my very impotency, shall become a greater excellency than all skill and toil."[15] Discovering possibility where Nietzsche would see only impossibility, Emerson in effect undertakes to speak with greatness and be silent at the same time. In the very magnitude of individual incapacity he posits individual power, converting imaginative poverty into imaginative plenitude. One reason the transparent eyeball epiphany in *Nature* and the catatonic breakdown in the opening pages of "Experience" have gained such notoriety is because they are so rare; it is far more common for Emerson to view himself "a pensioner; not a cause but a surprised spectator" (*W* 2:268), one who surveys "the awful gap" between the "promise of power and the shabby performance." Such distancing holds true for even the most ringing of *affirmations*. "Speak your latent conviction and it shall be the universal sense" is a sentence that does double duty, obeying even as it thematizes its own imperative. Emptied of content, the status of Emerson's "latent conviction" becomes synonymous with speaking on its behalf, thus precluding the need for further action. "Act if you like—but you do it at your own peril," he writes in Representative Men. "Men's actions are too strong for them. Show me a man who has acted, and who has not been a victim of his action" (*W* 4:266–67).[16] Every heart must also vibrate to that iron law: to invest one's words with the force of consequence, to shoot the gap from prophetic motive to living deed is a prelude to self-betrayal. Emersonian discourse, oppositely, will not fall prey to such betrayals, will not resign itself to the embarrassment of discovering its claims disproven the moment they are found to need asserting. Rather, as I suggested previously, he allegorizes this predicament by seeing it played out in the works of others. In what amounts to a remarkable transference, betrayal no longer identifies a threat impinging upon one's writing but is projected out and fully mastered in the aggressive act of reappropriation Emerson calls reading. Perusing the past masters, the self-reliant reader reads a fate which is the reverse of his own. Clinging fast to his poverty he finds in the deeds of genius a strength that weakens and finally enslaves. So it is said of Shakespeare that "he carries a wealth that beggars his own."

In undertaking to actualize "the great psalm of the Republic" Whitman, as we know, could rest content only in speaking *as*, not *of*, the Central Man. The poet's "every word ... must tell in action." From an Emersonian standpoint the consequence is as predictable as it is devastating: a musclebound bard seized with "Buffalo strength [but] choked by Titanic abdomen."[17] What Emerson glorifies as redundant deficiency Whitman finds rendered back into the vexations of a deficient redundancy. So section twenty-five accosts a voice surcharged with a wealth that beggars the poet's own. While it would be irresponsible to reduce the complexity of any author's work by threading it through the camel's eye of literary nationalism, the contrast can certainly be made that most American writers of Whitman's generation accommodated the imperative of fame by ironizing it— Hawthorne's Ambitious Guest, Melville's Pierre and such megalomaniacs as William Wilson are each in their own way grotesque overreachers whose overblown quest for commemoration merely dooms them to madness, suicide, or simple oblivion. Whitman, too, had begun his poetic career stuck head first in this vein, joylessly churning out commentaries on "The Punishment of Pride," "Fame's Vanity," and, of course, "Ambition." Yet in forging an aesthetic "as generous and as worthy" as the country it was to depict, Whitman came to perceive the need for a rhetoric purified of "ignominious distinctions." What remained for him to devise, in turn, was a structure of expression capable of fending off the disabling interaction between excess and deficiency as well as the disrelation between demand and response this interaction suggests.

Before going on to explore the impact of these issues on "Song of Myself," it might be useful to stand back and take stock of Whitman's affiliations to the background just outlined. Needless to say, he counted himself a staunch advocate in the drive for cultural independence and from his editorial post across the East River voiced his support for the Young America movement sweeping Manhattan in the 1840s. Firmly persuaded that "the top-most proof of a race is its own born poetry" (*PW* 2:474), he devoted essays to this "*sine qua non*" throughout the half-century of his writing career. (As a late as 1891 he was responding to yet another request from the *North American Review* for a piece on "American National Literature.") Yet it is worth noting that the author of "Song of Myself" was more than aware of the hopeless impasse that nationalism had turned out to be.

> *Caution*—not to blaart constantly for Native American Models, literature, etc., and bluster out "nothing foreign." The best way to promulge native American models and literature is to supply such forcible and superb specimens of the same that will, by their own volition, move to the head of all and put foreign models in the second class.

> I think today it would be best *not at all* to bother with arguments against foreign models or to help American *models*—but just go on *supplying American models.* (*N&F*, p. 30)

"Song of Myself" is scrupulous in honoring the spirit of such an injunction: it is careful to downplay the long-existent topos of *translatio studii* or the "Westering of Genius" (this being reserved for "Facing West from California's Shores"); it incorporates tableaux from American history (the storming of the Alamo; the old sea fight) with enough casualness to distance it safely from Joel Barlow's epic disasters; it abandons teleological narratives of cultural progress for the plotless adventures of a "kosmos"; it rewrites epic categories by subsuming them under the shared mythology of a celebrating self.

By 1855, then, Whitman did not need to be reminded that "literature comes not when it is bidden," that "you cannot force its growth." We can take this to mean something more than the fact that there will be no hailing of Columbia in Whitman's song by gaining a clearer sense of his cautious treatment of apostrophe at large. Few passages in *Leaves of Grass* succeed quite so brilliantly in coming to terms with this precaution as the opening lines of "Song of Myself," which eschew the ritual of invocation for a simple performative, "I celebrate myself and sing myself." The subject/object dualism conventional to address is here conflated for what appears as an inextricable fusion between the "I" that speaks and the "I" that is spoken, as if being claimed no permanence beyond the immediate moment it is uttered into existence.[18] There seems, in addition, no specifiable center or locus for this singing self, for, in what we can now recognize as a characteristic trait of Whitman's "arrivings and partings," no sooner does voice invest the speaker than it is dispersed through the landscape as so many "words ... loosed to the eddies of the wind." Words evoked in this way become stray interjections ("the belched words of speech"), passing reverberations ("echoes, ripples, buzzed whispers"), substances of sound and sight divorced from the abstractions of meaning and returned to the seductive power of a preverbal energy called the "lull" or "hum" of the soul's "valved voice." Their significance inheres in the random energies they release. The manner of speech is more epideitic than prophetic, content to luxuriate in the good fortune of "my respiration and inspiration ... the play of shine and shade." Thus it is worthwhile to note that as section three goes on to draw up a host of polarities—"beginning and end," "learned and unlearned," "I and this mystery"—these antithetical pairings are not so much subsumed as suspended. His lines want us to know that they are willing to countenance difference without wishing to absolve it: "Out of the dimness opposite equals advance, / Always substance ... always a knit of identity, always distinction, always a breed of life" (*CRE*, p. 31). To exclude nothing but exclusion, deny nothing but denial, allows the poet even to shrug aside, with a kind of wearied acknowledgment, the world-dividing logic of nationalism; it is enough for the time being to be told "showing the best and dividing it from the worst age vexes age."

The opening lines of "Song of Myself" continue to tantalize their ablest interpreters; so deeply assimilated have they become into the American grain that it is difficult now to imagine them as anything but inevitable. Part of that mystique, as I have intimated, indeed consists in the power of these lines to foster the impression that the work of prophecy *has already been done*. In the leisurely combination of engagement and withdrawal, liberation and restraint—both in and out of the game, leaning and loafing—utterance occupies a perspective unqualified by the demand for justification. His words are willing to risk obscurity in order to savor that imperturbability, for "to elaborate is no avail ... learned and unlearned feel that it is so ... while others discuss I am silent ... I have no mockings and arguments, I witness and wait" (*CRE*, pp. 31, 32). The point would not be that words fall short of the experience they seek to capture (for example, the poet's experience is "mystical") but that nothing could be added to a knowledge (call it "the perfect fitness and equanimity of things") that is not already enjoyed. (In this respect, to be told that "Backward I see in my own days where I sweated through fog with linguists and contenders" merely corroborates an inference already induced.) Adding to this sense that "my acceptation and realization" have been accepted and realized in the moment of being spoken is Whitman's use of the time-honored device of the Homeric legend or *pars epica*, by which the God or Numen is made present to the narrative through a recitation of its genealogical attributes, thus skirting overt supplication.[19] Though dusted off briefly in the opening lines ("My tongue, every atom of my blood, forma from this soil, this air, / Born here of parents born here from parents the same, and their parents the same"), the device receives its most extended treatment in the much-acclaimed "spiritual awakening," retrospectively told in the fifth section, where the soul's tongue is "plung'd to my bare-stript heart":

> Swiftly arose and spread around me the peace and
>   knowledge that pass all the argument of the earth,
> And I know that the hand of God is the promise of my
>   own,
> And I know that the spirit of God is the brother of my
>   own,
> And that all the men ever born are also my brothers,
>   and the women my sisters and lovers,
> And that a kelson of the creation is love,
> And limitless are the leaves stiff or drooping in the
>   fields,
> And brown ants in the little wells beneath them,
> And mossy scabs of the worm fence, heap'd stones,
>   elder, mullein, and poke-weed.
>
>   (*CRE*, p. 33)

Though the communion is said to surpass the earth, it seems fitting that we should be returned to its particularity. Though section five records what might be called a primal scene of voicing, its effect is not to hasten or individuate visionary powers but again to diffuse perception through the random, luminous commonplaces of the world.

"Not prophecy! NOT prophecy!" thunders William Carlos Williams, "no ideas but in things." If the verse discussed thus far hardly reaches so shrill a pitch, it does seek to mute the ambitious sweep of prophetic discourse by tracing out the metonymic deviations of "indirection." With respect to the latter scholarly opinion and the poet are in close agreement, for both see in the diffusion of Whitman's "limitless leaves" not only a "theme [which] is creative and has vista" but the distinguishing feature that sets "Walt Whitman, one of the roughs, a kosmos," apart from "the empty American parnassus" of his predecessors. In keeping with the prescription that "the great psalm of the Republic" is "to be indirect and not direct" most admirers properly extol "a strain of enthusiastic, receptive, indeterminate openness to experience which finds expression in a loose, unstructured form."[20] Under the terms of our discussion we could rephrase this to say, without too much forcing, that a poetics of indirection must consider itself to be neither a conversion nor an inversion of past values but something like a convocation of them. "Not to repel or destroy but to accept, fuse, rehabilitate" (*CRE*, p. 196) defines the "profound lesson of reception," an integrative, paratactic discourse (the rhetoric of "tallying") which, as we have seen, excludes nothing but exclusion. "Indirection" finds its calling in suspending evaluative acts altogether; it manifests its "indeterminate openness to experience" by abiding in a timeless present, thrusting aside "all talk of the beginning and the end." At the same time we have noted how "Song of Myself" 's "profound lesson of reception" is predicated on one essential exclusion: it situates the moment of proof before or beyond the present act of writing, variously thinking of it as antedating the text (poetic election being recast as a remembered event, the coupling of body and soul) or postdating it (awaiting future validation, as in the pledge to "stop this night and day with me and you shall possess the origin of all poems"). Yet what we have come to sense in our reading is the enormous strain of upholding such mediations, a strain evinced as the present shrinks into the fusions and confusions of beginning and end.

What is the direction of indirection? In posing this question under the guise of another ("What is the grass?"), Whitman responds with a series of propositions designed to show, as might be expected, that no (single) answer is possible. As with Ishmael's Leviathan, there are as many significances to Whitman's "uniform hieroglyphic" as there are consciousnesses to interpret it. Electing to "guess at" its multiple connotations, the speaker's tour de force combines a number of associations, ranging from the personal ("the flag of my disposition"), metaphysical ("the handkerchief of the Lord"), political ("sprouting alike in broad zones and narrow zones") to, lastly, a meditation on death ("the beautiful uncut hair of graves"):

> Tenderly will I use you curling grass,
> It may be you transpire from the breasts of young men,
> It may be if I had known them I would have loved them,
> It may be you are from old people, or from offspring
>   taken soon out of their mothers' laps.
> And here you are the mothers' laps.
>
> This grass is very dark to be from the white heads of
>   old mothers,

Darker than the colorless beards of old men,
Dark to come from under the faint red roofs of mouths.

                                              (*CRE*, p. 34)

Something of being "both in and out of the game" persists in this delicate
revery, though at least one subtle change in emphasis is worth noting. For
the first time in the poem voice is invested with a signifying force; as the
speaker soon "perceive[s] after all so many uttering tongues" and remarks
that "they do not come from the roofs of mouths for nothing," utterance
takes on a prominence that extends beyond the subliminal resonance of a
"lull" or "hum." Now hoping to "translate the hints" of the grave, the
speaker exchanges the pose of receptivity for hermeneutic appeal. It is as if,
in passing from the autoerotic communion of tongue and heart to the
broader question of genealogy, Whitman is acknowledging that self-creation
is not enough, that legitimation, to be true, requires sources of validation
outside the self. What this source consists of is, unsurprisingly, the principle
of reproduction, the power of his leaves to prevail over closure.
Consequently, as the poet next discovers that the furtive "hints" of his leaves
remain inscrutable, so far from lamenting this he presently launches into
ringing affirmations of life outlasting the grave: "All goes onward and
outward, nothing collapses":

What do you think has become of the young and old men?
And what do you think has become of the women and
    children?

They are alive and well somewhere,
The smallest sprouts show there is really no death,
And if ever there was it led forward life, and does
not wait at the end to arrest it,
And ceas'd the moment life appear'd.

                                              (*CRE*, p. 34)

But what materializes out of this ceaseless regeneration of meaning is,
paradoxically, meaning's fixation. Distinct from the accumulating sprouts of
section twenty-nine, where the temptation to symbolize is carefully resisted,
here we do find the poet editorializing on what "the smallest sprouts show."
His protests notwithstanding, there is a sudden effort to "translate the hints"
of "so many uttering tongues" and this effort is not without a discernible
strain, as suggested in the tortuous anacoluthon of the last two lines cited

above, whose congested phrasing, syntactical inversions, and confusing shifts of tense carry the reader anywhere but forward. The vision of unarrested flux staggers under the weight of sheer assertion.

Viewed from a broader perspective it is clear that the section registers a split between a mood of random, contented surmise and blunt, contentious expostulation. In "this inextricable hodge-podge you find at once beautiful phrases and silly gabble," charged one commentator eight years after Whitman's death in 1892; "tender imagination and insolent commonplace" collide so as to perpetrate "literary anarchy and a complete confusion of values."[21] Others have more recently deplored Whitman's "prophetic shrillness" at this stage in the poem,[22] though we need to go beyond simple condemnation and ask why such overinsistence occurs. That the section should be so divided against itself denotes, it might be said, a sudden rift between a poetry of diffusion whose signifier (the grass) ranges effortlessly through a field of significances and a poetry of reduction which seeks relief from such indeterminacy. Yet, as was noted in the discussion of the rivalry between the silent latency of "folded buds" and the tyrannies of "Speech," this view too swiftly polarizes what can be more profitably seen as a dialectic exchange. For what is striking about the end of section six is the way that it enacts what it appears to prohibit, the way it protests against reductiveness in a manifestly reductive fashion. The defiance of death and all terminations works to overdetermine indeterminacy. His lines, in effect, subvert what they cannot ultimately condone: a self-evolving chain of correspondences, "behavior lawless as snowflakes, words simple as grass ... laughter and naivete." The wish for this diffusion cannot be sustained any more comfortably than the drive to uphold its significance can be resisted. Stranded somewhere between both impulses, the myth of "free growth" threatens to harden into dogma.

"To impose is not to discover," Stevens warned. And once the uncompromising force of *that* imposition nears consciousness we fend it off by cleaving all the more adamantly to possibility. Cleave to it, in effect, with a bitterness that seems to only further drain it of significance: "It is possible, possible, possible. It must be possible." The difficulty facing Steven's predecessor, more easily resolved in theory than practice, is both obvious and acute. How does one propound the ideology of "free growth" without betraying its principles? How does a discourse that forswears the categorization of all value establish its own? To trace out the evolution of section six is to witness Whitman's struggle to accommodate his text to, in Richard Poirier's succinct definition, an aesthetic "so devoted to the *activity* of creation that it denies finality to the result of that activity, its objects and formulations. Art is an action and not the product of an action."[23] As an attempt to characterize "the place of style in American literature," this readily names the central aspiration of indirection: that no element in the text predetermine the course of its outcome. Yet while Poirier's generalization can certainly stand as an accurate paraphrase of Whitman's *ambition* it remains an equivocal account of his *achievement*. The quest for a "style continually fluid, leading on to shapes not yet apprehended and never to be fixed,"[24] identifies the project "Song of Myself" is pressed against, here more prosecuted by than prosecuting. Peering into the ominous richness of the grave, Whitman sees not only the simulacrum of womb and tomb but their composite in the macabre figure of "offspring taken soon out of their mothers's laps." What appears to presage the quickening of a new birth suggests as well its simultaneous demise.[25] Halted at a threshold which may be no threshold at all, the development of Whitman's conceit, itself something of a stillbirth, gropes toward an imagined bodily totality but succeeds in listing the *disjecta membra* of the grave: breasts, heads, laps, mouths, and tongues. Swerving from this phantasmagoria the poet concludes that nothing may conclude, and in the stridency of these assertions we overhear the anxiety that has set them in motion. The nemesis of foreclosure—"and did not wait at the end to arrest it and *ceas'd the moment life appear'd*"—persists. As we noted in reference to "Scented Herbage of My Breast," closure, because it is feared to have come too soon, will therefore not come at all.

The American writer, observes Leslie Fiedler, "is forever *beginning*," which is of course another way of saying that the American writer neither begins nor ends but is endlessly doing both at the same time.[26] I have been arguing that the drama of the excluded middle takes on a special urgency in "Song of Myself" since it marks that moment when Whitman's text confronts its "final merit" or "plenum of proof." Something thought to have pressed before or beyond the margins of representation breaks back into the present moment of writing, shutting down the chances for free growth before they can be set in motion. Proof wreaks havoc on temporality not by unraveling the continuity between beginning and end (this Whitman has already claimed to have done) but by condensing these terms with a swiftness that elides any middle ground capable of sustaining indirection's "indeterminate openness to experience." Time will always be out of joint for the revelations of proof so far as it underwrites that value which, like the grave's "so many uttering tongues," must and must not be translated. Representation is not thereby defrauded of its claims to legitimacy so much as it is preempted by the knowledge that any such claim can have no *place* in this song. As discourse falters between the imperative for autochthonous growth ("just go on supplying native models") and the prohibition against coercion ("you cannot force its growth"), prolepsis consumes metonymy, disclosing the end of every quest in the moment of its inception. Clearly, there can be little advantage in devising ways to anticipate the onset of this crisis since anticipation—the specter of foreclosure—itself defines the nature of that crisis. Looking back on section three, we read:

> I am satisfied—I see, dance, laugh, sing;
> As the hugging and loving bed-fellow sleeps at my side
>   through the night, and withdraws at the peep of day
>   with stealthy tread,
> Leaving me baskets cover'd with white towels swelling
>   the house with their plenty,
>
> Shall I postpone my acceptation and realization and
>   scream at my eyes,
> That they turn from gazing after and down the road,
> And forthwith cipher and show me to a cent,
> Exactly the value of one and exactly the value of two,
>   and which is ahead?
>
>   (*CRE*, pp. 31–32)

Much as this asks to be read as yet another instance of the kind of good-humored histrionics displayed in Whitman's expostulation with "Speech," there is genuine panic in it as well. We see the cross-purposes at once: value, to be secured, must be banished; its sanction will be its disappearance—"in the ground out of sight." This is not of course the explicit burden of Whitman's mocking question, whose satire we may imagine to be leveled at Lowell's witless crew of nationalists impatiently clamoring for cultural vindication, "as if it were some school exercise to be handed in by a certain day." And yet, as the fiercely overwrought denunciation called down upon the eyes attests, Whitman too wants not only proof but ocular proof. The godly insemination swelling the house with its plenty—perhaps harking back to the "houses and rooms" of the opening page or ahead to "the faint red roofs of mouths"—again lays bare the collusion between prolepsis and proof. Characteristically, postponement is not equated with the mere deferral of action but a kind of fast-forwarding of vision that prefigures the outcome of the journey before it has gotten under way. Voice screaming at vision is in this context scarcely distinguishable from vision berating Speech, each gesture standing as a self-reproach against the fetishizing of "proof," the overvaluation of "value.

Later editions saw fit to drop the explicit reference to "God" as that "hugging and loving bed-fellow" who steals away at daybreak, though this deletion should not entirely obscure awareness of the topos being toyed with in this vignette. The petition to draw down a God from the heavens so as to authorize and guide the poet's calling has a rich heritage in English prophetic tradition. So Milton calls on his muse ("Descend from Heaven, Urania") as another loving bedfellow who "visit'st my slumbers nightly" and who is requested "still govern thou my song ... when morn purples the east." This "harrowing of the skies" persists through various odes of the eighteenth century and certain Romantic lyrics with enough prominence to be labeled "the descendental theme" by Geoffrey Hartman.[27] It stands behind the voyeuristic glimpse of the mating of God and the Enthusiast Fancy in Collins's "Ode on the Poetical Character" as well as Blake's striking image of Milton entering Los's left foot. Whether Whitman had this cast of allusions in mind is at best uncertain, though as Abrams has established the topos in all likelihood reaches back to the apocalyptic marriage of heaven and earth, a Biblical precedent with which Whitman was certainly familiar.[28] Yet however he chanced upon this conceit it remains paradigmatic of Whitman's song that no sooner is this sign of election made manifest than anxiety over its *accreditation* takes hold. Because there is little or no interval between the promise of divine conception and the judgment to be passed upon it, vision never takes flight but turns back on the text to take stock of a value still in the throes of development. And in turning back it must be turned aside, as if there could be no alternative between value as an invisible immanence ("Do you not know O speech how the buds beneath you are folded?") and its fate as redundant energy ("Come now you conceive too much ..."). Thus it is hard to say whether Whitman's dalliance with this prophetic theme breaks off because it has lost its efficacy for him or because he wants too much from it.[29] Preferring description to invocation, the speaker does not of course petition his god; here as with his duel with the sun he makes good on his pledge of "not asking the sky to come down to my good-will, / But scattering it freely forever" (CRE, 41). But that is because the object of his calling is no more Urania than the "Me Myself." His true muse is "the value," the one element in his discourse which cannot be invoked.

Fetishism, from this standpoint, may be too inexact a term to apply to the quandary laid open by these ciphering eyes. From the "bard Elect" of *The Prelude* we learn of comparable misgivings over the tyranny of sight, "the most despotic of our senses," and by this we understand Wordsworth's need to coax the growth of his mind beyond a slavish adherence to external stimuli. To the untrained sensibility the "bodily eye," abstracted from the other senses and "thus sitting in judgement," wields "absolute dominion," often resulting in "that false secondary power, by which we create distinctions, then / Deem that our puny boundaries are things / Which we perceive, and not which we have made."[30] Fetishism on this showing involves a solipsism that outwits itself; the mind enthralled in the worship of "graven images" fails to recognize these as its own invention. A Wordsworthian poetics aspires to counter this deadening syndrome by pursuing a declared symbiosis of mind and Nature that "half perceives and half creates." As we have learned from Hartman the outer, "bodily eye" must be harmonized with inner illumination.[31] (A roughly analogous partnership is evoked early on in "Song of Myself" when Whitman, in speaking of "my soul" and "all that is not my soul"—"I and this mystery"—declares "lacks one, lacks both, and the unseen is proven by the seen, / Till that becomes unseen and receives proof in its turn" [(CRE, p. 31].) Yet, leaving aside for the moment the tendency of objects to surge past the "fluid and attaching character" with a swiftness that precludes visual fixation, the problem of perception in Whitman requires different emphasis. To stigmatize "that false secondary power" of the mind is to entertain, however provisionally, a detachment sufficient to isolate and analyze its proclivities, to posit a hierarchy of values serviceable to "this our high argument." Always sensitive to the twin threats of a entranced passivity before Nature or an aggrandizing mastery over it, Wordsworth's mature verse incorporates a finely wrought system of checks and balances capable of adjudicating between what may be credited as authentic vision and what may in turn discredit it. In Whitman the terms for any such metacommentary undergo a double fate, hardening as they dissolve. Just as proofs dismissal insures the persistence of its return, so does this recurrence touch off the panic of further denial. Given the extraordinary compression of this dialectic and the frightening rapidity with which it is set in motion, it becomes apparent that the feared reduction of value (whether through the idolatry of "graven images" or the "bald literalism" that "forthwith cipher[s] and show[s] me to a cent") cannot be attributed solely to the despotism of the eye. Rather, this fear permeates the world of "Song of Myself" at large; irreducible to any single dramatic encounter, it is most discernible as a prevenient, prospective energy, if not quite in the poem then visibly looming *before* it. Indeed, because no external image or "companionable form" gets attached to "the value" in the passage above, fetishism remains a danger in prospect only—not so much the product of a deluded, erring imagination as it is for Whitman something already ingrained in the starved expectations of a culture breathless to proclaim "An American bard at last!," the undissuable force of whose "native models" will "move to the head of all and put foreign models in the second class."

"To foretell our literature would be to create it," Everett had declared, as if word and deed, wish and fulfillment could be joined together in one irrevocable stroke. If political independence had been "spoken into existence," might not cultural liberty enjoy a similar fate? For, as Everett goes on to reason, he who could give shape to the anticipation of our literary destiny would perforce lay that anticipation to rest, just as "the gorgeous vision of the Iliad" was realized not in "the full detail of circumstance" but precisely in that moment when its "dim conception ... burst through the soul of Homer."[32] The instant translation of the "dim conception" into its finished structure identifies the dream and the peculiar burden of "indirection," which takes up the formidable task of conferring instant credibility for its own dim conceptions while insuring that each fresh "start" will not be its own "finish." In later years, once enshrined as the Good Gray Poet, Whitman would strike a more equable pose on the matter, patiently reminding his listeners in 1881 that "long, long are the processes of the development of Nationality. Only to the rapt vision does the seen become the prophecy of the unseen" (PW 2:486). Still, it is measure of the uneasy and often tortuous alliance between perception and validation in the Leaves that when the 1855 Preface turns to the visionary powers of the poet emphasis does not fall on the privileged vastation of the seer. Sight is instead called forth as that supreme source of acknowledgment, insusceptible to disconfirmation precisely because it tolerates no gap between what it sees and what it confirms. Seeing is believing: "Who knows the curious mystery of the eyesight? The other senses corroborate themselves, but this is removed from any proof but its own and foreruns the identities of the spiritual world" (PW 2:438–39). Broadly speaking, this is the "curious mystery" that prevails throughout the sections, predominantly visual in character, that intervene between the encounter with the grave's "uttering tongues" in section six and the subsequent encounter with the sun in section twenty-five. In them Whitman's "commission," his "acceptance and realization," is to harness the eye's pre-judicial energy, to get proof out of sight—in the sense of both deriving immediate confirmation from the eyes and of thereby removing the question of confirmation altogether. Following the shrill declamations against the "collapse" of life into death at the end of section six, section eight starts off by recouping some semblance of narrative continuity in the triple image of birth ("the little one sleeps in its cradle"),

sex ("the youngster and the red-faced girl"), and death ("the suicide sprawls
on the bloody floor"), each scene registered without comment by the
witnessing "I." Seemingly everywhere and nowhere, the speaker soon yields
to the vicarious delights of vision, beholding "the marriage of the trapper in
the open air in the far west," observing a "handsome and richly drest" lady
observing "Twenty-eight young [who] bathe by the shore," admiring the
"calm and commanding" poise of the Negro drayman. The divide between
perception and cognition is conscientiously maintained; like the "impassive
stones that receive and return so many echoes," the spectator for the most
part is content to "witness" and "note." Ciphering eyes have been set aside
for what are called in "Give Me the Splendid Silent Sun" "interminable
eyes." In the copious flow of scenes unfolding before it, "not a person or
object missing," the "I" no more pretends to disappear into these vistas as
omniscient narrator than it aspires to stand beyond them as a "transparent
eyeball." Identity appears as the interpenetration of all these activities which
"tend inward to me [as] I tend outward to them" (*CRE*, p. 44). This last quote
rounds of the first of the famed catalogs, whose additive appetite names
whatever it sees, from the "pure contralto in the organ loft" to the "canal boy
on the tow-path"; from the flat-boatman, spinning girl or fare-collector to
the lunatic connoisseur or half-breed. As commentators as diverse in outlook
as de Selincourt, Lynen, and Ziff have helped us to appreciate, these
constructions are not the wild effusions of someone "ranting and frothing in
my insane crisis" but a delicately arrayed stream of associations, with each
description and gesture by turns interlocking with or resonating against the
other.[33]

> The pedler sweats with his pack on his back, (the
>   purchaser higgling about the odd cent,)
> The bride unrumples her white dress, the minute hand
>   of the clock moves slowly,
> The opium-eater reclines with rigid head and just
>   open'd lips,
> The prostitute draggles her shawl, her bonnet bobs
>   on her tipsy and pimpled neck,
> The crowd laugh at her blackguard oaths, the men jeer
>   and wink to each other,
> (Miserable! I do not laugh at your oaths nor jeer at
>   you;)
> The President holding a cabinet council is surrounded
>   by the great Secretaries,

On the piazza walk three matrons stately and friendly
  with twined arms,
The crew of the fish-smack pack repeated layers of
  halibut in the hold ...

                                                      (*CRE*, p. 43)

With each snapshot flashing momentarily before the eye, action ceases the moment the line ends even as we are propelled forward by the paratactical momentum of the syntax. Just so, it is the "law of perfection" in the organic nature of things that any object's "finish is to each for itself and onward from itself."[34] The panoramic realism of the bard's "interminable eyes" releases an interminable series of images, separate but equal, which are as heterogeneous in content as they are undifferentiated in structure. In bringing America's "vast, seething mass of materials" to the page, Whitman's song of occupations here aims as well to bring the treacherous merger of scarcity and plentitude into workable form. Rather than the paralyzing collapse of end into beginning we find a procession of brilliantly etched, end-stopped lines that provides immediate closure for each utterance as well as the impetus for a fresh beginning. The effect is a structure that is radically open (the list being conceivably inexhaustible) and radically closed (each line being, imagistically speaking, a poem in itself). Excess can never be too much in such constructions, given their dexterity in harmonizing repetition and closure.[35] Because Whitman's tallying forbids granting visual salience to any one scene or individual (not even the "caresser of life" who absorbs and is absorbed by them), totality is both localized and refused. To the degree that there is no distinguishable "whole" to which the sum of these parts harkens, each part takes on the provisional appearance of that whole, though distributed along a contiguous chain of complementarity. "From the eyesight proceeds another eyesight, from the hearing proceeds another hearing and from the voice proceeds another voice eternally curious of the harmony of things." Value is held to strict account: voice will not go beyond what the eyes cannot reach; the eyes will not outstrip vision's advance. In the *concordia discos* of the catalog images are thus set forth "with scrupulous exactness," as Emily Dickinson wrote in another context, "to hold our senses on."

Exactness may seem the last word to describe the freewheeling euphoria of a Proteus, "hankering, gross, mystical, nude" who "can resist nothing better than [his] own diversity." The Jamesian injunction that the true artist is one upon whom nothing is lost takes on near maniacal proportions in the wake of section fifteen, with the "I" now "of every hue and caste ... every rank and religion, / A farmer, mechanic, artist, gentleman, sailor, quaker, / Prisoner, fancy-man rowdy, lawyer, physician, priest" (*CRE*, p. 45). Yet out of this apparent chaos of roles the rule of "opposite equals" predominates. Pledged as the poet is "not [to] have a single person slighted or left away," every thesis is promptly weighed against its antithesis for one who is not only "the poet of the Body" but "the poet of the Soul," of the "woman the same as the man," of the wicked as well as the good; "who play[s] not marches for accepted victors only ... [but] for conquer'd and slain"; no more "modest than immodest"; "stuff'd with the stuff that is coarse and stuff'd with the stuff that is fine." What seems a random dispersal of the self is on deeper reflection governed by a thoroughgoing attention to the apportionment of its energies. Thus while the poet appears to dilate to a breadth that defies all measurement—"not contain'd between my hat and boot-soles," his "orbit cannot be swept by the carpenter's compass"—he is also quick to insist that this amplitude can have no meaning unless measured by others, for "all I mark as my own you shall offset it with your own, / Else it were time lost listening to me" (*CRE*, p. 47). Like the catalogs in their closed openness, the self is presented as defiantly self-complete ("I know I am august ... I exist as I am, that is enough") and infinitely extendable ("In all people I see myself, not more and not barley-corn less"). The constitutionalism of the many into one and one into many does not melt the world, as Lawrence would have it, into "the awful pudding of One Identity."[36] The more we attend to "the afflatus surging and surging," the more we observe that its seemingly boundless lust for possession is marked off by countervailing impulses. "To see no possession but you may possess it" (*CRE*, p. 156) may be an article of faith for Whitman but it has little value unless the possessions of sight can be released or instantly expressed onto the page. An implicit economy of exchange applies throughout these sections: whatever this verse takes in must as readily be "let out," this being "the thoughtful merge of myself and outlet again" which "breath[es] the air but leave[s] plenty after me." The "kosmos" who commands "unscrew the locks from the doors, / Unscrew the doors themselves from their jambs" has himself become a revolving door, with every fresh "influx" of power partaking of its "efflux." This, too, is the fantasy of abundance without surfeit, of a capaciousness that will not incapacitate itself.

In this way the catalogs aim at a marriage of speaking and seeing which protects the poet against the perplexing condition of finding either sense "unequal to measure itself." Despite their notoriety as a radical innovation, they carry an essentially conservative appeal in the sense of restraining the pressure of human demand, of carefully tallying whatever is to be "let in" with whatever is "let out." While this particular feature of the catalogs is easily overshadowed by the comedic exuberance of a poem like "Song of Myself," it comes into sharper focus in a more composed lyric, "There Was a Child Went Forth," which offers the best account we have of the cataloging self and which is for this reason worth pausing over briefly. In its fusion of perceiver and perceived and in its flawless give and take of response and counterresponse, the poem unfolds a virtual allegory of consensus where the spoken and the seen are seamlessly and movingly joined.

> There was a child went forth every day,
> And the first object he look'd upon that object he
>   became,
> And that object became part of him for the day or a
>   certain part of the day,
> Or for many years or stretching cycles of years.
>
> (CRE, p. 364)

One thinks, momentarily, of Ahab on the quarterdeck, scanning the Doubloon for images of his omnipotence. But this is not, as it happens, a lyric about the solipsism of projection and before long we discover that the "object he became" is in fact simply all the objects that "became part of him." The omission of the relative pronoun in Whitman's Quaker-sounding title subtly reinforces this discovery by making whatever identity we can attribute to this child indistinguishable from his act of going forth, so that, in Charles Feidelson's graceful phrase, he "speaks the world that he sees and sees the world that he speaks; and in doing so *becomes* the reality of his vision."[37] As a result, the processional litany of sights and sounds, in taking on the appearance of speaking pictures, suffice in themselves to tell the story of poetic development, expanding outward from the burgeoning of plant and animal life, the sphere of primitive social distinctions, familial ambivalence, metaphysical doubts, to a final, valedictory scene at sunset. Untouched by nostalgia for a lost harmony that haunts comparable treatments of this subject by Wordsworth, Blake, or Shelley, Whitman's psychological idyll chooses to evoke an endlessly renewable reserve of forms, with objects and events permeating consciousness "then, now, and always."[38]

But even as this portrait recreates an ongoing commerce of "influx" and "efflux" which we have seen at work in the catalogs, it also hints at a necessary inhibition governing this poetic of reception. Whitman himself, no doubt unwittingly, strikes at the heart of the real poignance in the poem when, years later, he half-jokingly confided to Traubel that "there is really nothing in it at all—nothing at all.... It is a mere looking about at things"

(*WWC* 5:310). One could indeed say without prejudice that "There Was a Child Went Forth" succeeds so well because it asks so little. The reiterated emphasis on those things that "became part of him"; the peculiar reminder that the parents who fathered and conceived him "gave the child more of themselves than that, / They gave him afterward every day"; the hurried zeugma in a line like "the family usages, the language, the company, the yearning and swelling heart"; glancing references to the "affection that cannot be gainsay'd": these are in reality suppressed apostrophes, petitions so muted as to suggest apprehension over any mode of address that would too sharply individuate need against response. What "can be used can be used up" is how Geoffrey Hartman describes "*the anxiety of demand*," an anxiety "generated by the very pressure of demand we put upon things, and the resultant fear that they cannot 'beat' us."[39] Thus the declared correspondence between "I" and all the things composing the "I" never opens out into the glories of the egotistical sublime but functions precisely as a means of delimiting demand. Critics struck by the tantalizingly brief family portrait that straddles the middle of the poem have made this the center of their reading, finding this brevity suggestive of some profound rupture in emotional development that is quickly diffused into the generalized "doubts of the daytime and doubts of the nighttime." This no doubt is the case, yet the ambivalence observable in this scene is not finally distinguishable from the treatment of any other in the poem, all of which share the common trait of not evoking more than can be accounted for. Like the outpouring of people and places in the catalogs, the metonymic parade of details, in precluding visual fixation, also works to ensure that consciousness will not overspecify the objects of its attention any more than those objects will overextend it.

In the course of reflecting on various "systems of connection" or "types of union" which philosophy draws upon to structure human experience, William James hypothesizes that the "lowest grade" of connectedness would consist in "a world of mere *withness*, of which the parts were only strung together by the conjunction 'and'."[40] This essentially describes the world of the catalogs, whose components are strung together in the hope of realizing the lowest common denominator of Union—a world which lays to rest the dissension of competing values by setting the Secretaries at their cabinet meeting and the matrons in the piazza on an equal footing. What "There Was a Child Went Forth" reveals, in turn, is how this "world of mere *withness*" serves also to deflect or minimize the pressure of demand, in this case by diffusing the child's quest to locate the "affection that will not be gainsay'd" into a "mere looking about at things." Ordinarily, the two issues isolated here would appear to be unrelated, but only until we recall that an essential feature of the poet's demand in "Song of Myself" is to silence the dissension of value through the self-evident truths of his art. The catalogs represent one attempt to satisfy this demand, yet we are now in position to note that in suspending the issue of value and the vexed question of justification that goes along with it the catalogs do not finally settle these issues but wind them to a keener pitch. Thus, picking up "Song of Myself" where we left off, we read in section twenty-four: "By God! I will have nothing which all cannot have their counterpart of on the same terms"—an oath which gives vent to a rage for response so relentless in intensity and so overmastering in scope as to precipitate one section later the stifled potency of a voice "unequal to measure itself." For precisely because Speech is designated as that principle of excess forever overextending itself, its very redundancy triggers as well the fear of its own depletion. Held in check by what we have seen Emerson call a redundant deficiency and by what we can recognize as the disrelation between demand and response, Speech incarnates a demand doomed to recoil back upon its owner who, containing too much, contains not enough.

NOTES

1. See Whitman's letter to Emerson in 1856, reprinted in *CRE*, p. 739.

2. See Garry Wills, *Inventing America: Jefferson's Declaration of Independence* (New York: Vintage Books, 1978), p. xiv. My treatment of Lincoln's perception of a "moral hiatus" between Declaration and Constitution is also indebted to Dwight Anderson, *Abraham Lincoln: The Quest for Immortality* (New York: Knopf, 1982).

3. Fisher Ames, "American Literature," in *The American Literary Revolution: 1787–1837*, ed. Robert Spiller (Garden City, N.Y.: Anchor Books, 1967), p. 86; Harriet Martineau, *Society in America*, 3 vols. (London: Saunders and Otley, 1837), 3:206.

4. R. W. B. Lewis, *The American Adam: Innocence, Tragedy, and Tradition in the Nineteenth Century* (Chicago: University of Chicago Press, 1955), p. 45. On the relation between the American Renaissance and literary nationalism William Hedges justly notes that "we are seldom made to feel that there is any *vital* connection between the great writers of American literature and the literature of the years that are supposed to have prepared the way for it" ("The Myth of the Republic and the Theory of American Literature," *Prospects* 4 [1979]: 102).

5. I paraphrase the opening sentence of Margaret Fuller's "American Literature; Its Position in the Present Time, and Prospects for the Future," reprinted in *The American Transcendentalists: Their Prose and Poetry*, ed. Perry Miller (Garden City, N.Y.: Anchor, 1957), pp. 189–94. Whitman was much taken by Fuller's essay, first issued in 1846 among her *Papers on Literature and Art*. See his references to her "high-pitched taunt" (*PW* 2:539, 666–67), as well as William Carlos Williams's ironic adaptation of it in *Paterson* (New York: New Directions, 1969), p. 140.

6. D. H. Lawrence, *Studies in Classic American Literature* (New York: Viking Press, 1969), p. viii.

7. *The Native Muse: Theories of American Literature*, ed. Richard Ruland (New York: Dutton, 1972), pp. 313, 310, 312. For a comprehensive account of this period, the reader is referred to Benjamin Spencer, *The Quest for Nationality: An American Literary Campaign* (Syracuse, N.Y.: Syracuse University Press, 1957). Robert Weisbuch also provides a lively and informative overview in *Atlantic Double-Cross: American Literature and British Influence in the Age of Emerson* (Chicago: University of Chicago Press, 1986).

8. *The American Literary Revolution*, p. 309.

9. *The Native Muse*, pp. 86, 90.

10. Ibid, p. 143.

11. *The Will to Power*, ed. Walter Kaufmann, trans. Kaufmann and R. J. Hollingdale (New York: Viking Press, 1968), p. 3.

12. *The Native Muse*, p. 147.

13. See Perry Miller, *The Raven and the Whale: The War of Wits and Words in the Era of Melville and Poe* (New York: Harcourt, 1956), p. 207.

14. *The American Literary Revolution*, p. 74.

15. *The Journals and Miscellaneous Notebooks of Ralph Waldo Emerson*, ed. William Gilman and Alfred Ferguson, 16 vols. (Cambridge, Mass.: Belknap Press, 1960–), 7:521. Fisher Ames's opinions regarding "a right perception of genius" may be found in *The American Literary Revolution*, p. 75.

16. Or, as Frank Lentrichhia more bluntly states, "There can be no Emersonian action." See his discussion "On the Ideologies of Poetic Modernism, 1890–1913: The Example of William James," in *Reconstructing American Literary History*, ed. Sacvan Bercovitch (Cambridge, Mass.: Harvard University Press, 1986), p. 241.

17. See n. 2, Part 2.

18. Responding along similar lines, Donald Pease describes "an interlocutive process" whereby the poet's presence is not "identified with a psychological identity that existed before these songs.... Instead ... when Whitman wrote 'I sing myself' he literally meant that his singing brought a self into being" ("Blake, Crane, and Whitman: A Poetics of Pure Possibility," *PMLA* 96 [1981]: 77).

19. For a succinct description of this form see Northrop Frye, *Anatomy of Criticism* (Princeton, N.J.: Princeton University Press, 1957), p. 294. "Pars epica" I borrow from Kurt Schulter's study of *Die Englische Ode* (Bonn: H. Bouvier u. Co. Verlag, 1964), p. 31.

20. Richard M. Adams, *Strains of Discord: Studies in Literary Openness* (Ithaca: Cornell University Press, 1959), p. 181.

21. Barrett Wendell, *A Literary History of American Literature* (New York: Macmillan, 1900), p. 468.

22. Ivan Marki, *The Trial of the Poet: An Interpretation of the First Edition of "Leaves of Grass"* (New York: Columbia University Press, 1975), p. 137.

23. *A World Elsewhere: The Place of Style in American Literature* (New York: Oxford University Press, 1966), p. 21.

24. Ibid.

25. Commentators frequently cite the influence of Isaiah ("the son of man is as the grass") as standing behind Whitman's meditation on "the beautiful uncut hair of the grave." Yet as this familiar conceit modulates into the "faint red roofs of the mouth," the proximate source may be found in the Psalmist's curse "let them be as the grass on the

housetops that withereth before it groweth up," a curse which again plays upon the proleptic convergence of start and finish that I have been discussing.

26. *Love and Death in the American Novel* (New York: Criterion Books, 1960), p. xix.

27. See *The Fate of Reading* (Chicago: University of Chicago Press, 1975), p. 152.

28. *Natural Supernaturalism: Tradition and Revolution in Romantic Literature* (New York: Norton, 1971), pp. 37–56. We have of course already seen Whitman's variation on this "apocalyptic marriage" at the end of the twenty-fourth section of "Song of Myself."

29. In 1871, Whitman would have his way with the muse of the Old World Epic, charmingly beseeching her "To cross out please those immensely overpaid accounts, / That matter of Achilles's wrath ..." But that would come later.

30. *The Prelude*, ed. E. de Selincourt, 2d ed. revised by Helen Gardner (London: Oxford University Press, 1959), bk. 2, line 221, *passim*; bk. 13, lines 199–205. A useful discussion of Wordsworth's treatment of this issue and its bearing on subsequent nineteenth-century literature may be found in David Simpson, *Fetishism and Imagination: Dickens, Melville, Conrad* (Baltimore: Johns Hopkins University Press, 1982).

31. *Wordsworth's Poetry, 1787–1814* (New Haven, Conn.: Yale University Press, 1964).

32. *The American Literary Revolution*, p. 296.

33. See Basil de Selincourt, *Walt Whitman: A Critical Study* (1914; reprint, New York: Russell and Russell, 1965), pp. 124–55, 149–51; Lynen, *The Design of the Present: Essays on Time and Structure in American Literature* (New Haven, Conn.: Yale University Press, 1969), pp. 290–95; and Ziff, *Literary Democracy: The Declaration of Cultural Independence* (New York: Viking, 1981), pp. 233–34.

34. *The 1855 Edition of "Leaves of Grass,"* ed. Malcolm Cowley (New York: Viking Press, 1959), p. 11.

35. I therefore cannot agree with Quentin Anderson's contention that the catalogs, "at their brilliant best, are successful efforts to melt things together, to make the sum of things ring with one note ... he dowers his world with only so much quiddity as he can dissolve, or cants each created thing on the slope of process down which it will slide to oblivion." Anderson's "poet of decreation," whoever it may be, is certainly not Whitman. See *The Imperial Self* (New York: Knopf, 1971), pp. 95, 94.

36. *Studies in Classic American Literature*, p. 218.

37. *Symbolism and American Literature* (Chicago: University of Chicago Press, 1953), p. 25.

38. David Cavitch points up this aspect of Whitman's originality in remarking that "the figure of the child in Whitman's poetry conveys neither the challenging innocence of Blake's radical infants nor the natural piety of Wordsworth's 'best philosopher'. Whitman's child is not Rousseau's animal with perfectly balanced instincts.... Whitman is less sentimental than most writers who participated in the aggrandizement of childhood in the nineteenth century" (*My Soul and I: Whitman's Inner Mystery* [Boston: Beacon Press, 1985], p. 36).

39. "I. A. Richards and the Dream of Communication," *The Fate of Reading*, p. 38.

40. William James, *Pragmatism* (Cambridge, Mass.: Harvard University Press, 1975), pp. 76–77.

DAVID BROMWICH

A Simple Separate Person

When Whitman described himself as a *kosmos*, he may have meant that he contained a good deal of prose. But apart from *Leaves of Grass*, the only writing he brought to a finish went into two books, *Specimen Days* and *Democratic Vistas*. The first of these is entirely composed of moments: the vigils that Whitman kept over the dying or the wounded during the Civil Was; and his intervals of solitary repose in nature. Both kinds of moment show Whitman's absorbing concern with sanity—literally, with the cleanliness of the body and of the soul—and the same concern seems to have been a leading motive in his defense of American democracy. These works share a common premise with his poetry as well. They imagine a more than empirical character, the self, whose existence is prior to the soul's aspirations, and whose fate is untouchable by the reverses of daily life. This self Whitman thought of as the product of American society at a certain time, the years of the successful fight of the Union against the slaveholding interests. Personal independence to him was the natural accompaniment of the self's assurance of survival, through its union with others; and such assurance could not be had in all the possible circumstances of a society: it would be ruled out, for example, in a society moving toward a more rather than a less restricted franchise. But Whitman had given a social definition of self-trust which he felt that the war itself vindicated. It proved that all

From *A Choice of Inheritance: Self and Community from Edmund Burke to Robert Frost.* © 1989 by the President and Fellows of Harvard College.

inherited goods began in custom but ended in enslavement. This was another way of saying that the individual self had an exception-making power to any claim urged by others, a tendency to resist impositions which derived from its very knowledge of the body. Thus the liberating recognition of American political life turned out to be the same as that of American personal experience. All of Whitman's prose explores what he called "personalism," its moments and prospects, and all of it exists to help readers in bearing out the prophecies of "Song of Myself."

How far a single purpose animates his works ought to emerge now more plainly than ever before, with the appearance of his *Notebooks and Unpublished Prose* in six volumes edited by Edward Grier, together with the Library of America edition of his *Complete Poetry and Prose*.[1] Whitman filled more notebooks than anyone suspected. Apart from the short stories written in early youth, a temperance novel, and the miscellaneous contents of the *Collect* and *November Boughs*, he kept jottings of his moods, friends, false starts and late honors, eulogies to himself and paraphrases of other people's eulogies. In these pages one may discover him teaching himself the learned pronunciation of "insouciance" (een-soo-se-áwns); contemplating a Banjo Poem and a "*Poem of Large Personality*," of which he remarks in passing, "make this poem for women just as much as men"; compiling lists of the men and women he meets, but the men chiefly, and later the names of the Union soldiers he has talked to. There are also notes for various prefaces and at least two drafts of a last will and testament. Some of the most interesting entries try out versions of lines which one knows from their subsequent life in "Song of Myself." Such a detail as, "And a mouse is miracle enough to stagger sextillions of infidels," did not come all at once: it took Whitman some time to arrive at a number with the appropriate weight. But the most susceptibly erotic passages of the "Song" were still more so in draft:

> Fierce Wrestler! do you keep your heaviest grip for the last?
> Will you sting me most even at parting?
> Will you struggle even at the threshold with spasms more delicious than
>   all before?
> Does it make you ache so to leave me?
> Do you wish to show that even what you did before was nothing to what
>   you can do
> Or have you and all the rest combined to see how much I can endure?
> Pass as you will; take drops of my life if that is what you are after
> Only pass to some one else, for I can contain you no longer.
> I held more than I thought

> I did not think I was big enough for so much ecstasy
> Or that a touch could take it all out of me.[2]

A few entries like this are enough to justify the publication of the *Notebooks*; and the paragraphs that follow will quote many more. But alone, they give a false impression of the general quality of the material. For these two editions of Whitman suggest, both as to purpose and utility, opposite approaches to the experience of reading.

The *Notebooks* are only the latest of those massive and licensed editions in which every last scrap of an author (including in this case his games of animal—vegetable—mineral) is dutifully reproduced and annotated, everything but (though the omission may be accidental) his contests at tick-tack-toe. Presumably, if Whitman's hand could be detected in the noughts and crosses, these too would appear; along with the entry, occupying a whole page, which runs in full: "The Daylight? magazine? annual? monthly? quarterly"—one line of doodling, escorted into posterity by five lines of notes indicating the paper on which it was written and the date to which unfortunately it cannot be assigned. The typical page of these volumes is half empty, and what there is of print has been given over to notes of insertions and deletions, fourteen such notes to eight lines of print being a not uncommon proportion. By whom will it be used? The responsible scholar needs to look at the papers and microfilms anyway, while the interested reader cares for Whitman's words and not his subliterary *disjecta membra*. Of course, researchers exist who belong to a class between these two: word-counters and deletion-counters, the behaviorists of the writing process, for whom rough specimens of their subject will do. Their toil is harmless, though it ought not to be humored or paid for. And yet, the sheer size of this edition can only have been determined by a considerate projection of their needs.

By contrast with the *Notebooks*, the Library of America *Whitman* prints everything of prose as well as poetry that Whitman cared to see survive. It is meant for the study rather than the vault, and is agreeable to handle besides being pleasant to read. Since Whitman thought of his words as an almost physical extension of himself, one can imagine him ranking these merits high. Two features of the book also make it preferable to any combination of earlier editions: the inclusion of a complete text of the 1855 *Leaves of Grass*, and a section of "Supplementary Prose" with Whitman's pamphlet on the eighteenth presidency. In the latter document, as nowhere else in his writings, one sees with Whitman's eyes the look of the depraved men from whom Lincoln redeemed the nation. "WHENCE," he asks, "DO THESE

NOMINATING DICTATORS OF AMERICA YEAR AFTER YEAR START OUT?" "From lawyers' offices," he replies, "secret lodges, back-yards, bed-houses, barrooms; from out of the custom-houses, marshals' offices, post-offices, and gambling-hells." In answer to the next question—"WHO ARE THEY PERSONALLY?"—he pictures the nominators of Fillmore .and Buchanan according to their works:

> Slave-catchers, pushers of slavery, creatures of the President, creatures of would-be Presidents, spies, blowers, electioneers, body-snatchers, bawlers, bribers, compromisers, runaways, lobbyers, sponges, ruined sports, expelled gamblers, policy backers, money-dealers, duelists, carriers of concealed weapons, blind men, deaf men, pimpled men, scarred inside with the vile disorder, gaudy outside with gold chains made from the people's money and harlot's money twisted together; crawling, serpentine men, the lousy combings and born freedom sellers of the earth.[3]

This is done in Cobbett's style, with as sure a sense as Cobbett's of the mutually strengthening effects of the allegorical cartoon and the simple name. But it is strange to realize that Whitman was here addressing the same audience he hoped would listen to "Song of Myself": an audience of the shockable, haters of the unclean deed and the unclean side.

After the assassination of Abraham Lincoln, he knew of their existence as a certainty, because the news brought evidence of their feelings. "As to the other Presidents," he writes in a notebook entry, "they have had their due in formal and respectful treatment, in life & death. But this one alone has touched the popular heart to its deepest. For this one alone, through every city, every country farm, the untouch'd meal, the heavy heart & moistened eye & the sob in private chambers." The image of Lincoln dying seems to be associated throughout Whitman's writings with a more abstract conception: that of the "sane and sacred death" of a person, in the presence of whose body the mourners become conscious of their sanity, and of their sacredness to each other. Social obligations like personal ones thus follow from a recognition of sacrifice. The master-image for this, in his prose and poetry alike, is the passage of breath from a father to a son.

Whitman, however, was apt to dwell on one detail of the scene. In the lecture he used to give about the death of Lincoln, he ended his dramatic account of the murder by observing how "the life blood from those veins, the best and sweetest of the land, drips slowly down, and death's ooze already begins its little bubbles on the lips." In the great poem "As I Ebb'd with the

Ocean of Life," the observer is Whitman himself, but the dead man has become his father, whose broken career the poet must resume:

> Me and mine, loose windrows, little corpses,
> Froth, snowy white, and bubbles,
> (See, from my dead lips the ooze exuding at last,
> See, the prismatic colors glistening and rolling).

Here the passage from death to life is marked by a return of all aspirations to a material trace, the oozing of a spirit into the air. But for Whitman the consciousness of such a moment exalts rather than degrades. It recalls the soul to the things it is composed of, and points to their recoverability by others.

Our usual mistake about immortality, as Whitman sees it, is to imagine our survival as the extension of a single entity. We can avoid this, he thinks, by supposing that we continue in time only as an author's words continue in the minds of his readers. They create a benefit that is inconceivable to the benefactor. Our extension in space, through our moral relations with others, implies continuity of another sort. But to explain it, Whitman suggests that we can appeal only to what we know of existence (physical existence). This side of Whitman's thinking seemed to D. H. Lawrence praiseworthy beyond all the rest since it released us from the tiresome superiority of the soul. "Whitman was the first heroic seer to seize the soul by the scruff of her neck and plant her down among the potsherds. 'There!' he said to the soul. 'Stay there!'"[4] The soul's coincidence with the body is announced in a line of "Crossing Brooklyn Ferry" which captures all Whitman's doctrine: "That I was I knew was of my body, and what I should be I knew I should be of my body." This belief forms an implicit apology for his verbal innovations as well. Grammar and habitual usage agree in enforcing a firm, if conventional, division between verbs and nouns. But in Whitman a redefinition of language, by which common verbs are shaped into nouns, brings with it a redefinition of experience, by which the human joins the divine. "Dazzling and tremendous, how quick the sunrise would kill me, / If I could not now and always send sunrise out of me." In any poetry but Whitman's this would be an instance of bathos. "Earth of the vitreous pour of the full moon just tinged with blue! / Earth of shine and dark mottling the tide of the river!" Again, in any other poetry this would be merely an overconspicuous metaphor. As one reads "Song of Myself," however, both gestures seem accurate representations of the constant and radical connection of soul with body.

Paul Zweig in a recent and engaging biography, *Walt Whitman: The Making of the Poet*, allows his subject a more narrowly literary originality.[5] Whitman here is not what Lawrence called him, a great changer of the blood in the veins of men, but rather a man "genuinely at ease with the moralizing idiom of Victorian America." Whitman's adaptability, as Zweig understands it, enabled him to act subversively in another way; and on the last page of the book, Zweig asserts that Whitman "assaulted the institution of literature and language itself, and, in so doing, laid the groundwork for the anti-cultural ambition of much modernist writing. He is the ancestor ... of all who have made of their writing an attack on the act of writing and on culture itself." Elsewhere, in a similar vein, Zweig is rather careless of nuance: he sums up Whitman's belief that the self responds to experience as a "fundamental belief in the malleability of human personality." Still the summary statement, when placed beside the earlier suggestion about Whitman's congeniality to Victorian moralism, does make an interpretation of his career. Zweig invites us to look at Whitman as a theatrical personality whose bold experiments in language were aimed at destroying culture for the sake of a religious ideal. How well does this tally with the things Whitman said or did?

In his personal deportment, he appears not to have sought much conformity with the practices of his time and place. The sexual emphasis of the "Children of Adam" and of the "Calamus" poems in particular was thoroughly remarked by his contemporaries; but he did not follow the prudential advice to change or suppress them, even when it came from Emerson. It is true that he shared in a popular opinion whenever he could, and always avoided insulting a popular favorite. There may be a conventional ease, too, in his respect for such idols of the day as Longfellow and Whittier. But was his respect much more than tolerance? Whitman pointed out the good they did; and in Longfellow's case it certainly had to do with culture, in any possible sense of the word. But he never pretended to compare it to his good. As for Whitman's general "attack on the act of writing," what evidence is there of this? He writes in his notebook, "Make no quotations, and no reference to any other writers." But that is less an attack on writing than an echo of every great writer's demand to be read for his inventions; in short, a faithful and literal rendering of Emerson's admonition: "Meek young men grow up in libraries, believing it their duty to accept the views which Cicero, which Locke, which Bacon have given; forgetful that Cicero, Locke, and Bacon were only young men in libraries when they wrote these books." Such an attitude may turn to iconoclasm in the end; yet Whitman habitually instructs himself in a manner that could never be used by an iconoclast of writing: "In future *Leaves of Grass. Be more severe* with the final revision of the poem.... Also *no ornaments*, especially no *ornamental adjectives*, unless they have come molten hot, and imperiously prove themselves. No *ornamental similes at all—not one: perfect transparent clearness* sanity and health are wanted—that is the *divine style*."[6] Whitman's hope was that, in America, the dignity of social life would reach a height at which this style expressed nothing more than the experience of the "divine average."

Zweig paraphrases the divine average as "the mystery of the ordinary," but they are not the same thing. For Whitman's idea relates to a godlike self-sufficiency that may be achieved by each person from his contact with every other, and from the impalpable modifications of his experience by theirs. There is nothing mysterious about it; and more than a point about usage is at stake. Whitman preferred democracy to feudalism (the latter being his name for everything before America) only on the ground that it promoted this sort of contact. "We will not," he says in *Specimen Days*, "have great individuals or great leaders, but a great average bulk, unprecedentedly great." He naturally admired Carlyle as an unsettler of outworn customs, but saw that his effect was vitiated by the cult of the hero. Later in the same book, he puts down the fault to a physical indisposition, "dyspepsia," from which Carlyle did in fact suffer, and which has for Whitman the significance of a bodily lapse from sanity.

> For an undoubtedly candid and penetrating faculty such as [Carlyle's], the bearings he persistently ignored were marvelous. For instance, the promise, nay certainty of the democratic principle, to each and every State of the current world, not so much of helping it to perfect legislators and executives, but as the only effectual method for surely, however slowly, training people on a large scale toward voluntarily ruling and managing themselves (the ultimate aim of political and all other development)—to gradually reduce the fact of *governing* to its minimum.[7]

The personalism, however, which America uniquely fostered, began for Whitman as an imaginative premise. It would join the practice of democracy later, with the widening of the franchise in the thirteenth, fourteenth, and fifteenth amendments to the Constitution. In this sense the future proposed by "Song of Myself"—"I concentrate toward them that are nigh, I wait on the door-slab"—could not speak for itself without looking back at the war.

Specimen Days carries out the task of retrospect for the author alone. (One of its provisional titles was *Autochthons ... Embryons*.) But to the extent that this, and indeed all of Whitman's writings, are judged as an estimate of

America, they have to be read in the light of *Democratic Vistas*. From its opening allusion to the *Areopagitica*, the book concerns the possibility of realizing a "copious, sane, gigantic offspring" among the aggregate persons in a democracy, though till now that has been an achievement reserved for nations as a whole. No literature before America's—which still lay mostly in the future—had recognized the people as its subject. Even Whitman did not seethe depth of the error, he admits, before he visited the Civil War hospitals, and saw the courage of the individuals who suffered the agony of a nation. Yet the suffering that isolates strength and, in consequence, gives a first self-image to individualism, is only half of democracy: "There is another half, which is adhesiveness or love, that fuses, ties and aggregates, making the races comrades, and fraternizing all." Following the declaration of these two principles, Whitman asks that we change our idea of culture to bring it into keeping with both. The attempt will be not to overthrow but to civilize culture, so that we take "for its spinal meaning the formation of a typical personality of character, eligible to the uses of the high average of men—and *not* restricted by conditions ineligible to the masses." Throughout the argument Whitman insists on two facts about democracy: that it is an affair of daily experience and not simply of elections; and that its future is threatened, but need not be ultimately darkened, by the coming of the machine. He warns his reader emphatically against the "depravity of the business classes" whose authority has been tightened by the rationalization of labor. The weapon that the people can still use to defend themselves comes from their own sense of "the average, the bodily, the concrete, the democratic, the popular." These last, Whitman hopes to have shown, are different aspects of a single thing.

It has never been clear what it would mean to read Whitman just for the poetry. Readers who think they are doing so, either are not getting the poetry, or they are getting something more. Because he writes from a crisis in the history of American democracy, it may seem odd that he should implicate those who can take its victories for granted. And yet, because it was a crisis that defined the character of America, far more than the Revolutionary War ever did, he still seems to speak to us intimately. "What thought you have of me now, I had as much of you—I laid in my stores in advance." The attitude in which readers today are likeliest to find him objectionable is not that of the sage but that of the sympathizer. He cannot, they feel, sympathize with the runaway slave without reducing him to a victim, and at this point his sympathy is exposed as pity. But such an objection misunderstands Whitman's purpose in the narrative episodes of "Song of Myself" and elsewhere. These are not exchanges of identity, followed by a judgment, but experiments in a possible identity, followed by a *Stand back!* Even so, the resistance to Whitman's sympathy betrays the extent of the accommodation to another of his ideals. His individualism has done so well that readers want to forestall, as a trespass against themselves, any word or gesture that wears a momentary look of adhesiveness.

Lawrence said that the compulsion to love was at the bottom of Whitman's troubles, and he gave the illustration of the Eskimo in the kayak. Let Whitman see him sitting there and at once he will become the Eskimo though he does not know what a kayak is. It is a true picture; and in fact Whitman is routinely capable of stranger extravagances. In a passage of the *Notebooks* which he rephrased, rather obliquely, for "Song of Myself," he stands in the way of the man who is about to take his own life: "O despairer! I tell you, you shall not go down, / Here is my arm, press your whole weight upon me, / With tremendous breath I force him to dilate." He does this while staying quite free of the assumption he is charged with making, that he supposes the objects of his sympathy to be virtuous or reformable by himself. He does assume that "the universal and fluid soul impounds within itself not only all the good characters and heroes but the distorted characters, murderers, thieves." Impoundment is a long way from sympathy as most people interpret it, just as the divine average was a long way from the mystery of the ordinary. The most moving thing about Whitman after all is that he teaches, instead of an absolution from sins, a sort of patience with deformities from which a human charity might begin. A plausible further charge, that even acts of charity infringe on the rights of others, he has met by anticipation in an anecdote:

> "Tell them," said the agent to the interpreter, "that the poet-chief has come to shake hands with them, as brothers." A regular round of introductions and hearty hand-claspings, and "How's!" followed. "Tell them, Billy," continued the agent, "that the poet-chief says we are all really the same men and brethren together, at last, however different our places, and dress and language." An approving chorus of guttural "Ugh's!" came from all parts of the room, and W. W. retired, leaving an evidently captivating impression.[8]

He wrote the news story himself; but it is not recorded that any of the Sioux Indian chiefs afterward complained of this treatment by the poet-chief. As usual, he had laid in his stores in advance.

NOTES

1. Walt Whitman, *Notebooks and Unpublished Prose Manuscripts*, ed. Edward Grier, 6 vols. (New York, 1984); *Complete Poetry and Collected Prose* (Library of America, New York, 1981).

2. Whitman, *Notebooks*, I, 77.

3. Whitman, *Complete Poetry and Prose*, pp. 1313–14.

4. D. H. Lawrence, *Studies in Classic American Literature* (New York, 1961), pp. 171–172.

5. Paul Zweig, *Walt Whitman: The Making of the Poet* (New York, 1984).

6. Whitman, *Notebooks*, I, 385.

7. Whitman, *Complete Poetry and Prose*, pp. 892–893.

8. Whitman, *Notebooks*, II, 881.

MARK BAUERLEIN

Reading

The poem immediately following "Song of Myself" in the first edition (later called "A Song for Occupations"[1]) begins with a simple, direct entreaty:

> Come closer to me,
> Push close my lovers and take the best I possess,
> Yield closer and closer and give me the best you possess.
> This is unfinished business with me .... how is it with you?
> I was chilled with the cold types and cylinder and wet paper between us.
>   (ll.1–5)

He "*was* chilled." Henceforth, we may dispose of print, paper, and other "cold" mediations and enjoy the thrilling warmth of emotive bodily contact. But even though, presumably, writing now is committed to the past—that is, to the previous poem, which has, through its self-effacing signs, carried poet and disciple beyond technique and artifice and mediation—still there remains "unfinished business." The mutual swapping of "the best," occurring only through intimate "contact of bodies and souls" (l. 6, later deleted), is still pending. Further instruction is required:

From *Whitman and the American Idiom.* © 1991 by Louisiana University Press.

There is something that comes home to one now and perpetually,
It is not what is printed or preached or discussed.... it eludes discussion and
    print,
It is not to be put in a book.... it is not in this book,
. . . .
You may read in many languages and read nothing about it;
. . . .
I do not know what it is except that it is grand, and that it is happiness,
And that the enclosing purport of us here is not a speculation, or bon-mot or
    reconnoissance,
And that it is not something which by luck may turn out well for us, and
    without luck must be a failure for us,
And not something which may yet be retracted in a certain contingency.

(ll. 44–58)

In both style and subject matter, these didactic lines parallel Section 50 of "Song of Myself," the uplifting hymnal climax wherein Whitman affirms "eternal life" and "happiness" for all "brothers and sisters." But although both passages eulogize this "perpetual" "home-like" presence in all its transcendent benevolence, what stands out in each description is its inaccessibility to language. Appearing in the first edition within a few pages of one another, both sections speak of the "grand" but unspeakable truth lying at the base of all metaphysics, deny its representation by "utterance or symbol" and "discussion and print," refer to "it" in vague, negative terms— "There is something," "I do not know what it is," "It is not"—and then give to it the frankly inadequate name "happiness" (or perhaps "happiness" is merely a signifiable concomitant of "it"). But whereas in "Song of Myself" Whitman confidently attributes "it" to himself—"There is that in *me*"—in "A Song for Occupations," he regards "happiness" objectively: "something that comes home *to one*." Whereas the first poem emphasizes the poet's difficulty in *expressing* the "happiness" surging within him, the subsequent poem points out the impossibility of *reading* it in the word. "It is not what is printed or preached or discussed"; it is not in any language. Therefore it cannot be read or communicated in any ordinary sense of the term.

He "knows" it because it *affects* him. To Whitman, the encounter with "happiness" is a moment of nonlinguistic seizure by some organic medium of presence (call it "magnetism," "vocalism," "*live feeling*," and so on), an arresting penetration that overrides human will and permeates the soul. Conversely, reading, in his view, involves a calculated interpretation of lifeless transmissions no longer continuous with their authoritative provenance, an attempt to decipher original feelings from their exterior, errant representations. If those signs turn out to be inadequate to their source or if the reader lacks the necessary sensitivity and native breadth, reading will degenerate into critical appropriations more or less responsive to the poet's creative impulse, "leaving each reader eligible to form the resultant-poem for herself or himself" (*NUPM*, I, 335). Notwithstanding the language's magnetic attraction, its intended effect is left to the reader's arbitrary choice. In consequence, reading is indeterminate, a matter of chance, "something which by luck may turn out well for us, and without luck must be a failure for us."

Rather than letting *ananke* lapse into *tyche*, rather than offering up his inviolate, soul-inspired songs to capricious interpretations, Whitman insists that "the enclosing purport of us here is not a *speculation*, or *bon-mot* or *reconnoissance*." This italicized grouping names three types of reading that do violence to what is given, what is natural, what lives in the present. Specifically, "speculation," financially considered, is a self-serving projection into an unknown, random future, an investment of the signs of one's resources into a fluctuating, ineffable marketplace of percentages and interest rates and gains and losses, an attempt to take account of innumerable variables to add to one's store of possessions. Philosophically considered, speculation relinquishes concrete reality for the airy heights of abstraction and pursues absolute knowledge, theory, and proof, not realizing that the answer lies in the ground below: "I swear there can be no theory of any account, unless it corroborate the theory of the earth!" ("A Song of the Rolling Earth," l. 93).

A "bon-mot"—a literary parody of "the password primeval"—is the condensed result of "dandified" criticism, a witty epithet encapsulating but trivializing profound, sublime utterance (for example, Kenneth Burke calling Emerson's *Nature* a "Happiness Pill"). A "bon-mot" converts inspiration into the pithy phrase admirable more for its nifty sounds or clever ironies than for its sincere and direct meaningfulness.

And "reconnoissance"—that is, "scouting ahead," reading beyond the due confines of poem and poet—forsakes the proper locus of feeling and truth for pointless, extravagant meanderings into future representations. In other words, "*speculation*, or *bon-mot* or *reconnoissance*" needlessly supplements Whitman's language of the soul and adds to it irrespective of its organic wholeness. A proper reception of *Leaves of Grass* pays heed to "the law of [Whitman's] own poems" (*PW*, I, 210) and "tallies" faithfully their emotive permutations, lives and breathes in harmony with Whitman's "respiration and inspiration ... the beating of [his] heart" ("Song of Myself," l. 23), and thus incorporates his "meaning" directly, without alteration or "contingency." Unlike ordinary discourse, which can be refuted by arguments, disproved by facts, or qualified by future discourse, Whitman's poetry, once circulated, cannot be modified or "retracted" by inhospitable readers. His words carry feeling vigorously and ineluctably to those whose hearts are primed for it, those who need not "read" in order to understand.

These are Whitman's ideal (non-)readers, the "yous" whom he addresses in so many of the poems following in the wake of "Song of Myself." Indeed, apart from the tiresome catalog poems commemorating democratic life in the New World, the most prevalent motif in the second and third editions is that of Whitman, with more or less trepidation, counseling readers in how to interpret his poems. As in "A Song for Occupations," he usually expresses his acute consciousness of coming interpreters, of "Whoever You Are Holding Me Now in Hand," and then advises them to turn off their analytic apparatus and free themselves for an immediate, palpable incursion of emotive magnetism. He admits, "I know very well these [poems] may have to be searched many times before they come to you and comply with you. / But what of that? Has not Nature to be searched many times?" (*NUPM*, I, 263).

This preoccupation with reading marks a considerable step beyond the major issue of "Song of Myself"—composition—although both develop out of Whitman disquiet over the arbitrariness of the sign. Supposedly having surmounted "writerly" mediations in his preparatory epic, Whitman considers next the other side of communication—response. "Song of Myself" initiated Whitman's flight from the arbitrary sign by exploring the possibility of writing a natural language of pure sound or physiognomy; successive poems extend his "language experiment" by attempting to circumscribe not the inscription itself but its reception. Reading, not composition, becomes the central concern of Whitman's poetics, the dominant anxiety revealed by numerous explicit directives and supplications to far-off anticipated readers:

> Whoever you are, now I place my hand upon you, that you be my poem,
> I whisper with my lips close to your ear,
> I have loved many women and men, but I love none better than you.
> O I have been dilatory and dumb,
> I should have made my way straight to you long ago,
> I should have blabbed nothing but you, I should have chanted
>   nothing but you. ("To You," ll. 6–11)

Let the paper remain on the desk unwritten, and the book on the shelf
    unopened! ("Song of the Open Road," l. 216)

You bards of ages hence! when you refer to me, mind not so much
    my poems,
Nor speak of me that I prophesied of The States, and led them
    the way of their glories;
But come, I will take you down underneath this impassive
    exterior—I will tell you what to say of me:
Publish my name and hang up my picture as that of the tenderest lover,
The friend, the lover's portrait, of whom his friend, his lover was fondest,
Who was not proud of his songs, but of the measureless ocean of
    love within him—and freely poured it forth ... ("Recorders
    Ages Hence," ll. 1–5; the second line was later deleted.)

I am a man who, sauntering along, without fully stopping, turns
    a casual look upon you and then averts his face,
Leaving it to you to prove and define it,
Expecting the main things from you. ("Poets to Come," ll. 7–9)

See, projected through time,
For me, an audience interminable.
With firm and regular step they wend—they never stop,
Successions of men ...
With faces turned sideways or backward toward me to listen,
With eyes retrospective towards me. ("Starting from Paumanok,"
    ll. 29–36)

I myself make the only growth by which I can be appreciated,
I reject none, accept all, reproduce all in my own forms. ("By
    Blue Ontario's Shore," ll. 10–11)

To this list of verse passages dealing with the prospects of reading, one
could add dozens of quotations from Whitman's various prose writings. For
example, he writes, "I suppose it is hardly necessary to tell you that I have
pitched and *keyed* my pieces more with reference to fifty years hence, & how
they will stand mellowed and toned *then*—than to pleasing & tickling the
immediate impressions of the present hour" (*Cor.* II, 310). This rejection of
"immediate impressions" and admission of rhetorical calculation, written in
1874, shows the extent to which Whitman has modified his poetics.

One recognizes in the lines above several Whitmanian strategies abounding in the 1856 and 1860 editions. In the first quotation, Whitman, on the one hand, desires to inseminate readers with his seductive "lispings," to make them one with his poems, and, on the other hand, he fears that his "chant," too self-centered and peculiar, falls on benumbed ears. In the second, he tells readers to cast away their books and pens and join the bard on the open road (theoretically, the last thing Whitman wants readers to do is produce more writing) and apprehend with him "something better than any and all books, and that is the real stuff whereof they are the artificial transcript and portraiture" (*NUPM*, I, 188). In the third, he sets clear-cut prescriptions for future poets and critics to consult when memorializing him and his poems. In the fourth, he places responsibility on readers to complete his poems, "to prove and define" the inarticulate feelings he has rendered to them, although he will, in fact, denounce their results, a reaction not merely whimsical and personal but entirely consistent with his anticritical poetics. In the fifth, he positions himself at the head of a genealogy of "men-poets" who maintain a venerating attitude toward their patriarchal origin. And finally, he casts himself as "the only growth," the only aesthetic guideline or evaluative criterion, by which his poems are to be judged.

The various references or intentions here all share a common provocation—the anxiety of misreading. Because every expression is complete only after it has made its intended impression, Whitman's ideal poetic communication of soul and feeling rests on proper reading just as much as it does on proper composing. His poetics compasses two sites: the poet "auto-graphing" the blank paper, inscribing feeling into notation; and the reader de-inscribing the printed page, lifting the embedded content up into its ideal emotive sphere. The first scene the poet can moderately control; the second he cannot. This is especially distressing to Whitman; for, having burdened the sign with so much "meaning," having charged his words not merely with representing other words but with administering the impenetrable depths of his soul, he thereby implicates not only his poems but also himself personally in every act of reading. What if his language has too little poetic-emotive power to override readers' critical biases and probe their enclothed souls? What if nineteenth-century American literary culture proves too canonical and exclusive to tolerate any radical departures from its stylistic and material norms? What if the sign is such only according to its interpretation, not its intention?

First, one might ask why reading comes to assume so prominent a place among Whitman's concerns, and why writing, which was predominant in "Song of Myself," seems to become a secondary issue? Early in 1856, with his first effort having been printed and distributed and reviewed (with wildly mixed results), Whitman suddenly finds himself entangled in the vagaries of reader responses, baffled and dismayed and angered by imputations of licentiousness, stupidity, and impiety (notwithstanding his liberalism, Whitman maintained a deep puritanical conviction regarding many moral and religious questions), and immensely elated by expressions of favor and thanks (by Emerson, Charles Eliot Norton, Moncure Conway, Fanny Fern, and others). Relishing any praise he received (he carried Emerson's letter in his pocket for months), he felt emboldened to even more power over his audience. In one sense, the huge satisfaction Whitman got from positive notices made him realize just how important reception was to him. They caused him almost as much anxiety as the negative responses.

As to the "insults," Whitman was somewhat at a loss to explain how a volume overflowing with "happiness" and "love" could evoke abuse. What knowledge or custom or faculty stood in the way of mutual enjoyment? Why did readers adopt such fruitless skeptical habits? Where did they learn to interpret altruism as narcissism, joy as hedonism, and sentiment as sentimentality? Something unaccountable (and unnatural) must be at work in certain interpretations—something, he thought, that sympathy and compassion could not contend with. If so, then more passion poetry, more democratic celebrations, would only excite more vilification. Hence he initiates his notorious self-promotions and partisan criticisms, polemical gestures that engage hostile criticism on its own malevolent terms.

Seeing Whitman placed firmly in the canon, modern scholars regard his attacks and defenses and inverted plagiarisms (that is, passing his own evaluative statements off as someone else's) as an embarrassing and pathetic spectacle. But to the poet in 1856, ambitious for fame, presuming to be the voice of America, and obsessed with his reputation, the thought of misconstruction, of biased judgments of his private merits and unfair characterizations of his poems, fills him with despair and drives him into these literary hoaxes.

It is true that, as many point out, praise from Emerson, Alcott, Thoreau, and others marked a high moment in Whitman's life and probably encouraged him to try to master his readers. But still, their responses fell short of the universal welcome he envisioned. They convinced him he was "right" and hostile critics were "wrong," but that only indicated further cultural division, the very antagonism Whitman wished to end.

For him, then, the question is not one of ethics, but one of rhetoric: Will his criticism influence his reception any better than his poetry? Will criticism make future interpretations any more congenial than present ones?

Based upon his first experience of critical reviews, the outlook is uncertain; for, having endured the fickle assessments of public scrutiny, Whitman can easily project himself into a distant future in which *Leaves of Grass* is merely a pawn in a conflict of interpretations past and present. Then, there will not even be an author to authorize revision and counterattack and ghostwriting, no living origin to guarantee the right response to his work. His self-criticism will stand merely as one interpretation among many others (was there ever a time when it did not?).

At that point, only his poems will speak for him. To do so effectively, they must manifest his presence palpably and reliably, magnetically enough to preclude analysis and silence criticism, vigorously enough to substantiate Whitman's claim that "this is no book—but I myself, in loving flesh and blood" (*NUPM*, IV, 1465). But, as Whitman realizes in 1856, poetry is not enough; ultimately, it is the reader who vindicates the poet. No matter how much his language succeeds in transmigrating his living soul across "vast trackless spaces ... projected through time" ("Starting from Paumanok," ll. 25 and 29), if it does not evoke a corresponding feeling or experience in the reader's soul, if it is unable to exact an immediate intuitive affirmation of truth and empathy, the poem has failed.

Although Whitman's songs come from the heart, readers still may condemn them as the formless sentiments of an unskilled hack, the bestial bellowings of an uncultured brute, and banish them from literary discourse. In other words, culling an array of natural, transparent signs from the rampant dross of conventional literary language in order to found a natural poetic language appropriate to the human soul only raises another problem, one less governable than that of the poet's choice of words—the possibility of *natural reading*. That question forces itself upon Whitman when he turns his attention to posterity, when he realizes that the future of *Leaves of Grass* depends not upon particular truths being discovered and memorialized (who Walt Whitman was, what was happening in Brooklyn in the 1850s, what experiences or beliefs motivated this or that poem, and so on), but instead upon the vicissitudes of interpretation, upon the inconstant and uncontrollable reception of the sign, upon reading correctly or incorrectly the scattered traces of Whitman's being.

A correct reading would, of course, follow the natural guidelines (yet another oxymoron) Whitman sketches variously in his poetry and prose. He assumes that "his contempt for the 'poets' and 'poetry' of the day, his presentation of thoughts and things at first hand, instead of second or third hand, his sturdy and old-fashioned earnestness, and his unprecedented novelty, make him a capitol target for the smart writers and verbal fops engaged in manufacturing items and 'criticism'." So, "like all revolutionists and founders, he himself will have to create the growth by which he is to be fully understood and accepted" (*NUPM*, II, 898–99[2]). Because Whitman presents "thoughts and things at first hand," without stock ornamentation, the "smart writers and verbal fops" who dominate the literary milieu and believe such adornments to be the essence of poetry can only ridicule him with "slur, burlesque, and sometimes spiteful innuendo." Or they "emasculate" Whitman by turning *Leaves of Grass* into a mere topic of polite conversation, a poetic subject to be bandied about: "A talent for conversation—Have you it? If you have, you have a facile and dangerous tenant in your soul's palace" (*NUPM*, I, 295).

In either case, these glib reviewers degrade inspired poetry, dismissing it because inspiration is un- or pre-aesthetic. It is up to Whitman to vanquish readers who praise or blame according to a poet's skill in handling literary conventions and who rest content in limiting their analyses to the level of decorum instead of delving into the underlying feeling. He himself must bear the responsibility of fostering the "growth" of natural reading and carving out his own fit audience (although, in the same paragraph, Whitman notes his own "scornful silence, never explaining anything, nor answering any attack," a strategy he scarcely adhered to from 1855 onward).

To promote natural reading, Whitman first must break readers of their conventional "Book-learning" habits of inquiry and reorient them to the proper way of reading and experiencing nature. Put simply, a natural reading of Whitman's poetry would repeat, on the reader's part, the same experience Whitman has when he interacts with nature. His "poems ... [are] to be perceived with the same perception that enjoys music, flowers, and the beauty of men and women" (*NUPM*, IV, 1443). The physical exhilaration he felt when listening to Alboni sing Verdi (see *PW* II, 694), the desire to coalesce with eternity that draws him to the sea, where, he says, "I wended the shores I know, / As I walked with that eternal self of me, seeking types" ("As I Ebb'd with the Ocean of Life," ll. 16–17), the passive inquisitiveness leading him to bend "with open eyes over the shut eyes of sleepers" ("The Sleepers," l. 3) and enter into their dreams and nightmares—all such natural impulses and responses should motivate and delimit a proper reading of *Leaves of Grass*.

Readers should approach Whitman's poetic language as they do the sensuous living language of leaves and rivers and sunshine, of human countenances and slang speech, real-life signs that are reacted to with all one's being. The true language of life can be touched, tasted, and smelled, as well as heard and seen:

Earth round, rolling, compact—suns, moons, animals—all these
    are words,
Watery, vegetable, sauroid advances—beings, premonitions,
    lispings of the future—these are vast words.
Were you thinking that those were the words—those upright
    lines? Those curves, angles, dots?
No, those are not the words—the substantial words are in the
    ground and sea,
They are in the air—they are in you.
                              ("A Song of the Rolling Earth," ll. 2–4;
                              the first two lines were deleted after 1871.)

A reading focused upon "curves, angles, dots," upon print's uniform black
and white, confines itself to a textual configuration and checks the kind of
feeling interaction Whitman faithfully proposes between author and
reader. Instead of attending to human origins, reading lapses into mere
decoding, into translating prosaically these imageless stick figures back
into their perceptible references and then evaluating the poet's
"invention," his poetic translation of certain ideas or truths into verse.
Scholarly or dilettante readers approach poetry by studying linguistic
embellishments of the things themselves and classifying a work, usually
from the perspective of a restrictive literary history, according to its
superficialities (its decorum, poetic diction, obedience to "unities," and so
on). Instead of incorporating "beings" and "premonitions," they merely
annotate a text and leave those "substantial words," the realities,
untouched. Whitman would often righteously point out to his adoring
votaries how far their idle criticism deviates from an honest human
apprehension of nature's wonders!

  He also suggests that these pale men of letters read and write in such
an abstract, irrelevant manner not only because of local socio-historical
factors but because of linguistic conditions as well. Instead of blaming
perverse reading practices simply on arid scholarly influences and the
imaginative defects of routine readers, Whitman also censures the
representational distance between percept and sound and sound and script.
He condemns any sign that makes possible interpretive errancy, which
cushions the immediate sensible impact of natural phenomena and screens
individuals from a direct intuition of feeling. The tenuous progress from
perception to print, from image to sound to letter, is, of course, prone to the
mischievous effects of translation, not only to the translator's interestedness
and ideological slant but to translation itself, the leap from one sign system

to another, which necessarily works transformative operations upon its "content." In simple terms, with every translation, that content is adapted to a new grammar—that is, a new temporality, spatiality, history, and so on—undergoing resignification that amounts more to a mutation than an adaptation.

Only a privileged few have the natural genius and selflessness either to withstand the seductions that this dangerous substitution offers or at least to render it innocuous and read the sign aright. They form with Whitman an inner circle of interpreters, "a conference amid Nature, and in the spirit of nature's genesis, and primal sanity. A conference of [their] two Souls exclusively, as if the rest of the world, with its mocking misconceptions were for a while left and escaped from" (*NUPM*, IV, 1452). The stinging prevalence of "criticism" and "mocking misconceptions" in his social and literary worlds causes Whitman to demand that readers school themselves in the language of nature, the "vast ... substantial words" comprising the universal poem. Though textual—the "Earth; "suns, moons, animals, "ground and sea, "air," and "you" are "words"—their meaning is unique and immanent, unequivocally there for our physical and emotional pleasure, not for our intellectual wit and discernment. "Words" of/in nature are not traces; they are unified entities.

Composition reorders and resignifies those self-evident materializations of truth or spirit, imposing a secondary, man-made textual machination upon nature's sensuous presentations. It thus impoverishes the colorful display of beauty and warmth by submitting it to a skeletal notation. Too often, instead of rescuing nature and all its sublime manifestations from composition's excesses, reading only produces more outward signs, more camouflaging layers of artifice. Conventional reading proliferates verbiage and thus fosters the linguistic departure from nature. Natural reading, however, produces (or, rather, reproduces) nothing more than what is there. Much like his own restless attempt to translate the "meanings" of nature (albeit an effort he often regards as faulty) and opposed to his critics' arrogant, treacherous attempt to translate the "meanings" of his poems, natural reading retains an innocent, subdued receptivity to the pure thing before it. It halts any modifying tendencies. It constitutes both the poetic language and its interpretive (non-)methods as transparent—the former a vehicle of feeling, the latter a passive admittance of feeling. As a result, the poem remains intact, free to work its emotive power on and in its own terms without being mutated into an alien language.

This is, for Whitman, the preferred reading situation, the natural context wherein readers commune with writers and accommodate themselves to writers' passionate turns and innovations. The book functions as a provisional gathering place or scene of reading that suspends interpretation. Ideally, readers perceive without analyzing, apprehend without judging, repeat without annotating, experience texts viscerally, and leave interpretation to critics caught up in the trivial game of classification and exegesis. As the poet would have it, by its distorting and generally self-serving actions, interpretation undermines a healthy, rightful appreciation of life, of the "miracles" of "Seeing hearing and feeling" ("Song of Myself," l. 523) and the bare "things" in which "All truths wait" (l. 648). When Whitman stands and faces the sublime limitlessness of earth and sky or the "democratic average" of American society, the sea off the shores of Paumanok or Broadway at noon, he simply allows their sights and sounds to pour into his exposed senses. When recording his impressions, he assumes the voice of nature and America and merely echoes ingenuously the tangible "words" they spoke to him before. When readers come upon that voice, they are to respond in the same noninterpretive, spongelike way that Whitman did when he sauntered along the beach or down the avenue, except that instead of becoming another voice of nature, readers are to become the voice of *Leaves of Grass* (Whitman would say they are one and the same), sounding in a unitary paean the natural truths therein.

Presiding over a sensuous, uninterpreted world and an undomesticated society, addressing a familiar gathering of sympathetic confreres, the poet serves as "the answerer," the irrefutable "sayer" who bears the Logos. He is the purveyor of truth—"He puts things in their attitudes" ("Song of the Answerer," l. 18)—and the arbiter of conflict "Him all wait for.... him all yield up to, ... his word is decisive and final" (l. 8). He gains access to private passion—"He has the passkey of hearts" (l. 28)—and he levels social rank—"The gentleman of perfect blood acknowledges his perfect blood, / The insulter, the prostitute, the angry person, the beggar, see themselves in the ways of him.... he strangely transmutes them" (ll. 50–51). The "answerer" legislates and inspires, mirrors and "transmutes," in each case serving to naturalize relations, to bring the deviant back to purity. His power to compel an audience to "yield" or "acknowledge" and his capacity to "settle justice, reality, immortality" (l. 58) lie mainly in his ability to propagate faithfully and adequately the language of nature:

> Every existence has its idiom .... every thing has an idiom and tongue;
> He resolves all tongues into his own and bestows it upon men..
>   and any man translates.. and any man translates himself also:

One part does not counteract another part.... He is the joiner....
   he sees how they join.

(ll. 31–33)

The poet-answerer "resolves" particularized local idioms into the universal voice of being and "bestows it upon men" who "translate" it back into a personal, idiosyncratic language. This Babel-like fragmentation, however, does not dissever the communal bond, for the poet (as "joiner") holds individuals together, reminds them of their common cause, and keeps them unified and compassionate by wielding a vernacular glue. He has "all lives, all effects, all hidden invisibly in [him]self" (*NUPM*, I, 239). "Behind [his] talk stands the real life of all who hear [him] now" (*NUPM*, IV, 2047), and so he remains the oracle to whom those who seek truth and comfort appeal. The mediator and focal point of man and man, and man and nature, he gives vent to what all feel and touch and see and love, and makes interpretation and conventional reading an encumbrance.

But what presuppositions does this scheme of pure reading rest upon? The first presuppositions is that objects or "real life," whether natural or invented, can be perceived as extralinguistic givens immediately present to the senses or as discrete identities manifesting themselves apart from any system of reference. Second, there is the assumption that voice works no instrumental changes upon what it describes, and that it represents adequately and transparently the nonlinguistic reality inspiring it. The third presupposition is that translation either from sensation to language or from one language to another occurs without deforming the original referent, that the substitution of one sign for another may be smooth and innocent. And fourth, it is assumed that readers will be willing to adopt this reading attitude against interpretation and welcome *Leaves of Grass* as they would experience ordinary natural phenomena. "Song of Myself," being Whitman's struggle to preserve natural expression during the composition process, investigates the first three issues, resolving them through a metaphysics of perception and expression. Many later poems, involving his struggle to ensure a natural perception during the reading process, also ponder the first three, but from the explicit, anxiety-ridden perspective of the fourth issue, treating it as a problem of ideology (though this in no way excludes metaphysics).

Given Whitman's desire to found a natural language of feeling and his acute understanding of the dangers of reading, his anxiety makes perfect sense. It also makes more poems. Never one to flee from his distresses without first writing about them (directly or indirectly), Whitman converts his anxiety into more poetic material, more ideas and feelings to express, deny, analyze, metamorphose, subdue, and appease. One could, as some have, group together Whitman's polemical utterances against interpretation and perform a thematic reading of them, paraphrasing his statements in a critical vocabulary and extrapolating their general content, even though many of them are already so categorically critical that they baffle any translation from their putatively creative mode.

But whereas a thematic analysis, be it psychological, political, or philosophical, might furnish students of *Leaves of Grass* with certain interests and ideas preoccupying Whitman during his lifetime, it would not reveal the textual transfigurations those "real" concerns undergo both during composition, when they leave the cloudy, ephemeral space of Whitman's mind and assume definite shape in the book, and during reading, when the reverse process takes place. "Song of Myself" probes the former, later poems the latter, but not only in a thematizing manner. Instead of simply allegorizing, in the conventional sense, a preexistent content in a narrative or image, instead of simply constructing a poetic equivalent of truth, "Song of Myself" and succeeding poems dramatize that construction, recounting the poet's search for and readers' acceptance of natural signs. That is, Whitman gives his language a performative as well as a cognitive dimension, staging repeatedly scenes of writing and reading, and these scenes question the very nature of translation. They pose in a much more forceful and interesting way than do the abstract statements against active interpretation (which themselves must be subject to interpretation) the fate of reading, its inevitable *clinamen* from authorial intention.

In examining Whitman's canon, it is easy to find dozens of reading situations, moments where the poet scans a landscape or physiognomy for its "meaning," but such scenes are difficult to analyze because they so often appear in conjunction with explicit renunciations of reading. In "Song of the Open Road," for example, Whitman declares, "You road I travel and look around! I believe you are not all that is here! / I believe that something unseen is also here" (ll. 16–17). He goes on to ponder the "objects that call from diffusion [his] meanings and give them shape!" (l. 26) and to realize that they "express [him] better than [he] can express [him]self" (l. 47). That is to say, the "open road" is a numinous text made up of seen and "unseen," material sign and spiritual "meaning," the human truth Whitman treasures but which, though it dwells in his own soul, he can apprehend only by reading it through the object. Initiating the coalescence of a subject with an object and, ultimately, with itself, reading, then, is a fortuitous moment in an emotive dialectic, a natural step on the "open road" to contentment and "Happiness."

In these phrases, there seems to be no worry over any possible missteps reading might lead one into. And yet, a few lines earlier, Whitman writes, he is "Done with indoor complaints, libraries, querulous criticisms" (l. 6). But how else to characterize his approach to nature and its latent "meanings" than as "querulous" inquisitiveness, his attacks upon "philosophies and religions" (l. 83) and "the preacher preach[ing] in his pulpit! ... the lawyer plead[ing] in the court, and the judge expound[ing] the law" (l. 219) as defensive, contemptuous "criticism"? To save the poet from contradiction (on this issue Whitman wishes to be decidedly consistent), we must accept Whitman's differentiation between the kind of reading that is carried out in "libraries" from that which he performs in nature. As we have seen, it would appear that the reading of books, of verbal signs arranged horizontally on pallid leaves of paper, is to be qualitatively distinguished from the reading of natural objects, of tangible things that invite participation in their actions.

To understand why Whitman considers such a distinction necessary, we turn to "Crossing Brooklyn Ferry" (originally entitled "Sun-Down Poem"), not only the most profound and sustained lyric of the 1856 poems (the one Thoreau singled out, along with, "Song of Myself," as Whitman at his best) but also the poem most clearly about reading.[3] With its Heraclitean waters and Wordsworthian sunsets, its poignant apostrophes to "you who peruse me" (l. 112) a hundred years hence, and its lament for the "bitter hug of mortality" ("Song of Myself," l. 1288)—"myself disintegrated, every one disintegrated" ("Crossing," l. 7)—the poem overtly addresses the temporal human predicament and its tragic effects: aging, loss, death, oblivion.

Yet, what stands out in "Crossing Brooklyn Ferry" are not Whitman's ethical or philosophical conclusions regarding the human condition, but rather his articulation of the question of reading and what role it plays in an individual's development and in human history. Specifically, in the hope that it will assuage the dread of annihilation (as well as the threat of misinterpretation, which is annihilation for a poet), the poem tries to establish a comforting, stable identification between the way future generations, "you that shall cross from shore to shore years hence" (l. 5), perceive the scene and the way Whitman does in the poem:

> It avails not, neither time nor place—distance avails not,
> I am with you, you men and women of a generation, or ever so many
>   generations hence,
> I project myself, also I return—I am with you, and know how it is.
> Just as you feel when you look on the river and sky, so I felt,
> Just as any of you is one of a living crowd, I was one of a crowd,

> Just as you are refreshed by the gladness of the river, and the
>   bright flow, I was refreshed,
> Just as you stand and lean on the rail, yet hurry with the swift
>   current, I stood, yet was hurried,
> Just as you look on the numberless masts of ships, and the thick
>   stemmed pipes of steamboats, I looked.
>   (ll. 20–26; the third line was later deleted.)

Through this imaginative amalgam of souls all correspondingly taking in the landscape, Whitman's sensations, already fading into memories that must be recorded in order to endure, are rescued from mutability and obliteration. If their reading of Brooklyn at twilight, of the river, the boats and passengers, parallels his own (and if the poem about his reading is kept in mind), then the poet escapes misinterpretation. His experiences will become their experiences. The thoughts and feelings he suffers at the transitory crossing moment from the "tall masts of Mannahatta!" to "the beautiful hills of Brooklyn!" (l. 105), from day to night, from "The similitudes of the past [to] those of the future" (l. 8), from life to death, readers also will suffer. They, too, will see their reflection flicker, "Diverge," and be left behind in the "fine spokes of light ... in the sunlit water" (l. 116).

As others behold the fluctuating landscape while crossing on the ferry (or reading the poem) and relive sympathetically the poet's moving recognition of eternal becoming, a precious continuity of human experience will be established—what Whitman believes to be the true American history, he being one of its founding fathers. What sustains this continuity, as the poem makes clear, is this genealogical interpretive community's adherence to natural reading, an implicit agreement among readers to confine interpretation to the salutary limits set forth in the archetypal reading experience—Whitman on the ferry.

Whitman solidifies this orthodox chain of interpretation later in the poem, clarifying in his own mystifying terms how his reading is to be passed on to his descendants:

> Now I am curious what sight can ever be more stately and
>   admirable to me than my mast-hemm'd Manhatta, my river
>   and sun-set, and my scallop edged waves of flood-tide, the
>   sea-gulls oscillating their bodies, the hay boat in the twilight,
>   and the belated lighter,
> Curious what gods can exceed these that clasp me by the hand,

and with voices I love call me promptly and loudly by my
    nighest name as I approach,
Curious what is more subtle than this which ties me to the
    woman or man that looks in my face,
Which fuses me into you now, and pours my meaning into you.

We understand, then, do we not?
What I promised without mentioning it, have you not accepted?
What the study could not teach—what the preaching could not
    accomplish is accomplished, is it not?
What the push of reading could not start is started by me
    personally, is it not?
> (ll. 92–100; the last line was deleted after 1871 and
> the preceding lines were extensively rearranged.)

These lines turn upon two traditional philosophical oppositions crucial to
Whitman's metaphysical outlook: the sensible versus the intelligible (in the
first stanza) and what can be intuited versus what can be spoken (in the
second stanza). First, Whitman favorably opposes the vast panorama of
"Manhatta," the friendly handclasps of comrades, the "vocalization" of his
"nighest name," and the captivating physiognomic "look" of "the woman or
man," to whatever transcendent realities may lie beyond his sight, touch, or
hearing.

He wonders contentedly, What need has one of anything more than
what is perceived? Why let a perverse curiosity about the ineffable spoil
delight in the tangible and visible? Although the immediately present
assuredly fills his entire being with warmth and comfort and security, the
unperceivable can only appeal to abstract faith or pure reason, contemplative
faculties assumed to provide wisdom and restrain the senses in their desire
for excitement. But Whitman finds sensation true and sufficient unto itself;
only the pointless supposition of a supersensible reality characterizes
sensation as phenomenal delusion. In fact, he implies, it is conceptualization
that deludes, that uselessly depletes the display of life and robs it of its
energetic particularity in a restless pursuit of abstract, universal knowledge.

In the following stanza, Whitman favorably opposes the unutterable
"meaning" that is "understood" or "accepted" (in other words, assimilated
extralinguistically) to what is "mentioned," "studied," "taught," or
"preached"—all of which necessitate indoctrination. Although the former
achieves in fantasy a semantic copulation as the poet "pours [his] meaning
into you," the latter amounts to a distanced interaction by means of the

factitious intermediary, an event susceptible to all the deviations and misappropriations arising from the absence of a naturally grounded medium. By adhering to the natural conditions required for an ideal communion of souls instead of resorting to conventional social or intellectual discourses, and by infusing listeners with his unmediated vision instead of invoking its arbitrary substitute, Whitman preserves his authority and avoids becoming merely another one of the scribes. Also, what he feels and what he makes readers feel need not and cannot be uttered, for any detour of feeling through the sign inevitably fractures that feeling, de-notes its song, and no dialectical recuperation or circuitous return can restore it to purity.

Feeling cannot be communicated. Like the "Wisdom" that "cannot be passed from one having it, to another not having it" ("Song of the Open Road," l. 78), feeling can neither be articulated nor read nor interpreted. Properly secluded in the soul and remaining in its inviolate self-presence beyond representation, feeling can only be acknowledged and felt by those who already possess it, who already intuit it and need merely the promptings of mesmerizing bards to reexperience it. The sign by itself has no power to awaken feeling in others.

The sign succeeds not simply by its being fortuitously chosen by the poet and accurately interpreted by the reader, but of more importance, by its functioning as a familiar token of something mutually recognized by and already present in both participants. Reading is narcissism, the emancipating apprehension of one's own innate but culturally suppressed truth and pleasure. What saves reading from selfishness and anarchy is the fact that though each man and woman counts as "a simple, separate person" ("One's-Self I Sing," l. 1), there is a subjective Logos, a "word Democratic, the word En-Masse" (l. 2), enunciated by Whitman that taps the natural roots common to all men and women and ensures a constant reception of his poetry. Reading is corrupted not by readers giving free reign to their emotions but by their restricting emotion and allowing learned habits of interpretation to guide their responses.

Herein lies an opposition more relevant to "Crossing Brooklyn Ferry" and to Whitman's poetics than the metaphysical oppositions noted above— reading as a sympathetic fusion of souls versus reading as an active interpretation of texts. The former signifies an unmediated, living empathy of "persons," the latter a detached examination of signs. Whereas criticism expends itself in detailing the extraneous ornaments of feeling and then adding further supplementary languages to it, empathy for "adhesiveness; "comraderie," "rapport," and so on), though it must also negotiate signs, reads them for their proper reference and returns them to their original emotive content, which lies within themselves as well as in the poet. When readers assume the correct empathic and auto-pathic posture of being openly receptive to the poet's heartfelt tones, semiosis, here a lineal descent of "meaning," remains within the purview of its creator. Representation and interpretation coincide perfectly; and the first signification, which, in Whitman's interpretive model, equals inspiration, survives through successive generations of interpreters (an ideal process that, of course, contradicts infinite semiosis and pinpoints the behaviorist problematics inhabiting Whitman's scene of reading).

But criticism honors no such ancestral regulation. Under criticism's arrogant scrutinizing, "adhesiveness" dissolves and, instead of meeting anticipated reader-disciples, the far-off but beguiled initiates he expects to "complete" the poem, the poet finds himself pitted against interrogating judges weighing his thoughts and words against their own capricious beliefs.

Faced with a philistine literary establishment, Whitman is obliged to reply to with conscientious disdain or to accept with smothered resentment other people's interpretations, their manipulation of his works to suit their convenience. Whitman's lies and schemes, the arrant manner in which he anonymously defends himself or uses his disciples to lead the fight against his "enemies," are sometimes despicable, sometimes pitiful. But they also indicate Whitman's sense of just how much is at stake in the way his poems are read. Irony would perhaps be a more effective means of coping with his disfiguration at the hands of shallow, unfeeling critics; but irony would force Whitman to disjoin himself from what he speaks, to exploit the incongruity between the language of the heart and the language of society, the very discrepancy between feeling and sign that set the poet up for misinterpretation in the first place.

For Whitman to employ the sign fraudulently and break the organic contiguity of soul and sound would be, of course, to violate his first commandment—to speak forthrightly, without calculation or imitation. As he says, "All poems, or any other expressions of literature, that do not tally with their writers actual life and knowledge, are lies" (*NUPM*, I, 265; "tally" here signifies a direct, isomorphic transition from feeling to sign). He prefers to keep his signs "personal" (although to claim to do so, he must overlook the fact that many of his writings appear beneath the disguise of another's signature), to express himself in a language subjectively especial enough to retain its unique human origin. If Whitman can adapt a social, democratic medium of communication to his idiosyncratic feelings, and prevent the reverse from happening, then reading will be not a disinterested interpretation situating the text within the main currents of contemporary literary discourse, but rather a compassionate understanding between inspired souls, an encounter that secures the unbroken pedigree of "divine literati" in the American grain.

This raises for Whitman (and for de Tocqueville) the fundamental dilemma facing the American poet: How can a unique subjective language, a language with its own personal grammar and history, be a medium of communication readily understood by others? Only when the "other" is identical to the poet will such a language have its proper effect; but if this is the case, then the poet is not a unique individual but rather an anonymous constituent of the "en masse." Consequently, the attempt to be a poet and the raw materials of poetry threaten the very singularity of self-hood that leads one to be a poet in the first place. When in practice, when trying to share his experiences and opinions with others, the poet in America always finds himself seduced into conformity, accommodating his identity to the least common denominator of democratic intersubjectivity—ordinary language.

What elevates that line of descent above compromise is the enduring presence of Whitman himself: "I and mine do not convince by arguments, similes, rhymes / We convince by our presence" ("Song of the Open Road," ll. 138–39). His constant nearness, not merely his printed words, keeps American history universal and uncommon: "What the push of reading could not start is started by me personally, is it not?" Reading must be grounded in his "person," in his soul and voice and flesh, not in the borrowed language that renders his "person" to absent readers. As Whitman says midway in *Democratic Vistas*, "If we think of it, what does civilization itself rest upon—and what object has it, with its religions, arts, school, &c., but rich, luxuriant, varied Personalism?" (*PW*, II, 392). A paragraph earlier, he writes, "[Personalism] is individuality, the pride and centripetal isolation of a human being in himself—," a "second principle" complementing "democracy, the leveler, the unyielding principle of the average."

"Personalism" respects the value and integrity of the individual soul and, although promoting community, protects the soul from a stifling submergence in the homogenous mass of democratic society. Under the humane guidelines of "personalism," reading regards the book as merely a preliminary entryway opening into an easeful inner sanctum where more intimate recognition takes place. It makes a comforting harbor of passion and truth where "the meal [is] pleasantly set" and the poet "tell[s] things in confidence" ("Song of Myself," ll. 372 and 387). This is the rightful setting of interpretation. Presided over by Whitman's "person," his "life's hot pulsing blood, / The personal urge and form for [him]—not merely paper, automatic type and ink..." ("Now Precedent Songs, Farewell," ll. 9–10), reading inalterably fixes upon its true subject, the heart and soul, where falsification and misinterpretation are impossible.

But what if the "Personalism" Whitman extols as the guarantor of individualism in mass society degenerates into self-absorption and disregard for the natural covenant of mankind? What if the signs available to statesmen and orators and poets, those who supply the cohesive validating myths to the community, prove to have a divisive rather than a unifying effect, leaving individuals introspective and frustrated, helplessly intent upon their souls' unrealized evolution? What if the only alternative to interpretation is noncommunication? Without a natural language, at once both universal and personal, to sustain a fluid transition from private desire to public good and to ground individual identity in a collective identity, "Personalism" collapses into solipsism. Signs and feelings are not exchanged; instead, they are reflected back to their source. The "Personal" soul, elsewhere a sensitive interpersonal constancy but here an ego engrossed in its own feelings, threatens to reduce the democratic community to Narcissus' clear pool in which each person makes love to his or her own self-projection.

Showing more critical awareness than many of his early critics, Whitman blankly confronts this possibility in "A Song of the Rolling Earth":

Each man to himself, and each woman to herself, is the word of
    the past and present, and the true word of immortality,
Not one can acquire it for another—not one!
Not one can grow for another—not one!
The song is to the singer, and comes back most to him,
The teaching is to the teacher, and comes back most to him,
The murder is to the murderer, and comes back most to him,
The theft is to the thief, and comes back most to him,
The love is to the lover, and comes back most to him,
The gift is to the giver, and comes back most to him—it cannot fail,
The oration is to the orator, and the acting is to the actor and
    actress, not to the audience,
And no man understands any greatness or goodness but his own,
    or the indication of his own.

(ll. 78–89)

The lines leading up to this passage—"The divine ship sails the divine sea for you" (l. 74); "For none more than you is immortality" (l. 78)—suggest that Whitman is here celebrating in others the same narcissistic exuberance that led him earlier to celebrate himself. But whereas in "Song of Myself"

Whitman's regressive excursions into self-centeredness are generally preceded or followed by unreserved outbreaks of gregariousness, in these lines from the next to last poem in the 1856 edition, self-centeredness continues unabated. Formerly, Whitman's seclusion was accentuated by a profound silence that seemed tantalizingly to withhold the truth, but here it is the attempt to break that silence, to "teach" or "give," that creates his seclusion. Even singing and oratory, two of Whitman's preferred forms of discourse, only confirm man's entrapment within either a subjective nutshell or a prison house of language: "no man understands any greatness or goodness but his own, or the indication of his own." The speech or behavior intended to silence debate, appease dissension, and harmonize opposing parties into a community of visionaries unconsciously acknowledging the natural foundations of democratic fellowship no longer has the power to do so. Indeed, action has fallen into crime—murder, rioting, slavery, expansionism—and language has only aggravated dispute and made government a matter of compromise. Because every utterance and every action returns to its origin without having truly engaged the souls of its "audience," communication (in Whitman's ideal sense) can never take place. And because the democratic community rests upon a self-projected communication, the self-interest resulting from this monologic practice undermines any firm beliefs in American ideals and corrupts American society.

To appreciate the extent and gravity of this conclusion, we must remember that it had been Whitman's proclaimed cardinal purpose to arrest this decline and reinstitute those natural truths and rights that the New World experiment properly rested upon. But to rejuvenate the primitive brotherhood of man required, in Whitman's eyes, first and foremost the annunciation of the divine energies of words, of signs and sounds that possessed a performative capacity to enact the things they represented, to participate in the evolutionary growth they signified. Only if semiosis were a progressive unfolding of the innate spirit of humanity, instead of being a channel of information open to the uses and abuses of rhetoricians and "contenders," could nineteenth-century Americans fulfill the promises afforded by both the founding Fathers and a naked continent.

Believing that the state of the language is both the index and precondition of the state of the nation, Whitman, at the time he is outlining his poetics and writing his best poetry (1855–1860), regards a poetic-linguistic revolution as the best way or at least as the necessary first step to remedy social inequality and political corruption and general alienation. In the above passage, however, which Whitman hardly touched in later editions, language (of all kinds) appears to be more a condition of than an antidote for alienation.

It is tempting to restrict Whitman's cynicism about expression to those usages that debase communication and suppress rather than arouse feeling—for example, the stale prose of scholars and academicians, the fanciful conversation of the literary salon, the stern admonishments and irksome repetitions of teachers and preachers. Obeying this temptation, one can then turn to *Leaves of Grass* and relish its corrective and refreshing vernacular utterance, rejoice in "the dialect of common sense" and "the repartee of workers" (*PK*, II, 457, 577). But whereas such recourse is invited by "Song of Myself," in "A Song of the Rolling Earth" (and many other poems from 1856 and 1860) any hope that a Whitmanian idiom might overturn the prevailing "dead" languages is foreclosed. Although Whitman directed the assertions in the above quotation toward abstract functionaries (the "singer," the "teacher," the "orator," the "actor and actress"), in the next section he turns upon himself and draws the same conclusion of impotence regarding his own expressions:

> I swear I begin to see little or nothing in audible words!
> I swear I think that all merges toward the presentation of the unspoken
>   meanings of the earth!
> Toward him who sings of the body, and of the truths of the earth,
> Toward him who makes the dictionaries of the words that print
> cannot touch.
>
> I swear I see what is better than to tell the best,
> It is always to leave the best untold.
>
> When I undertake to tell the best, I find I cannot,
> My tongue is ineffectual on its pivots,
> My breath will not be obedient to its organs,
> I become a dumb man.
>
> (ll. 98–107)

Whitman becomes a "dumb man," however, not because he wants the expressive capability "to tell the best," but rather because "The best of the earth cannot be told..." (l. 108). It is the telling itself, not the teller, that blocks Whitman's desire. Owing to their ineradicable metaphysical seclusion beyond the poet's oracular reach, the "meanings of the earth" will not admit to representation. The supplementary action of his words prevents them from broaching the thing itself and unveiling the essential truths of man and nature (this is the Orphic poet's calling), leaving those cherished "meanings" forever "unspoken" and unprinted. As a universal presence felt individually, a ubiquitous given inaccessible to linguistic reconstruction, "the best" is too near, too enveloping, too much ourselves to yield to articulation and cognition.

To recognize and articulate "the best" would require the poet to assume a reflective distance from his "meanings," an observant position mediated by a system of reference that objectifies and thereby perverts feeling and experience. In their pure state, "the truths of the earth" elude the signifying grasp of "audible words." "[T]he common air that bathes the globe" ("Song of Myself," l. 360) disdains possession or restriction by man and his interpretations. When submitted to interpretation, "the best" loses its self-evidence, its status as "understood," and becomes the focus of debate, the subject of predications and attributions to be proved or disproved depending upon the relative persuasive force of the contestants' rhetoric. When "the best" comes to be a tool of sophistry and rhetoric, when nature, god, the soul, and the body come to be managed and directed by their representatives, democracy will have abandoned its natural foundations. Man will have traded his natural energies for their enervating proxies, while the poet, self-appointed guardian of language, will guiltily discover himself participating in the perverse substitution of words for things and signs for feelings, and furthering America's degeneration.

The only alternative is "to leave the best untold." With his realization that language fails to penetrate to the essence of things, Whitman finds himself paralyzed: "When I undertake to tell the best, I find I cannot, / My tongue is ineffectual on its pivots, / My breath will not be obedient to its organs." The Orphic mastery he had affirmed in "Song of Myself" and in his anonymous self-reviews has lapsed into a stifling impotence. The spontaneous cooperation of "tongue," "breath," "organs," and "the best" has broken down. Rather than trying to cover over this incapacitating rupture in expression or making a futile attempt to remedy it through the use of language, Whitman simply acknowledges the sign's shortcomings and reaffirms his faith in a supracontextual, extralinguistic "meaning." The fact that Whitman must employ a self-defeating medium, a fabricated language severed from its transcendental reference, necessitating interpretation, and generating more language (even a twice-removed critical metalanguage), only enhances the value and mystery of what lies beyond it and strengthens Whitman's confidence in his poetry's ability to "indicate" reality, if not "tell" it.

This confidence, however, is short-lived, and poetry is only temporarily saved from condemnation, for it is inevitable that an elevation of the inexpressible (as in "A Song of the Rolling Earth") should soon be followed by a devaluation of expression. Momentarily, Whitman finds refuge in "indication"—"Every thing indicates" ("Crossing Brooklyn Ferry," originally line 7, deleted in later editions)—as a more natural means of communicating "meaning" than print or "book-words," a deictic semiotic gesture founded upon concrete, physical action, not conventional abstraction. But nevertheless, though not as representational as printed words (loosely assuming that representation is quantifiable), "indication" still presupposes a signifying space between sign and referent and between signal and receiver.

"Indication," therefore, is prone to become skewed like any other form of expression, to waver from its destination as it is given up to desire and interpretation. In other words, putatively natural gestures such as "indication," which seemingly achieve unmediated status by virtue of their independence from the spoken and written sign, are in fact also liable to the hazards of reading. No matter how transparent or organic or symbolic the sign may be, its success still must necessarily rest upon interest, ideology, prejudice, upon the interpretive virtues and vices of willful, desirous readers.

Where is the audience, Whitman asks, who will imbibe his songs like sunshine after a spring rain? Who has withstood the terminal lessons of "the head teacher or charitable proprietor or wise statesman" ("A Song for Occupations," l. 6) and the "formulas" of "bat-eyed and materialistic priests!" ("Song of the Open Road," l. 130)? Who has remained untainted by abstract thought, analysis, interpretation? They are the fit audience for which *Leaves of Grass* was intended, but by the late 1850s Whitman has begun to doubt their existence, and hence to question his ambitions.

This is not to say that the entire career falls apart, but only that the unmitigated verve, the self-satisfaction, and the grandiose playfulness have become somewhat blunted. The public assertiveness has lost its edge, the reason for that decline lying somehow in problems of audience, publication, and review. His including positive and negative reviews of the 1855 volume in the 1856 volume may suggest continued audacity, but it also shows an increasingly anxious awareness of how others treat his work, of the crucial importance of response.

Chase writes, "In the 1856 edition of *Leaves of Grass* there is a rather nervously assertive attempt to put the house in order, to impress upon the public that the poems are intelligible and have behind them a large-scale program." After discussing Whitman's tactless marketing of Emerson's congratulatory letter, Allen tells how, for many months, "he had been 'promoting' himself as a uniquely American poet." Zweig cites his troubles with Fowler & Wells, his publishers, and says, "The 1856 edition went almost unnoticed, and apparently he was too caught up in his writings to campaign for it as he had for the first book a year before."[4] By 1857, Whitman had written dozens more poems, yet he would not find any publishing support for three more frustrating years.

Whitman makes a revealing admission along these lines in a letter dated July 28, 1857: "My immediate acquaintances, even those attached to me strongly, secretly entertain the idea that I am a great fool not to 'make something' out of my 'talents' and out of the general good will with which I am regarded. Can it be that some such notion is lately infusing itself into me also?" (*Cor.* I, 45). That is, is Whitman's self-definition succumbing to what others require him to be, what publishers, critics, enemies, and even friends define him as?

This drift of self-expression into audience-anxiety is what makes poems like "Crossing Brooklyn Ferry," according to Larson's excellent summation of this reader response issue, "a gesture, summons, or petition."[5] But although petitioning may work to some readers, to others it only poses the question of why attempt to do so. Why worry, at this point, so much about interpretation?

Because now he senses that once interpretation has begun, it gathers momentum and surreptitiously insinuates itself into human nature as a second nature (Whitman would appreciate that oxymoron), implacable in its designs and incorporating all resistances. After interpretation has vitiated the senses and the soul, every thing, every person, every feeling becomes not a presence but a sign awaiting exegesis, a ghostly demarcation of some reality we must remain insensible to. The only way to restore the divided sign to its monadic preexistence is by resorting, with greater and greater frustration and nostalgia, to yet more signs. The afflictive fact remains that "no substantive or noun, no figure or phonograph or image, stands for the beautiful mystery" (*NUPM*, I, 191).

So, if the only way to satisfy one's craving for the infinite is to rely upon the unsatisfactory finite, if the means of restoration is itself the problem, what is the poet to do? Is he to persist in his Orphic mission, continue to seek a language of union, compose a hundred visions and revisions in the hope of canonizing himself and America, all the while knowing that his life is a fiction? Or will he simply recall his projections, renounce his ambitions, and fade into silence and death?

This uninspiring corollary to the previous conclusion is what Whitman faces after 1856 as he begins occasionally, but with an abruptness and intensity suggesting a decisive return of the repressed, to focus his generalized critique of expression upon his own work. Now grimly conscious of the pitfalls of being read, Whitman loses confidence in words' power to bring about an unmediated experience. Regret and resentment arising from the failure of 1855 to do so takes its place. Language more and more is regarded as a catastrophe, the cause and instrument of man's expulsion from a preinterpretive golden age. Many of the best lyrics of 1860—"Out of the Cradle Endlessly Rocking," "As I Ebb'd with the Ocean of Life," "Scented Herbage of My Breast," to name a few—and parts of several other poems dwell upon this eventful "mistake" and ponder the implications it has for Whitman's career. As Whitman realizes, these poems and what inspired them tragically signal the end of the project begun five years earlier.

Notes

1. I quote the first version of every poem noted, but I call them by their final title.

2. Whitman assumes the third person here, even though he is writing about himself, because these phrases come from notes for one of his anonymous self-promotions. This particular scrap dates from late 1871 and is intended as a defense of his public reading of "As a Strong Bird on Pinions Free."

3. For critical readings of "Crossing Brooklyn Ferry," see Miller, *Walt Whitman's Poetry*, 199–208; Quentin Anderson, *The Imperial Self: An Essay in American Literary and Cultural History* (New York, 1971), 119–65; Black, *Whitman's Journeys into Chaos*, 157–66; Thomas, *The Lunar Light of Whitman's Poetry*, 92–116; Hollis, *Language and Style in "Leaves of Grass,"* 100–106; Joseph G. Kronick, *American Poetics of History: From Emerson to the Moderns* (Baton Rouge, 1984), 106–17; and Larson, *Whitman's Drama of Consensus*, 8–13.

4. Chase, *Walt Whitman Reconsidered*, 99; Allen, *The Solitary Singer*, 181; Zweig, *Walt Whitman: The Making of the Poet*, 279.

5. Larson, *Whitman's Drama of Consensus*, 10.

JOHN HOLLANDER

Whitman's Difficult Availability

We have yet had no genius in America, with tyrannous eye, which knew the value of our incomparable materials, and saw, in the barbarism and materialism of the times, another carnival of the same gods whose picture he so much admires in Homer; then in the Middle Age; then in Calvinism. Banks and tariffs, the newspaper and caucus, methodism and unitarianism, are flat and dull to dull people, but rest on the same foundations of wonder as the Town of Troy and the temple of Delphi, and are as swiftly passing away. Our logrolling, our stumps and their politics, our fisheries, our Negroes, and Indians, our boasts, and our repudiations, the wrath of rogues, and the pusillanimity of honest men, the northern trade, the southern planting, the western clearing, Oregon, and Texas, as yet unsung. Yet America is a poem in our eyes; its ample geography dazzles the imagination, and it will not wait long for metres.

—THE POET

It did not. Eleven years after Emerson concluded his essay "The Poet," there appeared a remarkable volume, prefaced with an echoing declaration that "the United States themselves are essentially the greatest poem," and likening itself and its "forms" to "the stalwart and wellshaped heir" of him whose corpse has just been carried from the house. *Leaves of Grass* was published by the author himself during the week of Independence Day 1855,

From *The Work of Poetry*. © 1997 by Columbia University Press.

and a few days later the corpse of his own father, Walter Whitman Sr., left its house at last. Self-published, self-reviewed (more than once), self-proclaiming, self-projecting, self-inventing, the *corpus*, the *opera*, the body of work and life of Walt Whitman Jr. gave birth to itself in an astonishing volume, augmentations, revisions, and rearrangements would occupy the poet's creative life.

The 1855 *Leaves of Grass* comprised twelve long stretches of a new sort of free verse, untitled, unglossed, and generically unframed, including the great poems now known as "Song of Myself," "The Sleepers," "Faces," "I Sing the Body Electric," "A Song for Occupations," and "There Was a Child Went Forth." Its title was—and remains—as deeply problematic as its appearance. Are the leaves literally the pages of books—not "those barren leaves" that Wordsworth's speaker wanted shut up to free the reader for the texts of nature, but pages that were paradisiacally both green and fruitful? Or are they rather metaphors for the poems, here not the "flowers" of old anthologies, but green with newness? Are they the leaves that, broadcast by the wind, served the Cumaean Sybil for her prophetic pages? Are they revisions of the oldest poetical leaves of all, those figurations of individual lives in Homer, Virgil, Dante, Milton, and Shelley, and is the grass likewise also that of all flesh mown down by death in Isaiah and the Psalmist? Are they *leavings*—residues of the act of "singing," departures for worlds elsewhere that are always regions of here? And in what way are the leaves-pages *of* grass: made of, about, for, authored by? "Leaves of Grass"—hard words, putting body, life, text, presence, personality, self, and the constant fiction of some Other, all together.

The poetry, like its title, looks easy and proves hard. Who was this and to whom was he talking? Was this "you" he invoked variously a version of himself, a companion, a muse, a reader? Why should a reader care about "Walt Whitman," "one of the roughs," even if he did regard himself as being "so luscious"? What appeared difficult and problematic immediately included the centrality of body, the placing of *homo urbanus* at a visionary frontier, the homoerotic realm as a token of both independence and connectedness, the confused addressing of reader, body and soul by a nonetheless unfractured voice, the innovative formats for the framing of metaphor. Now, just a hundred years after the poet's preparation of the "deathbed" edition of his works, these issues seem virtually classical. Nevertheless, Whitman's growing and ongoing book, insisting on its role and nature as the poem of Democracy and the poem of the great poem of "these United States," defies easy characterization the more one reads it. The poet insists that he stands for all America—that he is America, and lest you not believe him, he will play out that theme in energetically crowded detail. It is difficult because of its celebration of self-possession in scattered multitudes of tropes of self-dispersion, or in confusing images of the incorporation of wonderful arrays of particulars; it is difficult in its propounding the song of body, in compounding a body of song. And, as always, it presents us with the perpetual problem of the Old and the New, the Early and the Late. When Milton at the beginning of *Paradise Lost* proposes that his adventurous song will accomplish "Things unattempted yet in prose or rhyme," his very words are those—as I have mentioned in the essay in this volume called "Originality"—of a successful precursor (Ariosto) flamboyantly making the same promise. Whitman implicitly allows that celebrations and singings had indeed gone on in the past ("the talkers were talking, the talk of the beginning or the end," by which he means the Bible was bibling); still, he declares,

> There was never any more inception than there is now,
> Nor any more youth or age than there is now,
> And will never be any more perfection than there is now,
> Nor any more heaven and hell than there is now.

He demands to be taken literally and requires to be taken figuratively. ("I and mine do not convince by arguments, similes, rhymes, / We convince by our presence," he chants, which has to be either a lie or a metaphor.) What the poet of "Song of Myself" invokes as "O perpetual transfers and promotions!" are his tropes and his hyperboles, his profoundly nonliteral tallyings and ecstatic reportage, his episodic pictures fading in and out of parable. Robert Frost—that most un-Whitmanian of major twentieth-century American poets—characterized the essentially poetic as "saying one thing and meaning another, saying one thing in terms of another, the pleasures of ulteriority." Whitman's metropolis of ulteriorities hums and buzzes with lives and busynesses, but below its streets are pulsing countercurrents. His proclamations of openness ("Unscrew the locks from the doors! / Unscrew the doors themselves from their jambs!") only concern outer layers of closure, for the most important matter inside the house remains ever safe, as he proclaims and concedes in "As I Ebb'd with the Ocean of Life,"

> ... before all my arrogant poems the real Me stands yet
>   untouch'd, untold, altogether unreach'd,
> Withdrawn far, mocking me with mock-congratulatory signs
>   and bows,

> With peals of distant ironical laughter at every word I
>   have written,
> Pointing in silence to these songs, and then to the sand
>   beneath.

This "real Me" or "Me myself" is an elusive being. For all the openings and accessions and outreachings propounded in the poems, it can never really bear to be touched, save by the mothering presences of night or the sea, perhaps, and thereby by death. Whitman's difficult ulteriorities are often reversals of this sort. When he announces his expansions, containments, and incorporations, he is frequently enacting a contraction and a withdrawal. Likewise with Whitman's varying figures of the filling and emptying of the Self and the Everything Else, the "I contain the XYZ" and the "I leak out into the XYZ." They are as easy to mistake as are his purported identifications of Self and Other, which D. H. Lawrence shrewdly observed had nothing to do with feeling and sympathy ("Agonies are one of my changes of garments, I do not ask the wounded person how he feels, I myself become the wounded person").

In "Song of Myself" the singer is very shifty about his mode of *standing for*, whether in the relation of the poet's "I" to the massive particulars he so ecstatically catalogues and inventories or to the other components of his being—his soul and his "real Me," not at all of one substance with the authorial father. The Personal, the Individual, instead of the Collective—but so overwhelmingly adduced that it is easy for the dulled reading spirit to glue all the vibrant particulars into a slab of generality. For enough people to be able to be in a crowd, each without losing self-identity, self-respect, and dignified particularity, would be to transform the meaning of "crowd" utterly. Whitman is a remarkable celebrant of dignity and confounder of shame; the only shame he feels is, manifestly, the moment at the end of "Song of Myself" (sect. 37): "Askers embody themselves in me and I am embodied in them, / I project my hat, sit shamefaced, and beg" where his riot of inclusions entraps him in the begging that would have been so sinful in his Quaker upbringing. (But it is this moment that leads to the remarkable self-recognition and recovery in section 38.) More generally, his implicitly pronounced shame is at shamefulness itself.

"Do I contradict myself? / Very well then, I contradict myself," he slantingly avers toward the end of "Song of Myself," but there is no paradox of self-reference here, and that is one of the things that makes this poem such a hard one. Starting out with the work of "loafing," which is more than the trivially paradoxical industry of idleness, the speaker poses quirkily, a *flâneur*, or dandyish observer of the life of the city street whose sympathies are always effortlessly outgoing:

> Apart from the pulling and hauling stands what I am,
> Stands amused, complacent, compassionating, idle, unitary,
> Looks down, is erect, or bends an arm on an impalpable
>   certain rest,
> Looking with side-curved head curious at what will come
>   next,
> Both in and out of the game and watching and wondering
>   at it.

Along with Whitman's celebration of bodily projection comes an ambivalence about old stories. "As if the beauty and sacredness of the demonstrable must fall behind that of the mythical!" he exclaims in the 1855 preface; but it is just the complex mythopoetic elevation and concentration of the "demonstrable" that his poetry effects. Wordsworth had, at a crucial moment in his preface to *The Excursion*, proclaimed the betrothal of ancient myth and the quotidian:

>   Paradise, and groves
> Elysian, Fortunate Fields—like those of old
> Sought in the Atlantic Main—why should they be
> A history only of departed things,
> Or a mere fiction of what never was?
> For the discerning intellect of Man,
> When wedded to this goodly universe
> On love and holy passion, shall find these
> A simple produce of the common day.
> —I, long before the blissful hour arrives,
> Would chant, in lonely peace, the spousal verse
> Of this great consummation.
>   The Excursion, 800–810

Whitman, subsequently but more audaciously, comes "magnifying and applying" in section 41 of "Song of Myself" as a collector of old images of "the supremes," the obsolete gods, buying them up at auction, reproducing them, "Taking them all for what they are worth and not a cent more, / Admitting they were alive and did the work of their days." He even uses them for a poetic coloring book: "Accepting the rough sketches deific to fill out better in myself (*by* myself, *with* myself), bestowing them freely on each man and woman I see.... / Not objecting to special revelations, considering a curl of smoke or a hair on the back of my hand just as curious as any revelation." By the end of the section's ode to the Olympus of Everything ("The supernatural of no account"), the poet himself, "waiting my time to be one of .the supremes," half-astonished, acknowledges his own role as the sole originator. In a powerful vision that colors in the rough sketches that both the first chapter of Genesis and the opening invocation of *Paradise Lost* have become for him, he feels his near rape of the primordial darkness and chaos into which prior myths of the universe have now sunk: "By my life-lumps! becoming already a creator, / Putting myself here and now to the ambush'd womb of the shadows." He can also move from the acutely "demonstrable"— the detailed vignettes of sections 10 and 12 of "Song of Myself"—to the puzzlingly "mythical," as in the beautiful parable of section 11, with its twenty-eight young men who are also days of the month, and the lunar lady who comes to join them in the spray.

Oddly enough, a chief difficulty of his poetry for every reader comes not from his ecstatic vocabulary, his self-descriptive "barbaric yawp" but in Whitman's hard ordinary words. These include basic verbs of motion, like "drift" and "pass," located somewhere between "sing" and "sally forth." There are also complex terms like "vista," which can mean (1) what is seen, (2) the point or place from which one sees it, (3) the structure of mediating or intervening opacity past or through which one does the seeing. There are rarer but stunning verbs like "project," which has both physical senses (to throw or cast out or away, to jut out from, to make something jut out from, to cast images or patterns onto a surface, etc.) and mental ones (transitively, to plan, contrive, devise; to put before oneself in thought, to imagine). The interplay of these senses helps energize that remarkable moment in "Out of the Cradle Endlessly Rocking" when he calls out to the bereft, widowed mockingbird, "O you solitary singer, singing by yourself, projecting me," (to which, darkling, he listens and reciprocates with, "O solitary me listening, never more shall I cease perpetuating you").

Most famously problematic has been the matter of Whitman's free verse and his formal innovations generally. A map of the "greatest poem," the United States themselves, shows us shapes formed by natural contours— seacoasts and lake shores, demarcating rivers and so forth—and by surveyed boundary lines, geometric, unyielding, and ignorant of what the eye of the airborne might perceive. Whitman's poem of America purported to have dispensed with all surveyors, with arbitrary strokes of a mental knife that score out legal fictions like state boundaries or city limits. It declared that all its component lines, stanzas, and structures would be shaped only by the natural forms they organically exuded. Which meant, as in every great poet's high ulterior mode, that the art that shaped them would teach older formal paradigms and patterns to dance, rather than negate them utterly. As a poet, you can only, in Wordsworth's phrase, "Let nature be your teacher" after yourself having taught nature how to speak. Very complex are the linear and strophic patterns in which Whitman would claim to "weave the song of myself" ("Song of Myself" section 15, where he fuses melodic lines and horizontal warp threads of a growing fabric), and their formal modes as well as their complex articulations of those modes are all in themselves subtle and powerful formal metaphoric versions of more traditional ones.

This revisionary character can be more easily observed at the level of trope or fiction than at the realm of scheme or formal pattern. Some of his greatest imaginative figures—leaf, grass, bird, star, sea, flowering branch, city, river, road, ship, the Wanderer, the Original—have all the freshness and imaginative power that only come from the revision of traditional figurations. And often the rhetorical deed of a poem or movement in a poem will be ceremoniously to enact such a revision, as when, for example, the poet substitutes his domestic, American, erotic, spring-blooming lilac for the more traditionally emblematic flowers on the funeral hearse of the Lost Leader in "When Lilacs Last in the Dooryard Bloom'd": "O death, I cover you with roses and early lilies, / But mostly and now the lilac that blooms the first." He is hereby also substituting his own kind of poetry (text and bouquet, poesy and posy, having been associated since antiquity); and the original gesture earns its memory of "Lycidas" and "Adonais" by also mourning a complex mythological personage on the occasion of the death of an actual person. Or there is the substitution of the native American mockingbird for the romantic nightingale and skylark. These are simple and manifest instances of a phenomenon occurring throughout Whitman's poetry.

In its formal aspect, Whitman adopts almost unvaryingly an end-stopped line, characteristically connected to its near companions by anaphora (formulaically repeated opening word or phrase) or parallel syntactic form in a ramified growth of subordinate clauses (the familiar formats of his fascinating array of modes of cataloguing). In context, his form is as identifiable as a quantitative or accentual syllabic line would be, not marked by a tally of its parts but by the way it is shaped to be part of an epigram, a strophe, an aria, or sonata-form like "movement," or a block of stipulations. There are his strophic forms, sometimes, in his later work (as in "Eidólons" or "Dirge for Two Veterans" or "Darest Thou Now, O Soul") suggesting in their format classical stanzas, more often some form of ad hoc rhythm developed by linear groupings, as in the opening of "Song of Myself" no. 6. (There a pattern of two and then one, three and then one, four and then one develops in the responsive suppositions rising in answer to the child's—and the reader's—"What is the grass?")

And always, there is the marvelous deployment, throughout lines and strophes, of the rhythms of speech as well as the totally unspeakable rhythms generated only by writing, the cadences of the inventoried, parallel modifying phrases and dependent clauses (who *talks* like *that?*); the mannered, Frenchified noun–adjective inversions; the rhythmic jolts provided by intrusions of weird diction. The rhythmic patternings of long and short lines, aligned, variously interjected, refrained, extended, receding were not exactly, as Whitman put it to his friend Horace Traubel, analogous to "*the Ocean*. Its verses are the liquid, billowy waves, ever rising and falling, perhaps wild with storm, always moving, always alike in their nature as rolling waves, but hardly any two exactly alike in size or measure, never having the sense of something finished and fixed, always suggesting something beyond." But the fixer and finisher, the poet himself, is far more crafty a puller of waves than the coldly regular moon. He might just as well have likened his long anaphoric catalogues to urban crowds through which the reader himself will pass, jostling, pushing, sometimes striding, sometimes pausing.

A word or two about Whitman's basic form of cataloguing: it exhibits a variety of structural modes. In the third strophe of "Song of Myself" no. 31, for example, the little list begins with the generality "In vain the speeding or shyness," then reiterates the qualifier "In vain" to introduce each item in the list of ascending entities (in archaeological time and humanly scaled space—from "plutonic rocks" to the auk). The conclusion is the burden of this song: "I follow quickly, I ascend to the nest in the fissure-cliff," which itself follows quickly on the last line, as well as on the whole series of ineffectually evasive beings, all of which the poet "follows quickly." But it is as if the particular following—the climb up to the high point to the nest of the great bird—becomes a momentary archetype of all the others. And one great function of the list may have been to explore fully the meaning of "the speeding or shyness." Without the array of instances, it could not be grasped; fully informed by the items of the catalogue and the musical patterning in which they are unrolled, it becomes a unique phrase, Whitman's—and the reader's—own. What is not a central matter is the extent of Whitman's lists, but rather their internal structure, the narrative of their development, the ways in which they are—as in this case—variously framed by enveloping initial predications or shape their own closures by the framing gesture of the last entry.

Consider the great catalogue of specifications preceding the "I tread such roads" in "Song of Myself" no. 33. Starting after the declaration that "I am afoot with my vision," there are nearly eighty lines of *wheres* ("Where the quail is whistling ... / Where the bat flies ... / Where the great gold-bug drops ... / Where the brook puts out ..." etc.), *throughs*, *upons*, *pleas'd withs* that make up subsections of their own. Through these and beyond, the whole passage itself treads roads of country, city, farm, factory, wild and domestic animal, marine nature and industry, and moves toward a hyperbolic envelopment. Its electrifying last entry functions like the dancing figures on Achilles's shield in *The Iliad*, which seem to sum up the whole story of the making and describing of the vision of human life represented on it:

> Speeding amid the seven satellites and the broad ring, and the
>   diameter of eighty thousand miles,
> Speeding with tail'd meteors, throwing fire-balls like the
>   rest,
> Carrying the crescent child that carries its own full mother
>   in its belly.

The concluding line is packed with complex figuration: the "new moon with the old moon in its arms" (from "Sir Patrick Spens" and Coleridge) invokes the barely discernible full sphere shadowed within the bright crescent, being connected—through the literal Latin sense of "crescent"—to the curved form of the enwombed fetus. It concludes, sums up, and reaches beyond the preceding elements in the list with a marvelous image of containment.

From the Homeric list of ships and the biblical genealogies, through the rhetorically rough inventories of goods; the blazons of erotic details of a desired body, the stacks of clauses and conditions and contingencies on a contract or lease; the inventories of rescued necessities by a Crusoe or Swiss Family Robinson or of what Tom Sawyer received in barter for the whitewashing; the wondrously detailed names of those who came to Gatsby's parties—the rhetoric of cataloguing in our literature has encompassed everything from the high heroic to the low quotidian. Whitman's catalogues often consist of lists of ramified predications. Sometimes their litanies of specimen instances are his sort of chanting of the laws—as only in biblical times and rituals—of the Great Poem of America as a self-acknowledged legislator of the world. Generally they are transcendental: they include and metaphorically revise these and other nonliterary modes of inventorying.

With Whitman, lists become basic topoi, places in, by, and through which his poems develop themselves. Through their internal structures and rhythms of syntactic and semantic grouping, they articulate their own boundaries and purposes.

Not only is Whitman the poet "afoot with his vision" in the poem, but throughout his life, in his constant textual revisions as well. The nine subsequent editions of *Leaves of Grass* after 1855 not only rearrange material in the preceding ones but add many new poems, subtract a good many, sometimes reinsert a previous subtraction. The leaves of the book remain green and growing throughout his life. There is an academic industry of interpreting the continual changes Whitman made in his work from 1855 to 1891, with a number of different interpretive agendas, each running roughshod over the partial applicability of the others. There is the school whose central agenda is the matter of varying explicitness about homosexuality; another of developing explicitness about poetic intention; those who see greater obliqueness, increased second-guessing of a growing audience, and so forth. Such impulses can indeed all seem to be at work differently, at different times and places in the text. Whitman's evolving thoughts on formal structures are reflected in his renumbering—and thereby reconstituting—of strophes and sections ("Song of Myself," unnumbered and unnamed in 1855, falls into 372 numbered strophes—ranging from couplets to full odes—in 1860 but does not acquire its calendrical division into 52 sections until 1867.) Likewise interesting in this regard are the opening and form of "Out of the Cradle": the sheer play of retitling generally, sometimes reframing, sometimes clarifying an intention, sometimes obscuring or transforming one; the addition of clusters in later editions; the segmentation, in 1856, into genres of poems, and so forth.

The history of Whitman's reputation seems to me to be less interesting than the history of any reader's reaction to the poetry. But generally one may say that the Poem gets reinterpreted into the Works of the Bard. "Song of Myself," with, again, the ambiguous resonances of the grammatical construction (composed of, by, to, about, for, myself? "of myself" as it might be "of itself?" etc.) starts out untitled in 1855, becomes "Poem of Walt Whitman, an American" (which introduces the ambiguous "of"), and "Walt Whitman" thereafter until 1881, when it assumes its familiar title. New leaf-forms—asides, communiqués from Parnassus, blurbs for the universe, position papers, self-commissioned laureate verses, ghosts of leaves that are really only *Albumblätter*, etc., start filling up the pages. They work their way into thematized sections—he calls them "clusters" from 1860 on—as part of a program to extend his formal metaphor of organic structure from line to strophe to poem to poem-group to the ever-growing oeuvre itself. "Chants Democratic," "Leaves of Grass" (a synecdochal subtitle), "Enfans D'Adam," "Calamus" (again, like "leaves," a complex figure, blending the stiff phallic rush or cane, the musically tuned pipe cut from a reed, the writing-reed, the green, growing, and emphatically fragrant plant, into an object of erotic, musicopoetic instrumentality), "Messenger Leaves," these appear in the 1860 text. Some fall off and die in later editions, others continue to flourish and are joined by newer ones, often when entire books, like the volume of Civil War poems, *Drum Taps and Sequel* of 1865, are subsequently "annexed" to later editions.

Sometimes putting a previously published poem into a new cluster in a later version of the book amounts to a gloss on that poem. So with, for example, the gnomic "Chanting the Square Deific" with its four strophes erecting a weird pantheon composed of (1) Jehovah-Brahma-Saturn-Kronos, (2) Christ-Hermes-Hercules, (3) Satan, and (4) a subsuming Santa Spirita identified with the bard himself, who ultimately squares the circle of "the great round world" itself. It first appeared, along with the beautiful little "I Heard You Solemn-Sweet Pipes of the Organ" in the *Sequel to Drum-Taps* (1865–66), but by 1871 it had been gathered into the cluster entitled, from the second poem in it, "Whispers of Heavenly Death," as if implicitly perhaps to avow its cold agenda. "As Adam Early in the Morning" originally appeared in 1860 as the last poem (15) in the "Calamus" cluster, but without the first two words; the added simile may only make manifest what was latent in the original use of the word "bower," but it certainly brings to the little poem an additional assertion of Originality—it is as if Whitman were now off to name all the animals for the first time. Sometimes it is only a privileged glance at a manuscript that reveals some of the heart of Whitman's revisionary process. That traditionally formed emblematic poem "A Noiseless Patient Spider" emerged from a passing simile in a meditation on unexpressed love on an occasion of unseized erotic opportunity; in the published poem, the matter of a street pickup is put through what Hart Crane called "the silken skilled transmemberment of song" and becomes a greater matter of the soul's far-flung "gossamer thread" catching somewhere, of the song being heard.

There is also the effect, noted earlier, of the many retitlings. In some of his notebooks, Whitman projects poems with titles like "Poem of Kisses" or "Poem of the Black Person," where, as in his overall title, the *of* is fruitfully ambiguous. Most original with him is the simple compound form, for example, "Sundown Poem" (the original title of "Crossing Brooklyn Ferry"; canceling it dims the prominence of the westwardness of the crossing from

Brooklyn to Manhattan underlined by the occasion and allows the alternative directions of so many trips and crossings to emerge) or "Banjo Poem" (one of these projected—what would that have been like?). The two great shore poems—odes of the figurative littoral—"Out of the Cradle Endlessly Rocking" and "As I Ebb'd with the Ocean of Life" that dominate the "Sea-Drift" cluster were differently titled. The first was originally published as "A Child's Reminiscence," then "A Word out of the Sea" (with the subtitle "Reminiscence" at the start of the second strophe, and with an additional line before the present third one: "Out of the boy's mother's womb, and from the nipples of her breasts," thus giving Whitman's familiar Quaker designation of September, "the Ninth Month midnight" an additional significance). The second was initially "Bardic Symbols," then no. 1 of the cluster entitled "Leaves of Grass" in 1860 (again, with the added opening "Elemental drifts! / O I wish I could impress others as you and the waves have been impressing me"), then "Elemental Drifts," and finally, when those two lines were canceled, the present incipit title it now bears.

But we also sort through Whitman's leaves and form our own readers' clusters, generic groupings that seem to emerge among the finished poems as if from unstated or unavowed intentions. Walk Poems; Panoramic Poems; Talk Poems; Optative Exhortations (including the brilliant and sardonic "Respondez!" an ironic inversion of that mode originally entitled "Poem of the Propositions of Nakedness," and dropped after the 1876 edition); Poems of Pictures—following the fragmentation of that never-printed early manuscript poem "Pictures" (it survives both as the tiny "My Picture-Gallery" and, more importantly, throughout all the poems, starting with the well-known vignettes of sections 9 and 10 of "Song of Myself").

Then there are the musical odes, such as the midpoint chant of "Song of Myself" (section 26), "Italian Music in Dakota," the splendid "Proud Music of the Storm," "That Music Always Round Me," "I Heard You, Solemn-Sweet Pipes of the Organ," section 5 of "A Song for Occupations," section 3 of "Salut au Monde!" and of course, "I Hear America Singing." These tend to use Whitman's catalogue format in a unique way; their prototype is a pattern of layered lines of verse each embodying a polyphonic voice, instrumental, vocal, or "natural" (the wind in the trees, birdsong, sounds of moving water, etc., to which Whitman adds the noises of human work and enterprise, constructive, destructive, or whatever). This is a device that persists from Spenser through the romantic poets. Whitman employs it in a poetic revision of musical polyphony, even extending the symphonic format beyond phonetic materials to include specimens of all human activity. Section 15 of "Song of Myself," for example, opens with a Whitmanian duet:

"The pure contralto sings in the organ loft, / The carpenter dresses his plank, the tongue of his foreplane whistles its wild ascending lisp" (and how Homeric this last half-line!), but then continues with about sixty varied glimpses of What Is and of What Is Done, musical relations between parts having been only an introductory paradigm for a more general organic assemblage of "the beauty and sacredness of the demonstrable."

Here and there throughout the poetry lurks a notion that the Poem of America—whether in the notion of the United States as "greatest poem" or in *Leaves of Grass* itself—had already been written by Walt Whitman in some earlier phase of consciousness and self-projection. It is not only among the animals, in whose selectively described moral condition ("Not one kneels to another, nor to his kind that lived thousands of years ago, / Not one is respectable or unhappy over the whole earth") the poet finds "tokens of myself." (It might nevertheless be added that Walt Whitman did not eat his young, or remain incapable of knowledge of death or acknowledgment of anything.) It is rather about all his inventoried and chanted phenomena that he surmises, "I wonder where they get those tokens, / Did I pass that way huge times ago and negligently drop them?" Still, his continuous "transfers and promotions" remain his greatest generosities and sympathies, his widest- and farthest-reaching hands or filaments: "And there is no object so soft but it makes a hub for the universe" means, of course, that the imaginative faculty that can construe as a hub a caterpillar, or a drop of sweat, or a hair on the back of a hand—and can construct the right concentric circles radiating from it—is the breath of Democratic life itself.

Democracy, for Whitman's poetry, begins with questions of "representation"—that is, of metaphor. His literal is elusively figurative, and his favorite figure—synecdoche, the part for the whole, the whole for the part, the container and the things contained variously figuring one another—is itself metaphoric, and even more ulterior. American democracy entails a representative government and a deference toward a body of opinion with a propensity to slacken toward self-identifications of the synecdochal sort. We clamor for public officials who are members of whatever group of which we constitute ourselves; we want to be represented by a lump of our region, district, race, sect, caste, or ethnic strain (but seldom of our intelligence, our moral nature, our imagination, our prudence, our regard for others). A system of metaphoric representation (and British Parliament, or perhaps our Senate—rather than our House of Representatives—has been more like this) would have us wish the best and most skilled advocate to argue and negotiate for us (which is a different business from singing), even if he or she were nothing like a neighbor, a workmate, a cousin, or a fellow congregant who would know our song by heart. Such a representative would *stand for* us in another way.

Whitman's affirmations thus always engage our Democratic paradoxes: that if there is to be no selfishness there must be true self-containment. Responsibility starts with the mutual obligations among the components of one's own identity; acknowledging the dignity of things and beings requires a zoom lens to home in on the minute and otherwise help get by the false worth of mere magnitude. Self-respect, as Whitman liked to say, mocks and dissolves aristocracies. American Democracy is both uniquely equipped for, and uniquely in need of, interpreting itself. Its own bodily and empirical constitution is framed anew in all the languages of many sorts of lives—from "the blab of the pave" to the complex poem of celebration that takes back with one hand what it gives with another, perpetually claiming that reading it poses no problems and thereby generating a multitude of them, yet always extending the ultimate perpetuating connection of poet and reader, interpreter and reinterpreter, citizen and citizen. Like his own great poem of poems, "Democracy" said Whitman in *Democratic Vistas* is "a word the real gist of which still sleeps, quite unawakn'd."

HELEN VENDLER

Poetry and the Mediation of Value:
Whitman on Lincoln

The Tanner lectures, as you know, is asked to consider questions of human value. I take as my texts today, to reflect on how the art of mediates value, Walt Whitman's four poems on the death of Abraham Lincoln. Lincoln was shot by John Wilkes Booth, in conspiracy with others, on April 14, 1865, while the Civil War was still ongoing. In the twenty days between the assassination and Lincoln's May 4 burial in Springfield, Illinois, many events occurred. There was first the shocked five-day interim following the assassination; then the thronged April 19 state funeral for Lincoln in Washington; then the seventeen-hundred-mile ceremonial journey of the funeral train bearing Lincoln's coffin through Baltimore, Harrisburg, Philadelphia, New York, Albany, Buffalo, Cleveland, Columbus, Indianapolis, Michigan City, and Chicago. On April 26 Booth had been apprehended and shot, and by April 27 eight conspirators were in jail (awaiting the trial that would end in the hanging of four of them on July 7). All of these events were available to Whitman as he wrote his four poems, as was the fact that the body of Lincoln's son Willie (who had died three years earlier) was exhumed from its grave in Washington and reburied in the Lincoln tomb at Springfield.

In order of composition, Whitman's poems on Lincoln are the following: the short occasional poem "Hush'd Be the Camps Today" (dated April 19,

From *Michigan Quarterly Review* 39 (Winter 2000): 1-18. © 2000 by The University of Michigan.

1865, the day of Lincoln's funeral service in Washington, and printed in the May 1865 edition of *Drum-Taps*); the formally rhymed poem "O Captain, My Captain" and the free-verse elegy "When Lilacs Last in the Dooryard Bloom'd" (both added to the second edition of *Drum-Taps*, September 1865); and the later epitaph "This Dust Was Once the Man" (1871). The assassination of Lincoln of course provoked a flood of writing—journalistic, biographical, poetic. Of the many poems then written, Whitman's memorials have lasted the best; and in considering what values they select, enact, and perpetuate, I want to ask by what aesthetic means they make those values last beyond the momentary topical excitement of Lincoln's death.

Most poetry mediates values differently from prose. In prose, values are usually directly stated, illustrated, clarified, and repeated. One has only to think of the classical form of the oration—and its descendants the sermon, the stump speech, and the university lecture—to see the importance placed, in an oral form, on reduplication of matter. Whitman's poetry retains many vestiges of the oration; and we can see such vestiges in "Lilacs." But most lyric poetry, being short, cannot avail itself of the ample terrain of oratory; it has consequently had to find extremely compressed ways by which to convey value. Readers of poetry not only become adept in unfolding the implications of a poetic language; they also learn to see—by exercising historical knowledge—what is being left out that might well have been present. In respect to the conveying of value, what is left out is always as important as what is put in. Let me give one quick example: Lincoln was assassinated on Good Friday, and commentary on his death quickly attached to him—probably for that reason—the word "martyr" with its overtones of Christ's sacrifice. Whitman offers no word placing Lincoln in the context of Christ's passion, Good Friday, or Easter Sunday. He does not put Lincoln in a Judeo-Christian frame at all—even though contemporary commentators such as Bishop Matthew Simpson at the Washington funeral compared Lincoln to Moses.

I will come back to what is left out by Whitman, but I want to return now to the main question—how we can examine poetry's mediation of value. To relate what is left out to what is put in is a task relatively easier with respect to narration than with respect to lyric. One can see that a novelist (say, Herman Melville in *Moby-Dick*) has included no female characters and suggest what effects and values are enabled by, and also prohibited by, this stratagem. But in lyric, there is no such obvious norm. A symphony score employing no violins would be visibly anomalous; but nobody noticed at first when Georges Perec wrote a novel (*The Void*) without the letter *e* because letters—and words—are less visible than women or violins.

It is imagination, then, that is our first recourse in thinking about poetry and value—the imagination of what is left out. This imagination operates not simply on the grosser level of images (such as the Judeo-Christian ones of Moses or Christ that I have mentioned) but also on the level of syntax—in what other manner could this sentence have been framed?—and of diction—what words might have occurred by contrast to the ones we have? The critical imagination must operate even in the realm of sound, especially at crucial poetic moments, asking what alternative phonetic effects might have been used instead of the given ones.

It is generally agreed that images and the semantic content of words mediate value, but syntax and sound are rarely conceded that potential. In prose, syntax and sound are generally less powerful than in poetry; in poetry they provide a crucial ground to the assertions of value carried by images and words. And, since a short poem is in fact a single complex word in which all individual components are bound together in an inalterable relational syntax, there is, strictly speaking, nothing that does not become a carrier of value in poetry (even such harmless-looking particles as the indefinite and the definite article).

Every lyric belongs to one or more anterior theoretical paradigms of genre. The paradigm may be a formal verse-whole, such as the sonnet, which brings with it certain values—those of courtly life—and general expectations (that it might concern, for instance, love or politics). Or the paradigm may be a formal stanza, such as *terza rima*, which brings with it overtones of Dante, the afterlife, and the value of spiritual self-scrutiny. Or the paradigm may be that of a genre that has no formal shape: the English elegy, for instance, can take any verse shape, but must reflect the death of one or more persons and must meditate on the value of a given sort of human life. Or the paradigm may be that of a genre which, while having no prescribed shape, does have a prescribed length and tone: an epitaph, for instance, must be short and impersonally phrased, and it must assert a final judgment. Or the anterior paradigm may prescribe only one part of the stanza: the presence of a refrain at the end of each stanza, for instance, suggests the value of folk-motifs and of incremental intensification of emotion. A poem can ally itself with the first-person singular paradigm (which is the most common lyric self-presentation, valuing individual experience), or it may depart from that norm by choosing a first-person plural paradigm, in order to claim collective utterance and, with it, collective value.

A poem is expected not only to inscribe itself within the subject-matter and values implied by its paradigms, but also to extend, reverse, or otherwise be original in respect to those very paradigms. It is in the use and critique of its own antecedent paradigms that a poem most fully reveals its own value-system. It is this that I hope to show in reflecting on Whitman's poems concerning Lincoln. The value-system of an original poet—and therefore of his or her poems—will be in part consonant with, in part in dispute with, the contemporary values of the society from which he, and they, issue. Were the poetry not intelligible with respect to those social values, it could not be read; were it not at a distance from them in some way, it would not be original. The most disturbing lyrics are those, such as Whitman's, in which so many shared social values appear that one is surprised when interior divergence manifests itself. Whitman's memorials of Lincoln are patriotic ones, devoted to the image of Lincoln, voiced in solidarity with the Union army, sharing the nation's grief at Lincoln's death and at the carnage of the Civil War, and (in "Lilacs") proud of the much-celebrated beauty of the American landscape. What is it, then, that makes them original? And what values does that originality consecrate? And why is "Lilacs"—the longest of Whitman's poems about Lincoln—also the best? What does it allow that the others do not?

"To have great poems, there must be great audiences, too," Whitman had declared in the 1855 preface to *Leaves of Grass*. His poetic depended on a close connection, even an erotic one, with his imagined listeners: he not only wished to be their spokesman, he wanted *them* to call out to *him* to *be* their spokesman, thereby legitimating his writing. It is not surprising, then, that Whitman's first literary response to Lincoln's death—after the wordless silence that followed the shocking news of the assassination—was to speak in the collective voice of the Union army, as soldiers call on the poet to "sing ... in our name ... one verse." They ask that the subject-matter of this verse should be "the love we bore him."

> Hush'd be the camps to-day,
> And soldiers let us drape our war-worn weapons,
> And each with musing soul retire to celebrate,
> Our dear commander's death.
>
> No more for him life's stormy conflicts,
> Nor victory, nor defeat—no more time's dark events,
> Charging like ceaseless clouds across the sky.
>
> But sing poet in our name,
> Sing of the love we bore him—because you, dweller in camps,
>   know it truly.

As they invault the coffin there,
Sing—as they close the doors of earth upon him—one verse,
For the heavy heart of soldiers

What the soldiers want is not a eulogy of Lincoln's personal life and actions, of the sort pronounced from the pulpit in Washington, but rather an articulation of their mourning. It is the soldiers themselves, as the poem opens, who devise the liturgy appropriate to the death of their commander-in-chief: "Let the camps be hushed, let the weapons be draped, and let us each retire"—to do what? to mourn, to muse, yes, but above all to "celebrate"—in the liturgical, not the festive sense—"our dear commander's death." Any human being can perform these personal acts of silence, weapon-draping, and musing, just as any human being can voice the consolation of the second stanza, as the soldiers say that Lincoln has escaped "time's dark events, / Charging like ceaseless clouds across the sky."

Only after they have invented a collective ritual, and offered a collective consolation, do the soldiers feel the absence of something necessary to their ceremony—an elevated, that is, sung form of utterance offered in their name. It is significant to them that it should be sung by one who, because he has been a "dweller in camps," knows the particular heaviness of soldiers' hearts. This short poem values collectivity in the voice it adopts, in the rituals it devises. It not only values—more than all pomp-filled state memorials—the love borne by the common soldiers, but it also views poetry as merely one ingredient in an indigenous ritual, devised by the people for the people. Why, then, do the soldiers need a verse at all? The poem answers by showing the omnimobility of words. The soldiers remain bound in their camps, but the poet's invisible verse, as the syntax shows, can insert itself into the very circumstance and moment of far-off burial: "As they invault the coffin there, / Sing—as they close the doors of earth upon him— one verse." Lincoln is valued in this collectively voiced poem less as president of a country than as beloved commander of a brave army, themselves accustomed to "time's dark events, / Charging" at them. Yet the view of Lincoln is still a hierarchical one—not in a feudal, but in a military, sense. He is not king or president, but he is the commander. It is not surprising that the democratic Whitman will eventually turn to valuing Lincoln outside a military hierarchy.

Now that he has written the collective call beckoning him to sing, Whitman can compose the verse that will show, from the inside, the army's love and their heavy hearts. "O Captain, My Captain" is sung in the voice of a Union recruit. He is a young boy; he has sailed on the ship of state with his captain, whom he calls, Oedipally, "dear father"; the tide of war has now turned and victory is in sight, as cheering crowds welcome the victorious ship. At this very moment the captain is shot, and dies. The moving turn of the poem comes two-thirds of the way through the poem. In the first two stanzas the boy addresses the captain as someone still living, a "you" who, cradled in the boy's arm, can hear the words directed to him. But in the third stanza the young sailor unwillingly resorts to third-person reference, marking his captain as dead: "My Captain does not answer, his lips are pale and still." The hierarchy of commander—remote from his troops—has been lessened to the hierarchy of captain—sharing a ship with his men—and then lessened to the familial hierarchy of father and son, as Lincoln's relation to others becomes ever more democratic, even intimate.

Two stylistic features—its meter and its use of refrain—mark "O Captain" as a designedly democratic and populist poem. In each stanza, four seven-beat lines (each the equivalent of two standard ballad lines of tetrameter and trimeter) are followed by a slightly changing ballad refrain. The refrain—after two trimeters—returns to the tetrameter/trimeter ballad beat. The poem, by its form, implies that soldiers and sailors have a right to verse written for them in the sort of regularly rhyming stanzas that they like best. And because Whitman has chosen to speak now as a sailor-boy, the diction of the poem offers the clichés of victory that such a boy might use: "Our fearful trip is done, / The ship has weather'd every rack, the prize we sought is won, / The port is near." Everything on shore adheres to the expected conventions of popular celebration—"For you the flag is flung—for you the bugle trills, / For you bouquets and ribbon'd wreaths." Even "the bleeding drops of red," the "mournful tread" of the sailor, and the captain "fallen cold and dead" come from the clichés of war-journalism.

Whitman was not, I think, hypocritical in writing such a poem; he was answering his first poem with the second poem that he thought the first had called for. But in adopting the voice of the young boy mourning his "father," Whitman had sacrificed his own voice entirely. Because he valued, and validated, the claim of his audience that he represent their heavy hearts, Whitman thought to do so by becoming one of them. Wanting to value democracy, he thought he had to exemplify it by submitting to the rhythms and rhymes and clichés of the popular verse prized by the soldiers, rather than inventing a democratic form of his own. Because he was bent on registering individual response as well as the collective wish expressed in "Hush'd Be the Camps," he took on the voice of a single representative sailor, silencing his own idiosyncratic voice. And wanting to show the sailor and his father-captain as participants in a national endeavor, he adopted the allegorical cliché of the Ship of State as the ruling metaphor of his poem.

Though we do not know, factually, that "O Captain" was composed before "Lilacs," it seems to me that the sailor-boy's dirge must have been the direct response to the call in "Hush'd Be the Camps." "Lilacs" is, by contrast, the outburst of individual voice following on Whitman's attempt to honor collectivity by writing in the voice of the heavy-hearted soldiers and to defend representativeness in verse by writing in the voice of the mourning sailor. He was valuing Lincoln as commander in the one and captain-father in the other; he was valuing poetry as a contributor to collective ritual in the one and as a form of populist expression in the other. When we come to "Lilacs," all the values change.

"Lilacs" is written not collectively, and not representatively, but in Whitman's own original lyric voice. In it, Lincoln is not placed in a vertical social hierarchy as president, commander-in-chief, captain, or even father, but is rather placed horizontally, as a fellow-man, even if one distinguished by superlative wisdom and sweetness. There is ritual in the poem—even received ritual, carried out by other mourners but even by the poet, as he lays conventional bouquets of lilies and roses on the coffins of the dead; but there are also strange new rituals, to which I will come, outnumbering the conventional ones. And—most striking of all—there is a suppression of the coincidence of the day of the assassination with Good Friday, as well as a refusal to echo the Christian rituals of services and sermons and hymns that pervaded the twenty days preceding Lincoln's burial.

In "Lilacs," the coffin-train indeed makes its long and mournful journey—in a funereal ritual unprecedented in American history, and therefore attractive to Whitman as an original event—but aside from the mentions of the mourning ceremonies attending the train at each of its stops, nothing in the poem depends on historical fact. The poem never mentions the assassination, the assassin, or the jailed and executed conspirators; the Emancipation Proclamation and other acts of Lincoln's presidency are passed over in silence. Even the startling fact of the reburial of Lincoln's son is omitted. We are given, instead of facts, three symbols—the lilac of this earth, the star of the evening sky, and the hermit-thrush of the dark swamp. By apportioning his poem among the classic three realms of upper-world, middle-world, and underworld, Whitman gives cosmic importance—rather than the political importance ascribed to it by historians—to Lincoln's death. The poem does not value facts: it does not value politics; it does not value Christianity; it does not value speaking in a voice other than one's own. It is written in free verse of the most original sort; it does not value debased popular taste in poetry. Has Whitman repudiated "Hush'd Be the Camps" and "O Captain"? Or does something of them linger in "Lilacs"?

What does "Lilacs" value? And how are its valuings enacted? And what aesthetic value do they exhibit? These questions have answers too complex to be fully enunciated here, but let me give some brief observations. "Lilacs" is a sequence constructed of sixteen cantos ranging in length from five to fifty-three lines. It builds up to its longest and most lyrical moment in canto 14, achieves its moral climax in canto 15, and ends with a coda of "retrievements out of the night" in canto 16. The nonreligious "trinity" that opens the poem (perennial lilac, Lincoln-star, and the "thought of him I love") will become, by the end, the trinity of "lilac and star and bird": that is, the bird and its carol become the equivalent of the opening "thought" of the poet. It is unusual for Whitman to establish such a firm symbolic constellation; his secular trinity is set as a memorable elegiac emblem of the formality that is one of the poem's values. This is not an intimate elegy: Lincoln is named a "friend," but he is also the "powerful western fallen star" who is due formal honor as a symbol of the ideal. That honor is given character in the symbolic trinity dedicated to his memory.

The first act of the speaker—after he has initially lamented his helplessness in the grasp of the "harsh surrounding cloud that will not free my soul"—is to break off (in line 17) a sprig of lilac from the lilac-bush growing in the dooryard. No explanation is given for this act; it is not until line 45 that we learn why he took the sprig. It is to have a flower to lay on Lincoln's coffin: "Here, coffin that slowly passes, / I give you my sprig of lilac." This is not the conventional sort of floral offering; it has passed through no florist's hands. The speaker knows the conventions of arranged "bouquets" made of the rarer "roses and early lilies" and indeed later observes these conventions, as his mourning becomes generalized to "the coffins all of you." Still, he prefers his roughly torn and unarranged lilacs:

> All over bouquets of roses,
> O death, I cover you over with roses and early lilies,
> But mostly and now the lilac that blooms the first,
> Copious I break, I break the sprigs from the bushes,
> With loaded arms I come, pouring for you,
> For you and the coffins all of you O death.

The poem dismisses the idea of personal immortality; when the star sinks, it is gone forever:

... I watch'd where you pass'd and was lost in the netherward
    black of the night,
As my soul in its trouble dissatisfied sank, as where you sad orb,
Concluded, dropt in the night, and was gone.

What the poet can confirm, as a principle of hope, is the natural vegetative resurrection from which Christ took the metaphor of the risen wheat: the funeral train, he says, passes "the yellow-spear'd wheat, every grain from its shroud in the dark-brown fields uprisen." And in the old woods, "lately violets peep'd from the ground, spotting the gray debris."

The chief stylistic trait of this first part of the poem is the long-withheld subject of its sentences. The run of sentences with postponed subjects begins in the one-sentence, six-lined canto 3: "In the dooryard ... / Stands the lilac-bush ... / With many a pointed blossom ... / With every leaf a miracle—and from this bush in the dooryard ... / With delicate-color'd blossoms ... / A sprig with its flower I break." In canto 5, with its seven-line sentence, the continuo is carried by a series of adverbs and participial adjectives—"Over ... / Amid ... / Amid ... / Passing ... / Passing ... / Carrying ... / Night and day journeys a coffin." We can see that this sentence-form imitates the long passage of the train across the eastern third of the North American continent. It is important to Whitman to ally his single tributary sprig of lilac with all the preceding civil and religious ceremonies honoring the dead man; and canto 6 is the poem's chief concession to factual reporting; but this canto is staged so that the public observances lead up to the poet's anomalous, solitary, and unarranged sprig:

Coffin that passes through lanes and streets,
Through day and night with the great cloud darkening the
    land,
With the pomp of the inloop'd flags with the cities draped in
    black,
With the show of the States themselves as of crape-veil'd women
    standing,
With processions long and winding and the flambeaus of the
    night,
With the countless torches lit, with the silent sea of faces and
    the unbared heads,
With the waiting depot, the arriving coffin, and the sombre
    faces,

> With dirges through the night, with the thousand voices rising
>   strong and solemn,
> With all the mournful voices of the dirges pour'd around the
>   coffin,
> The dim-lit churches and the shuddering organs—where amid
>   these you journey,
> With the tolling tolling bells' perpetual clang,
> Here, coffin that slowly passes,
> I give you my sprig of lilac.

The poem here gives what all the contemporary photographs of the journey cannot: movement, silence, sound, tonality, atmosphere. While other poems about Lincoln's death mostly contented themselves with abstractions of praise and grief, Whitman renders the very scenes of mourning in present-participial form, making them unroll before our eyes in what seems real time. The journey comes to a telling climax—after all the elaborate tributes of the cities—in the single lilac-sprig. The poem, it is evident, values showing over telling, and the senses over abstraction; it emphasizes the contribution of each individual act to the tally of mourning gestures. It also values drama—not only in the changing chiaroscuro tableaux of homage presented here, but also in the narrative syntactic drama of the sentence that presses toward the gift of the dooryard lilac.

One could think that the poem could end here. The poet has contributed his flower: is that not enough? We soon learn that it is not: he puts aside the summons of the bird heard in canto 9 to ask the three questions of canto 10: "How shall I warble? ... / how shall I deck my song? ... / what shall my perfume be for the grave?" The last problem is easily solved: the perfume will be the sea-winds and the breath of the poet's chant. But the first two are less rapidly answered. In fact, the first—"How shall I warble?" is not at this point replied to at all, while "How shall I deck my song?" mutates into the specific question, "What shall the pictures be that I hang on the walls, / To adorn the burial-house of him I love?" This question originates from Whitman's knowledge of Egyptian tombs, decorated on the interior with idyllic pictures of daily life. He will renew this convention in canto 11, making resonant pictures of American landscapes and action: "Pictures of growing spring and farms and homes ... / And all the scenes of life and the workshops, and the workmen homeward returning." He includes no religious iconography on the walls of the tomb; he employs only the iconography of the land, catalogued in terms redolent of aesthetic bliss: "With floods of the yellow gold of the gorgeous, indolent, sinking sun, burning, expanding the air ... / In the distance the flowing glaze, the breast of the river, with a wind-dapple here and there." The praise of the beauty of America and its "gentle soft-born measureless light" almost distracts the poet from the still-unanswered question "How shall I warble?"; and though he once again turns toward the chant of the bird, "limitless out of the dusk," and calls it, unexpectedly, a "Loud human song, with voice of uttermost woe," he represents himself as still held back from "the swamps, the recesses," by the star above, and the lilac beside him.

He is really held back by his prolonged cataloguing of beauty, which spills over into the beginning of canto 14, as the poet glosses "the large unconscious scenery of my land." Whitman values very highly, as a poetic structure, the accumulation of sentences of inventory. Beyond the formal triad of his symbols, beyond the conferring of cosmic significance on Lincoln's death by showing its consequence to upper and lower and middle worlds, beyond the drama of the periodic sentence pressing toward its climax, beyond the rendition of theatrically lit atmospheres, he valued the multiplicity and beauty of the world's objects, landscapes, and inhabitants, even in the moment of mourning. Inventories fill most of the poems of *Leaves of Grass* (and all parodies of Whitman begin with a swell of egotism followed by unbridled lists of categories).

But the beautiful categories of canto 13, though they overflow into canto 14, continue under a shadow. While the poet, ravished by the "heavenly aerial beauty ... / and the summer approaching with richness," watches the ample scene, "—lo, then and there, Falling upon them all and among them all, enveloping me with the rest, / Appear'd the cloud." The poet finds "the knowledge of death" walking on one side of him and "the thought of death" walking on the other side, "and I in the middle as with companions, and holding the hands of companions." He finally flees to the swamp, which is then revealed as an underworld of "shores of... water" and "solemn shadowy cedars and ghostly pines so still." This is not the Christian afterlife, but the underworld of shades and ghosts in the midst of the waters of Lethe and the Styx that we know from Greek myth. By annexing the afterworld of classical Greece to the tomb-decorations of Egypt, Whitman tells us that he prefers these ways of knowing and encountering death to those offered by the Christianity in which he had been raised. In 1891, the last year of his life, after he had suffered strokes and other disabling illnesses, he wrote: "The philosophy of Greece taught normality and the beauty of life. Christianity teaches how to endure illness and death. I have wonder'd whether a third philosophy fusing both, and doing full justice to both, might not be outlined" [*Collected Writings* II, *Collect and Other Prose*, ed. Floyd Stovall (New York: NYU Press, 1964), p. 708]. But when he was writing "Lilacs," it was the "normality" of Egypt and Greece, rather than Christian patience, that Whitman valued.

We have reached, in the second half of canto 14, the lyric center of "Lilacs," the song of the hermit-thrush, where one supreme aesthetic value of the poem—the value of free musical language—resides. Though this is the poetic center of the elegy, it is not its moral climax, which will come in canto 15, when the poet fully accedes to vision. However, we must ask ourselves first about this lyric center. "And the charm of the carol rapt me," says the poet: what is that charm? The "carol" is a hymn to a female deity, Death, and is therefore allied to the earliest lyrics we have, the Orphic hymns to abstractions such as Death and the Homeric hymns to the gods and goddesses such as the maternal goddess Demeter, mother of the lost Persephone in Hades. The song of the thrush, beginning in invocation ("Come lovely and soothing death"), and becoming a song of praise ("praise! praise! praise! / For the sure-enwinding arms of cool-enfolding death"), invents a celebratory ritual ("Dances for thee I propose saluting thee, adornments and feastings for thee") to replace the mourning ritual of somber dirges and tolling bells and shuddering organs invented by Christianity. Yet the repudiation of Christian melancholy, forceful as it is, is less memorable than the seductive oceanic rhythms of lyric loosed to be itself. Whitman "overwrites," with this rhythm, the dragging journey of the train. As the train moved across the land, we heard it go "Over the breast of the spring, the land, amid cities": now we hear the carol float above the train, over the same landscape:

> Over the rising and sinking waves, over the myriad fields and
>   the prairies wide,
> Over the dense-pack'd cities all and the teeming wharves and
>   ways,
> I float this carol with joy, with joy to thee O death.

As the song of blissful death "overwrites" the journey of melancholy death, lyric claims its right to the joy that resides in art, even in art of tragic import.

As the bird sings the acceptance of death, the poet, tallying the song in his soul, finds that as he lets go of his former fear and denial, his vision awakes: "My sight that was bound in my eyes unclosed, / As to long panoramas of visions." The painful silent moral visions, gifts of memory, replace, with a wrench, the aesthetic sights of the earth seen earlier by the eye of sense. Whitman first admits to a "screen vision" of mutilated battle-flags ("pierc'd with missiles / ... and torn and bloody, ... And the staffs all splinter'd and broken"). As he persists in his resolve to remember all, the splintered flags of the "screen vision" give way to the greater mutilations of flesh they were hiding:

> I saw battle-corpses, myriads of them,
> And the white skeletons of young men, I saw them,
> I saw the debris and debris of all the slain soldiers of the war.

At this point the elegy for Lincoln resumes in an explicit way its earlier guarded gesture ("For you and the coffins all of you O death") toward all those ordinary soldiers who have died in the war. This is the moment of highest moral value in the poem, as the poet allows himself to see all that the war has cost. At the same time, by resurrecting a word used earlier, apparently casually, in the mention of the violets that peeped from the ground, "spotting the gray debris," Whitman reminds us that debris is the compost of new growth. It was the Union that was to grow strong from the battle-corpses.

The drama of canto 15 is enacted in the style of a chronicler of apocalypse. I quote first the *Book of Revelation*:

> And I saw in the right hand of him that sat on the throne a book.... And I saw a strong angel proclaiming.... And I beheld, and to.... And I saw when the Lamb opened one of the seals.... And I saw, and behold a white horse. [*Revelation* 5, 6]

And now Whitman:

> And I saw askant the armies,
> I saw as in noiseless dreams hundreds of battle-flags ....
> I saw battle-corpses, myriads of them,
> And the white skeletons of young men, I saw them,
> I saw the debris and debris of all the slain soldiers of the war.

This style boldly claims, if implicitly, that Whitman expects his vision to be granted the same credence as that granted the *Book of Revelation*; the passage is his most blasphemous transvaluation of Christian value.

In the coda of canto 16, the poet resumes his earlier themes, and finds his trinity complete—"Lilac and star and bird twined with the chant of my soul"—but unexpectedly is not permitted to leave, in memory, the underworld. Though in real life the lilac is "there in the door-yard, blooming, returning with spring," the poet finds "Lilac and star and bird twined with the chant of my soul, / There in the fragrant pines and the cedars dusk and dim." Because the underworld is "there," the poet is by implication "here" in the normal world—but the poem cannot enact the "here" in which he finds himself. The living part of his soul is still there in the dusk and the dimness of Hades, twined with his trinity.

If we seek out the originality of "Lilacs"—beginning with its refusal to name Lincoln and its suppression of his civic and military roles—we can see that though it indeed obeys many paradigms of its genre, the English elegy, it wears its rue with a difference, subduing Christian symbols to those of Egypt and Greece, celebrating the natural beauty of life rather than the prospective beauties of heaven, finding its consolation in new joyous rituals of death, and asserting that its revelation of corpses and skeletons is as prophetically binding St. John's revelation of heaven. Its style asserts the value of showing rather than telling, the value of the idiosyncratic voice over the collective or representative voice, and—in its journeying sentences that climax in a definite halt the value of acceptance, rather than denial, of the full stop of death. Its other striking sentences, phrased not in the progressive pressure to end, but rather in arias ebbing and flowing without resolution, assert the fluctuating harmonies and contrasts of the expansive but inconclusive rhythms of experience:

> Victorious song, death's outlet song, yet varying ever-altering
>   song,
> As low and wailing, yet clear the notes, rising and falling, flood-
>   ing the night,
> Sadly sinking and fainting, as warning and warning, and yet
>   again bursting with joy,
> Covering the earth and filling the spread of the heaven....

After "Lilacs," Whitman wrote one other poem concerning Lincoln—the only one left to write, Lincoln's epitaph. It was published in 1871, six years after Lincoln's death. Lincoln is no longer friend or wise and sweet soul; he is reduced to dust. The poet grasps the dust to himself. "This dust," he says. He does not point to the grave, saying "That dust." This is not a poem gesturing outward toward the "there" of the lilac or the "there" of the underworld:

This dust was once the man
Gentle, plain, just resolute, under whose cautious hand,
Against the foulest crime in history known in any land or age,
Was saved the Union of these States.

The epitaph is massively imbalanced: a mere two words "This dust" make up the left half of the copula, while the right half requires thirty words. The proportion is therefore appropriate to the light dust versus the complex description of the consequential man. Lincoln, in becoming dust, becomes historical, "the man who guided the preservation of the Union." The initial adjectives are themselves complex, as the initial personal "gentle" is played off against the final official "resolute," while in between we see the "plain" of Lincoln's upbringing set against the "just" character of his legal profession. I hear the line with the emphasis on "and": "Gentle, plain, just—*and*—[when the hour came] resolute." The next adjective, applied not to Lincoln but to his guiding hand, is "cautious"—this speaks to his wisdom. What is most surprising about the epitaph is that it, unlike most such honorific inscriptions, gives no active verb to its subject. Lincoln is not said to be "the man ... Who saved the Union of these states." That would give him the power of a monarch. It was the thousands of soldiers, alive and dead, who saved the Union; the president, *primus inter pares*, was merely their supervising fellow-participant. But the soldiers are left unmentioned as such: they exist only subsumed within the passive verb. Yet they are the saviors, and as such they are the ultimate repository of individual value, even in an epitaph praising their leader. The very peculiar syntax of this epitaph reserves the main subject and verb of the subsidiary adjective clause—"The Union of these States was saved"—to the very end and inverts the normal word order to "Was saved the Union of these States," thereby putting the Union in the climactic syntactic position of national value, placed even above the actions taken to save it. Tucked in between the presiding cautious hand and its salvific agents is the averted horror: the continuation of slavery. Slavery is here named by euphemism, as though its proper name should never again be uttered in human hearing. It becomes, superlatively, "the foulest crime," and it is placed in a cosmic spatio-temporal field: it is "the foulest crime known in any land or age."

What makes this epitaph a poem? Above all, its tortured syntax, which tries to tuck into thirty words the personal, professional, ethical, and prudential qualities of a single historical personage; his relation to the Union Army; the soldiers' relation to the winning of the war; the chief result of that victory; and a description of the ancient, widespread, and evil crime against which both president and soldiers opposed their lives. Syntax, when tortured, becomes a sign of a complexity too great to be naturally contained within a single sentence and yet bent on being thus contained because all the elements of that given complexity are inextricable one from another and must therefore be named in the same breath. Whitman's last word on Lincoln emphasizes his historical greatness, based on greatness of character, while reserving to him merely a guiding role in the ultimate value, the salvation of the Union. This is a poem of Roman succinctness and taciturnity, betraying its depth of feeling chiefly in the implicit figure of the scales—in which a handful of dust is equal in weight to the salvation of the Union, with the copula serving as the needle of equilibrium. In it the poet speaks not collectively, not representatively, and not idiosyncratically and lyrically; he speaks impersonally, as the recording angel. This poem places value on the voice of history in final judgment. Walt Whitman, the man, is sublimed away; this poem is—to use Elizabeth Bishop's words—one of those "admirable scriptures of stone on stone." One can see its words chased on a tablet: it is itself a tombstone. But did any tombstone ever carry such an epitaph?

There is more to say about the values imaged and implied by these four poems. In attempting the subject of Lincoln from four different perspectives, Whitman (who had often seen Lincoln and had described him in prose of a journalistic and mimetic nature) turns away from personal and historic mimesis of the man and president to symbolic mimesis, framed for the conveying of value. In each case the aesthetic vehicle—the collective voice of the soldiers in the camps, the single voice of the grieving novice-sailor, the idiosyncratic voice of the poet coming to know death, and the impersonal voice of historic judgment—offers a different possibility of expression. The shorter poems show us, by contrast, how and why "Lilacs" reaches its heights and its amplitudes. All of the poems show us Whitman debating what stance the American poet should adopt when speaking of important national events. If each stance—collective, representative, idiosyncratic, impersonal—has something to be said for it, then we are shown that value can be mediated by poetry in any number of ways and that both the poet and his audience are modeled differently in each. We are warned, by the greater success of the most original of the four poems, of the dangers to the poet in attempting to speak collectively or within the bounds of popular taste—or even with the impersonal voice of historiography. It is chiefly when a public crisis evokes some crisis in the soul of the poet—here, Whitman's crisis in judging what could be truly said of human mortality—that a public poem takes on lasting aesthetic value.

ANGUS FLETCHER

The Whitman Phrase

"Notwithstanding the beauty and expressiveness of his eyes, I occasionally see something in them as he bends them upon me, that almost makes me draw back. I cannot explain it whether it is more, or less, than human. It is as if the earth looked at me—dumb, yearning, relentless, immodest, inhuman. If the impersonal elements and forces were concentrated in an eye, that would be it. It is not piercing, but absorbing and devouring—the pupil expanded, the lid slightly drooping, and the eye set and fixed.[1]

When John Burroughs in 1863 wrote about the experience of being looked at, in this case by Walt Whitman, he was indirectly drawing our attention to "something" we notice in the poetry as well, its scarcely definable close-up distance, its power to radiate an absorption. We need to be reminded, many times, that Whitman was one of the great gazers. He studies the vista, not just when he writes about the promises and corruptions of democracy. His work contains a complete philosophy of seeing and looking, extending all aspects of the sense of sight while maintaining the power to absorb. Like a Stoic, Whitman sees into things, although often he may appear merely to notice them in passing. Some have wished to say that he stares like a man cruising the streets, looking for a sex partner. That might be, but I would rather explore Whitman's sight in

From *A New Theory for American Poetry*. © 2004 by the President and Fellows of Harvard College.

terms of his wish for theory, a desire which historians would normally treat under the heading, "The Defence of Poetry." One cannot help feeling the influence or the affinity with Shelley's *Defence*, for example. Whitman, however, does not think poetry needs defending so much as expounding in the first place; he is very American. He knows what it is, and he is going to tell you. He believes poetry needs no defense as long as its visionary function is made clear. He reminds me of John Donne preaching a sermon on the text: "For now we see through a glass darkly, but then face to face; Now I know in part, but then I shall know, even as I am known." Clarity on earth comes from a way of thinking in vistas, including analogues to vista. Thinking in vistas is a general sight. As Donne says: "All the senses are called Seeing."[2] In his famed prose introduction to the 1855 *Leaves of Grass*, Whitman proclaimed the American bard would be a seer: "the expression of the American poet is to be transcendent and new," and when in the next sentence he rejects what he calls the "direct or descriptive or epic," he is imagining a new role for these traditional poetic impulses. Specifically, as we shall see, he loosens the idea of the descriptive, as Clare had done and Ashbery was later to do. *A Backward Glance O'er Travel'd Roads* (1888) celebrated the poet's sixty-ninth year by announcing the time had arrived "for democratic America's sake, if for no other, there must imperatively come a readjustment of the whole theory and nature of poetry."[3] In fact he had already achieved this readjustment, which depended upon his assumption of the role of prophet.

When the poem "Salut au Monde" (Sec. 4) begins line after line with the phrase "I see," the meaning clearly is "I imagine, I envision, I perceive in my memory, or finally, I behold," and this parallels a similar use of the formula, "I hear."[4] Such invocations of the senses are just that, invocations of the powers of prophecy. Invocation is then what the poet means to be doing, and after a while the "I see" formula ceases to strongly suggest the visual. In an unusual perception, like Galileo's father, Whitman grasped the importance of opera as another mode of seeing, seeing through sound.[5] Whitman is sharply concerned to show that he is actually looking at things in order to see them; he hears things because, in fact, he is listening to them. As a poet inventing his own tonalities, he is paying a special kind of close attention. A bird song, heard as aria in a lament, is something he might actually listen to, though it is hard to distinguish that warbling from his imaginary version of Rossini or Donizetti played by a brass band in South Dakota.[6] There is a problem, fundamentally, regarding imagination, which I note because of the status of the detached image in Whitman. In a purely hallucinatory way the imagery in Leaves of Grass recalls the definition of a thought in Shakespeare's Sonnet 27: "Like a jewel hung in ghastly night." How un-actual, one asks with Whitman generally, is any sense perception? He seems often to be *wondering at* what he sees and hears and touches, perhaps like a doctor diagnosing a patient's symptoms. The wonderment is critical, the experience of actually *having the percepts* always being felt to be the "main event." The idea of vista therefore remains curiously teasing; in John Burroughs' description of Whitman's eyes, his look, it is not easy to tell which of the two is Tantalus—Burroughs the new friend (it was 1863), or Whitman himself, gazing like earth as to a sky promising rain, desiring to absorb.

If such a sojourning sensibility is to issue in poetry, it will have to find a language of absorption to create poems of our climate. Climates, in fact, absorb us. The problem of climate and also of environment is that they resemble the galaxy: they are a soup of sameness and difference. In them, differences are absorbed by the recurring samenesses. To express these relations, Whitman shifts vista into *vision*. All the things he "sees" come to him then as what he calls "thoughts." Given this remarkable range of sculptural plasticity, and his meandering vision, we ask: what is their principle of order?—for poets as authors are so called because they seek to increase order in the universe. In this light, the following is the outline of theory for discussion.

Three initial points need to be made. First, when Whitman speaks of poetry and its theory, he means the theory of the making of poems, which are *made* symbolic objects, *poemata*. He does not mean interpretation, that is, he does not mean anything like what scholars have been calling "theory" ever since about 1965 or so. His concern is poetics, and *neither* rhetoric *nor* any sort of hermeneutics, immediately making it remarkable that he includes in his poetics the idea that "these United States are the greatest poem," hence raising the question: what is the poetic theory of this political union? We are left holding a most bizarre hybrid—unless we know Vico's work[7]—namely that the USA and "Song of Myself" are equally "poems."

The second point concerns politics, very broadly understood, namely, the assertion that Whitman's political vision was formed on the model, under the influence, within the culture, of Jacksonian democracy as it evolved during Andrew Jackson's two terms (1829–37). This claim should occasion no surprise. The Jacksonian model is obviously complex, the subject of numerous distinguished historical studies. I have only one thing to say about it. With Jackson, American politics changed from the end of the Federalist period in one major direction that surely no historian would ever think to identify as such: the politics and political order defining the country shifted from a hierarchical top–down structuring, with many natural chains of descending authority, to an utterly different model.

The third point is that this new model gives the picture or conceptual scheme of what I have been calling an environment. As soon as Jackson effectively established the full force and credit of universal suffrage—despite its restrictions as to race or gender—politics in America became, as a unifying fact, the ordering of a vast social environment. The implications of this fact, including its special pressure upon the Union of free and slave-holding states, will become clear as we proceed. The key question then becomes: what is the coherence principle for this or any other environment? What is post-Jacksonian coherence? John Quincy Adams was the last American president to wear knee-breeches, I have been told[8]—how could those breeches survive in the new environment fashioned by Old Hickory?

Whitman's call for theory takes a critical turn, of course, after Darwin. Our culture and politics must now, to quote the poet, "conform with and build on the concrete realities and theories of the universe furnish'd by science, and [science is] henceforth the only irrefragable basis for anything, verse included."[9] My argument may not seem to value Whitman's serious commitment to science as expressed in 1861. Darwin had understood his own theory of evolution already in the 1840s, but did not publish *The Origin of the Species* until 1859. The implication is clear, though I will not develop it here: an active interest in science and its methods would be ongoing for Whitman during all his years as a journalist, so that he *did not suddenly* become a poetical scientist in the early 1850s. To Thoreau or Muir or Burroughs, one would never ascribe a sudden scientific conversion, and so equally with Whitman. He was converted to the attitudes and to the observational methods of science, but not suddenly; always he remained true to his calling, to be the great Bard, the new poet of Democracy.

DEMOCRATIC VISTAS

Whitman's *poem-en-masse* cannot be a matter of conventional structures; this is not a matter of whim. According to *Vistas*, the old feudal order had used superior force as "the only security against chaos," whereas in Whitman's poetic view democracy embraced "many transmigrations, and endless ridicules, arguments, and ostensible failures" such that democratic man "may and must become a law and a series of laws, unto himself, surrounding and providing for, not only for his own personal control, but all his relations to other individuals, and to the State."[10] Whitman would like to see poetry take its part in promoting his idea that American democracy is "life's gymnasium."[11] He most often promotes the metaphor of the healthy body, but also uses the Enlightenment image of the machine. To express the balancing of the individual with the demands of the mass, he speaks of a "compensating balance-wheel of the successful working machinery of the aggregate American."[12] He knows that money and money-making will not preserve balance, for they are based on raw acquisition. If the larger aim is "preserving cohesion, ensemble of Individuality," then the only answer will be to "vitalize man's free play of special personalism." Like a Miltonic tract, the *Vistas* finally launch a violent attack upon "savage, wolfish parties."[13]

Yet the poet wonders at his own degree of balance. He asks himself if his thought is simply "the splendid figment of some dream," and he answers No: "we stand, live, move, in the huge flow of our age's materialism—in its spirituality."[14] The criterion for the poem must be a "scientific estimate." Whitman wants to make of politics a natural phenomenon, as opposed to a law-driven social conventionality. He wants citizens to be good steersmen, letting each soul voyage "with the accompanying idea of eternity, and of itself, the soul, buoyant, indestructible, sailing space forever, visiting every region, as a ship the sea." This voyager is to discover "the pulsations in all matter, all spirit, throbbing forever—the eternal beats, eternal systole and diastole of life in all things—wherefrom I feel and know that death is not the ending, as was thought, but rather the real beginning—and that nothing ever is or can be lost, nor ever die, nor soul, nor matter." Thus among us "must arise poets immenser far"[15] who make great poems of death, for "we sail a dangerous sea of seething currents, cross and undercurrents, vortices"—and what are these false tides, if not demagoguery and greed. He castigates the "blind fury of the parties" battening on "scrofulous wealth, the surfeit of prosperity, the demonism of greed"—excesses hardly to be redeemed by "new projections and invigorations of ideas and men."[16] His final focus is on the political sickness and disease caused by "the depraving influences of riches just as much as poverty." It is in this context of a mingled personal and political health that he invoked theory: "In fact, a new theory of literary composition for imaginative works of the very first class, and especially for highest poems, is the sole course open to these States."[17] This medical doctor is discovering a new doctrine, "the average, the bodily, the concrete, the democratic, the popular," notions providing the base for a good future. If we imagine the largest bound of such a medicinal art, it would have to be ecology, as studied and practiced by our environmental guardians of natural systems. What Whitman means by "adhesion" and "cohesion" comes finally to be what such scientists mean by ecological balance, what the Ancients meant by *philia*, the precondition of any working state, what Lucretius meant by saying that in the nature of things *amor* had to command the cosmos.

In the mid nineteenth century it was hard to imagine the laws of such outlooks, and we are not at all surprised that Charles Eliot Norton wrote thoughtfully of *Leaves* that it was a "curious and lawless collection of poems."[18] Thoreau wrote to a friend about "a great primitive poem," the verse "rude and sometimes ineffectual," while William Dean Howells equally discovered this lawlessness in *Drum Taps*. "The thought is as intangible as aroma; it is not more put up than the atmosphere."[19] Howells could not have been more percipient, for what he calls aroma and atmosphere are perhaps the defining cases of environment. He noticed subtle indeterminacies in the poetry: "memories and yearnings come to you folded, mute, and motionless in his verse, as they come in the breath of a familiar perfume. They give a strange, shadowy sort of pleasure." Unlike young Henry James,[20] Howells knew, of course, that Whitman had rougher democratic interests in mind, attenuated, he thought, by a delicate willingness to pull back from "spoken ideas."

In that age of Jacksonian influences there was more than ever a need to consider the Founders' distrust of natural acquisitive and aggressive drives, along with the constitutional balancing of powers designed to divert predatory political desires into channels of rational benefit. It is odd that as machines were rising in physical importance, the machine metaphor of the balance wheel of the clock was diminishing in political force. All through Edward Pessen's important study of the period runs the thread of a contradiction, as epitomized in his remark that "neither in word nor action did Jackson reveal a consistent interest in, let alone sympathy for, democracy and democratic social change, during the first 62 years of his life."[21] Yet Jackson presides over the massive change in our politics that occurred through the widening of the suffrage, although the right of the individual to vote was still radically curtailed—excluding women and blacks, for a start. A widened political place for the individual, even if only theoretical, was bound to destabilize. The historian Robert Remini tells us that "Madison regarded democracy as an 'unstable' effort to include every citizen in the operation of government." Chief among the consequences of polity would be the use of majority rule, which, Madison thought, could only "jeopardize the personal and property rights of the minority"—an established, often wealthy minority, the class and the culture represented by the Founders. In true Lockean fashion a validated identity, a proper governmental role for the individual, was to be defined in terms of property, a basis thought to be the guarantor of underlying political stability. The virtual opposite of this system would be the shift to an unpropertied individuality, and from the poet's vantage point this would require a new poetic expressive language whose grammar would reflect the different basis of speech and communication in the new political climate—a new grammar of status relations. Grammar implies the concept of the social mechanism. The American sentence will actually have to change.

It would not be until the 1890s that a knowledgeable English novelist, George Gissing, would find himself "insisting on the degree to which people have become machines, in harmony with the machinery amid which they spend their lives."[22] Gissing was going to call his book *Gods of Iron*, "meaning machinery, which is no longer a servant but a tyrannous oppressor of mankind. One way or another this frantic social struggle must be eased." In America, the changes marking the mechanistic assault upon the individual craftsman belong initially to the Jacksonian era, but for Americans they were masked by westward expansion, over which Jackson presided in no small measure. Industrial changes would accelerate vastly during the Civil War, but the link between "this frantic social struggle" and Jacksonian democracy can hardly be doubted.

Whitman in his formative years had occasion to learn all about many aspects of the complexities of a great age of personal independence. New York City, as Sean Wilentz has shown in great detail, long retained a variety of shops making endless arrays of different things; and although I myself remember remnants of this old New York in Manhattan, where we lived, today this individual entrepreneurial activity is almost unimaginable. Wilentz states that by mid-century New York's manufacturing cityscape demonstrated "immense diversity of scale and its complex range of journeymen, contractors, small masters, and independent producers bridging the gap between the largest manufacturer and the lowliest outwork hand. It was not, contrary to the most cataclysmic images of the early industrial revolution, a setting where all opportunity had been destroyed by invading merchant capitalists—where all artisans were plunged into the ranks of proletarianized wage labor.[23] On the other hand, the individual New York craftsman slowly came to participate in an incorporation of working men into large self-representing groups, encouraged by speakers and leaders like Fanny Wright or Robert Owen. Furthermore, as Wilentz and David Reynolds have also shown, the Jacksonian influence in New York had the effect of radically stimulating party politics, so that although a poet or a journalist like Whitman might see deep into the fate of the individual working man, the major shift gave power to organizations of political power groups, that is, to the parties dedicated to the game of colliding with each other, as groups. "Song of Occupations" reflects the legacy of craft and the small manufacturing businesses; meanwhile, when politics was imagined as craft, it remained an intensely local affair and hence occupied a middle ground between massive financial powers and the abject personal isolation of the poor. With the construction of the Whitman grammar, which was the chief artistic novelty of his 1855 *Leaves of Grass* and all his ensuing poems, we reach the area that chiefly concerns us, the imaginative vision that enabled him to become the poet of all these instabilities and changes.

THE WHITMAN PHRASE

The conditions and consequences, social and linguistic, of this new poetry may now be summarized under three headings:

> I. Whitman, known for inventing free verse, even more radically invented a new kind of poem, which we must call the *environment poem*. His poems are not about the environment, whether natural or social. They are environments. This generic invention, though not entirely without precedent, and not without affinities in certain nature writings, is a strange idea. Stranger than one might at first imagine.

> II. The principle of order, form, expressive energy, and finally of coherence for such environment-poems is the *phrase*, which I mean in a grammatical and in an extended gestural sense. The paramount use of phrase accounts for the Whitman style, and more important for his poetics, for the way he arranges the boundaries and the innards of his poems.

> III. The phrase, as it controls the shaping of the environment-poems that are required if he is to express any truths about a Jacksonian world—whether pragmatic, political, mystical, aesthetic, or otherwise—takes its physical correlate and its metaphysical function from Whitman's obsessive analysis of wave motions. To put it iconically: when John Ashbery wishes to overgo his own Whitmanian prose-poem, "The System," or his vastly complex *Flowchart*, he simply writes "A Wave."

A few ideas for Whitman have thus emerged and are worth repeating: (a) that for theory we must deal with poetics and not much with rhetoric; (b) that the world in which these poetics evolve is a Jacksonian world; (c) that

Whitman invents a new poetic form, the environment-poem; (d) that the chief method of such poems is the eccentric deployment of phrase-units, an extreme grammatical endeavor; (e) and finally, that the Whitman phrase is itself modeled on the virtually infinite translation of the wave—in nature, art, thought, and human experience. If one keeps these five avenues or vistas in mind, which are drawn from theory, politics, poetics, grammar, and physics, then one will begin to see what Whitman meant when he spoke of "a complete readjustment of the whole theory and nature of poetry."

Let us begin then with grammar in the poetic line. Virtually every single poem in his original manner is structured out of a single stylistic process: the *phrase*, but the phrase inflected in a particular way. Most readers of Whitman have seen his obvious discontinuities, but it seems no one has asked what larger structural principle is implied, in a formal sense, by the union of these discontinuities? It is as if readers delighted in saying Walt is just chockfull of colorful phrases, but they never ask what poetic principles of formation would allow the plethora to work. They do not ask how the coherence of the plethora is maintained. They do not seem to remember that Whitman writes poems which seem unbounded, but are in fact enclosures. The theory of poetry demands that we ask always what forming principles conspire to make the work into a poem, rather than a casual discourse or rhetorical exercise. The issue finally has to do with Union and Civil War. In a strict sense, every poem is a state. Leaving grammar aside for the moment, theorists should pay attention precisely to what Emerson may have meant by his colloquial expression, "part and particle,"[24] especially since for him, as for Whitman, states live only when they are always changing shape.

Theory demands that we isolate the phrase as the minimal life-unit of coherent expression. Hence, to construct modern literature's largest poetic environment, Proust built *Remembrance of Things Past* around the dynamics of the (musical) phrase, epitomized in *la petite phrase de Vinteuil*.[25] Broadly, by aggregating his own identity into an ensemble of parceled phrases, Whitman is able to insert his own personality into the drifting climate he invents, for ensemble is context in motion. Through the phrase and its clausal surrogates, the poetry gains particular control over the drift, the ensemble, the *en masse*, the average. Without subliming the grammar—a dangerous game, as Wittgenstein observed—let us consider more deeply what phrase does for Whitman.

Originally, the word comes from Greek *phrasis* and *phrazein*, to tell. A phrase is a short pithy expression, the shortest of telling expressions. In dance, it is a series of movements comprising a pattern. In Western music, Webster tells us a phrase is a short musical thought at least two, but typically

four measures in length, closing with a cadence. A cadenced thought, coming
through inflected cadenced melody. Most important of all, in grammar, it is
any group of two or more words that form a sense-unit, either expressing a
thought fragmentarily or as a sentence element not containing a predication
but having the force of a single part of speech—hence we have prepositional
phrases (*west through the night*), or participial, infinitive or gerundive phrases.
The key idea here is that without predication the phrase expresses a thought,
with the *effect* of the thought always being a fragment or part of a larger
union.

> My sail-ships threading the archipelagoes,
> My stars and stripes fluttering in the wind,
> Commerce opening, the sleep of ages having done its work,
>   races reborn, refresh'd,
> Lives, works resum'd—

When phrases like these pile up in "A Broadway Pageant," they are
employed in chanting a plethora of gifts, where number is the chief
metaphor—the metaphor of metonymy.[26] Classic philological skill and a
deep study of *stimmung* enabled Leo Spitzer to reach into the inner form of
the Whitman list, to show he is never simply itemizing things.[27] He is
itemizing things which occur to him, which is different. Spitzer called the
technique "chaotic enumeration," which he found also in the poetry of Paul
Claudel, Blaise Cendrars, Aimé Césaire, and Rubén Darío, and we might add
Pablo Neruda. He went on to show that instead of narrated events expressed
in conventional syntax, we find on the contrary that the poet's "nominal
style" employs a "coupling of nouns with adjectives or participles, without
benefit of finite verbs or copulas." In a way this yields an impressionist effect
because the style uses unconnected ingredients, touches of color, a general
suppression of superordinate control. Explicating "Out of the cradle
endlessly rocking," Spitzer wrote, "I see in these participles nervous
notations of the moment which serve not to re-enact actions, but to
perpetuate the momentary impressions which these have made on the boy
when he was perceiving them." Spitzer identified the present participial
ending, repeated over and over, with the rocking motion of the sea. Perhaps,
ironically, this undulant numerous lapping is also a harbinger of death, the
final message from the sea, a message borne upwards by the aria anchoring
the elegy. The sense of rocking has many dimensions, like the rolling of
images in Stevens's early homage to Whitman, "Sea Surface Full of
Clouds."[28] The undulant in that poem initiated a perpetual prelude, holding

and holding, while as the ocean imagined an end, "the water-glooms / In an enormous undulation fled."

With Whitman and *his* theory of poetry, however, Spitzer's chaotic enumeration is a thinking which expresses "the complexity of the modern world." Such thinking seems mainly a matter of individual consciousness, hence nonpolitical. But this is only an appearance; the politics run deep, right into the heart of grammar. Historical awareness underwrites an interrogation of the poet's "I," but simultaneously asks, purely pragmatically: what lies beyond the self? The limits of the present tense are obvious, in this historical perspective. A mindless favoring of the present tense (like the television commentator's use of the historical present) is bound to dissolve the sense of history, the sense of hierarchical concatenation or indeed any logically *enlinked* furthering of probable steps in a development—none of the hierarchical orders are supported any more, they dissolve, they liquefy, while complex enumerations in parallel quasi-biblical rhythms are allowed to verge on chaos. But, with Whitman, they do so in the interest of presenting a drama of the poet's own thinking, that is, the drama of his having what he called, systematically, his "thoughts."[29] It is apparent that among the few central theoretical questions to be raised regarding Whitman, none is more important than his paradoxical, elusive, and doubtless evasive relation to the problem of history.

Whitman seems early on to have found his phrasal method, not without influence from journalistic prose, and he clearly thought this linguistic method would neutralize interpretive problems of the relation between American and European history. Virtually unstructured sequences of phrase would allow for translation from the one conceptual scheme, to the other. A similar quest occurs with the fiction of Henry James, where a questioning recursive style betokens a pragmatic skepticism, whether about Europe or about American origins. Whitman seems to believe that these United States are engaged in a great transition, separate and yet not entirely detached from European custom, and therefore his poetry specializes in all forms of intransitivity. To "see" is his main occupation (and then to sing), and this means in general that his expression of what he sees almost never rests on transitive verb action. There is almost never any strong sense of subject, verb, and object, although transitivity is always a further implication on some level of *interest*, as we shall see in our discussion of the middle voice. Whitman's hammer never hits the nail. Instead, he catches, as in a snapshot, the hand holding the hammer in midair in all its intrinsic hammerness. The Zenonian trajectory is what counts, or if you wish, an arrested liminal passage between and between and between. The lack of transitivity is staggering in its consistency. On reflection, of course, this persistently intransitive manner would necessarily have to be the Whitman method, given that vision and the full range of sense perceptions is archetypally his mode of response to the world. Perception and the naming of percepts, as with the Wordsworth poems on the "naming of places," are not material action.

To say that Whitman thinks intransitively, veering always toward the middle voice, is to claim that he sees rather than narrates, taking the word *see* in its prophetic sense. It is also to claim that he finds this seeing a sufficient index to a possible action implied in the gesture, a Neapolitan gesture, caught by the instant photo of what is seen. We do not forget that when he put his own engraved photograph opposite the 1855 title page of his book, he meant to suggest to the readers to read his book in a new way. Besides the wide format permitting the long lines to remain long on the page, he meant us to follow those lines as a picture-taker follows a subject. Everything is a brilliant sketch, almost a cartoon (and again his journalism is an influence). We are invited to catch glimpses of outlines, and that requires us not to be trammeled by ideas of logical or material concatenation. To read Whitman aright, we have to remain perpetually intransitive, like the vast majority of his middle-voicing verbs, his verbs of sensation, perception, and cognition.

Wishing to intensify the phrasal unit, he insists on the phrase of the pure verb, the verb before it is locked down into predication. Whitman's favorite and most effective phrase is crafted from the present participle. Take one example, out of thousands, a fragment found among his uncollected manuscripts. As so often, the piece has no title and is unfinished—or is it unfinished? The method prohibits a definite answer. Whitman's usual title for two lines like these would have been, simply, "A Thought."[30]

> Undulating, swiftly merging from womb to birth, from
>   birth to fullness and transmission, quickly transpiring—
> Conveying the sentiment of the mad, whirling, *fallout*
>   speed of the stars, in their circular orbits.

Here the effect of the floating present participles is to enhance an unusually cosmic sense of activity, as Ezra Greenspan has argued, and yet also this is personally felt by the poet.[31] He wants to be able to express his belief, "I know that Personality is divine," hence must intensify his verbs of mental activity. He also wants these devices of presence to express ideas about the land and country where he lives, and we are surprised to discover that the phrase is a device of political implication as well as personal expression.

PHRASING JACKSONIAN DEMOCRACY

The "buried past" with all its power over the evolution of custom and government has somehow to find its language in Whitman's verse. Our theory must now widen its perspective, for it is not enough that the phrase permit a wondrous play of the present participle. In a more general way the phrase also allows ideas, images, and thoughts to be distributed across and within the boundaries of each environment being described, and since each phrase is such an elemental part of the grammar, composing whole poems out of each description, it plays a central part in the idea that for Whitman each poem constitutes a state.

Note then what follows. The chief rivals the phrase contends with are *clauses*. ("When it rains, I carry an umbrella.") As every schoolboy knows, or used to know, this sentence is composed of two clauses, and in English these are the main building blocks of predication. In grammar we call these the main clause and the subordinate clause. Our language is completely controlled and expressively driven by the chief property of these clausal forms, namely, that they express superordinate and subordinate relationships between the main parts of the predication. A language of this type is constantly seeking to affirm a system of subordination, that is, what we may call a top–down hierarchical order, which was the order for America the Founders believed to be best for the country.

The only way for a Jacksonian democracy and its refusal of subordination to thrive, in symbolic terms, would be to get rid of the clauses of sentences as much as possible. This excision of the clause is only partly possible. Whitman carries it as far as he can by assimilating clausal forms in phrasal gesture, thereby weakening the hierarchical stranglehold of traditional English literary grammar. If you read William Cullen Bryant's nature poems along side Whitman's lyrics, you will see that Bryant is virtually locked up inside the traps of clausal grammatical units. Whitman uses the phrase as if he were a student of the Sapir–Whorf Hypothesis—in *Colors of the Mind*, I showed that Edward Sapir regarded Whitman as an extreme case of idiosyncratic expression, the master "of a larger, more intuitive linguistic medium than any particular language" (263). We know to what lengths the poet studied and noted down his language experiments. The phrase provides the fundamental technique Whitman uses to become the poet of democracy. No phrase is ever *grammatically* superordinate, superior to, any other phrase, although vocal intonation may confer greater importance on this phrase rather than that phrase. Examples of this ordering by intonation abound in paratactic poetic languages, such as Old English, where we see that anarchy does not follow from the abandonment of the grammar of subordination. Through powers of intonation poetry thus may need to learn how to inflect complex relations without resorting to the hierarchical top–down structure, and probably the best model for such intonation is the wave. By empowering the phrase Whitman averts a secret vice foreseen by Proust. In a passage of *The Guermantes Way* about the survival of etiquette in a decadent aristocratic milieu and in "an egalitarian society," he asks, "Would not society become secretly more hierarchical as it became outwardly more democratic?" "Very possibly," he answers.[32]

We have to imagine the rhythms produced by a phrasal style, undulant rhythms. The wave and the participle are not things; they are virtually agencies of thought, like waves of reminiscence. Whitman composes so as to *assimilate* all his units of expression, no matter how clausal and hypotactic they appear, to the participial idea, to the phrase. Throughout *Leaves of Grass* one notices a resistance to poetic argument, which, on a local level, would require controlled predications along with their extension into further sequences of predication, leading in logical fashion to clear conclusions. The example of Christian epics such as *The Divine Comedy* and *Paradise Lost* tells us that logical consequence is not alien to poetry on a large scale, but in fact may severely control the fable through the argument. Whitman's desire for a phrasally expressed chorographic vision of himself and of America leads him away from argument toward a visionary simultaneity without progress toward an end. His conclusions are deliberately expectant, suspended in liminal space before any arrival at a permanently defining closure. Such closure as he achieves is given by the anthropologist's model of ritual ending to initiations, that is, the stage known technically as aggregation. If we imagine a poetry dedicated to the idea that life is primarily a passage from birth to death, anthropologists will teach us the precise structure of this conception, namely, that the passage has three phases—separation, liminal passage, and aggregation—where the final stage marks the arrival of the initiate at a completely new status. The initiate is aggregated into a higher group within the society, and by analogy the poem following this plan would reach closure and climax when the protagonist reaches a higher level of insight, status, or home and belonging. When this last stage is reached, the protagonist is free to move around within a new language of equality, no longer disturbed with doubts about his or her own subordinate position. These anthropological facts of social ordering are one of the ways in which any "social environment" comes to possess its structure.

Aggregation and the forming of the ensemble allow the phrase to become the centrally natural linguistic expression of democracy, for good or ill. The phrase bespeaks thought in its most immediate, unreticulated, even fragmentary form, which in a later chapter I will identify with Whitman's use of waves deriving from particles. When he entitles poems simply "Thoughts," he names his general procedure, almost as if he were Amy Lowell calling her famous imagist poem "Patterns." The Whitman procedure is to vary the shapes of the poems—the complete poetic enclosures—so changingly, with such architectonic variety, that he can find places for a seemingly infinite number and variety of previously unreticulated thoughts. A prior reticulation would have occurred only if the present thoughts had been shown to follow from a series of previous continuous predications from which the present thought logically derived. Participial thinking in Whitman's manner holds the grammar of his ideas in a continuous present, which frustrates all sense of historical continuations. At the same time, it enhances the orbital vision the poet wants, displaying him, in Emerson's words, as the "man behind the poem."

Such thoughts can only be spoken in the present tense, as thinkings, equivalent to collisions between Emerson's "atoms and their elective affinities," as Emerson alludes to Goethe's novel.[33] This allusion is packed with a revolutionary change in ideas about the forces binding or dispersing adjacent persons, whether in a love story or the founding of a nation. The ideal Goethean democracy would have to be a nationally constituted elective affinity. The landscape of wildness described initially in some of Thoreau's nature writing and most recently used as a model for preserving the environment could only suggest a parallel wilderness in politics. There was thus no conflict in Whitman's mind when he related his politically grounded poetry to the wildness of the Rocky Mountains, which he saw for the first time from the seat of a railroad train:

> "I have found the law of my own poems," was the unspoken but more-and-more decided feeling that came to me as I pass'd, hour after hour, amid all this grim yet joyous elemental abandon—this plenitude of material, entire absence of art, untrammel'd play of primitive Nature—the chasm, the gorge, the crystal mountain stream, repeated scores, hundreds of miles—the broad handling and absolute uncrampedness—the fantastic forms, bathed in transparent browns, faint reds and grays, towering sometimes a thousand, sometimes two or three thousand feet high—at their tops now and then huge masses pois'd, and mixing with the clouds, with only their outlines, hazed in misty lilac, visible.[34]

The above passage could almost be notes for a version of Shelley's *Mont Blanc*. Along with the artless wild plenitude goes a sense of the mathematical sublime. Whitman seems most himself when he notes not simply the numbers, but more important, the "uncrampedness." He assimilates the mountain scene to pulsations of free movements, breathings of rock and gorge. Such wild is the external terrain of a vast natural heartbeat pulsing in the world's body—a thought from Wordsworth perhaps, but more closely tied to the thought that in nature one finds the "law" of an art. To a degree, this is High Romantic doctrine, employing Bloom's American sublime.[35] Since the Renaissance, it had been customary to believe that art would tell nature what it was to be natural, but now in Colorado nature will tell art what it is to be artistic, so that a complete art/nature reversal has occurred. Whereas the English Romantics would still have to subordinate their interest in nature to a higher concern for hierarchical political order, Whitman's new world dream of America would permit him to fuse ideas of nature's sublime external power with the genuinely wild forms and actions of the new and often adolescent American polity. He admitted liking the society of roughs, but only on condition that they would not descend into "the herd of independent minds," as Harold Rosenberg ironically labeled the new fakery of yuppie freedom.[36] Abraham Davidson's book, *The Eccentrics and other American Visionary Painters*, shows what real artistic independence looked like during Whitman's lifetime; notably, the artists in question all looked for new "light" in the wilderness of nature.[37] Description here demands luminism.

It was left for Whitman to discover the wildness of the city. His early manhood was spent in a jungle of personality, his newspaper world, and democratically he made a theory of poetry centered on the idea that if the poet could only express his thoughts so as to insert them into a larger vision without claiming logical necessity for the insertion, the result would be a new social coherence, which I have identified with the coherence of a living environment. Man was to him a sublime animal, whose society could only be understood in the ecological terms of a grand scale, whose terror was essential.

In *Democratic Vistas*, Whitman spoke up against the mainly urban commerce in shams and simulacra. In "Our Real Culmination," a final story in *Notes Left Over*, the poet makes a plea for "comfortable city homesteads and moderate-sized farms, healthy and independent, single separate ownership, fee simple, life in them complete but cheap, within reach of all."[38] He attacks excessive wealth and its "anti-democratic disease and monstrosity." Late in life, Whitman has had his fill of "immense capital and capitalists, the five-dollar-a-day hotels well fill'd, artificial improvements, even books, colleges, and the suffrage." Behind his acute dismay and outrage at the side-effects of Jacksonian democracy, one perceives an older or more radical thought. His love of the machine had always been keen, but one hears another understanding here when he tells us "there is a subtle something in the common earth, crops, cattle, air, trees, &c., and in having to do at first hand with them." His feeling for the diurnal could not be more powerful. This may be a utopian version of agriculture, "the only purifying and perennial element for individuals and for society," but he is not wrong to glamorize this laboring utopia. Remembering he is a city dweller, one has to include in this cultural account an awareness that one of the most popular American poems ever written was Edwin Markham's dismal elegy, "The Man with the Hoe."[39] Yet Whitman at least asks the right question: "What fortune else—what dollar—does not stand for, and come from, more or less imposition, lying, unnaturalness?" He finally had to worry about the decline of craft in the Jacksonian legacy. He had always been a more serious thinker than his idling manner suggested, and when the Civil War left him shocked and saddened by a carnage that reached its tragic scene in the death of Lincoln, he could only accept the dark side of his initial optimism. Three years before the poet died, Oscar Wilde wrote a review, "The Gospel according to Walt Whitman," where he commented, "If Poetry has passed him by, Philosophy will take note of him."[40] This was often a primitive natural philosophy, of the kind I associate with the Presocratics. "He has begun a prelude to larger themes. He is the herald to a new era. As a man he is the precursor of a fresh type. He is a factor in the heroic and spiritual evolution of the human being." This makes the poet a virtual demiurge.

Although Whitman discovers how his poetry could fit democracy, he never writes as if the two institutions were all there is. That was much of his message, his continuously praising the things humans do, in all walks of life. When, as I claim, he invented the poem-as-environment, he never believed this was a literal fact. The environment-poem is, as any good poet would know, an imaginative discovery and an imaginative product. Given the form invented, that would be enough. But what a strange belief it involved, this belief in the mystery of the vastness of our ecological home, as if the earth momentarily looked at us!

NOTES

1. From *The Life and Letters of John Burroughs*. The naturalist wrote two books about Whitman, and knew him well. My citation comes from Burroughs' notebook used in

compiling Notes on *Walt Whitman as Poet and Person* (1867)—from *Whitman in His Own Time*, ed. Joel Myerson (Iowa City, 1991), 311–12.

2. John Donne: *Sermons*, ed. Evelyn M. Simpson and George R. Potter (Berkeley, 1956), vol. VIII, 221. This Easter sermon of 1628 was preached on the text of *I Corinthians* 13.12, "For now we see through a glass darkly, but then face to face." "Then" is a day of resurrection.

3. I have generally used, for Whitman prose texts, *Walt Whitman*, ed. Justin Kaplan (New York: Library of America, 1982) (henceforth *LA*). As here, 662. For the verse I have mainly used the *Norton Critical Edition* (henceforth *NTN*) of *Leaves of Grass*, ed. Sculley Bradley and Harold W. Blodgett (New York, 1973). This edition uses the editors' 1965 *New York University Edition*.

4. Whitman, "Salut au Monde," *NTN*, 137. The order counts: in line forty-one Whitman asks, "What do you see Walt Whitman?" and in line forty-three answers, proceeding for another fifteen consecutive anaphoric lines, with "I see." His method is established subtly in Section One, but directly in Section Two, which begins, "What do you hear Walt Whitman," and builds eighteen subsequent lines, all beginning, "I hear." The question for poetic history is simple-seeming in theory: how does the Whitman line, based on his phrase, lead as model to the loosened line-shapes of later poets such as Ashbery (and he belongs in a virtual galaxy of American poets)? My view, as detailed in later chapters, is that by metonymic détente such later poets substitute their merely accumulated, i.e., not anaphorically linked, image-clusters in sequent lines and paragraphs. E.g., in "Grand Galop," in John Ashbery, *Self-Portrait in a Convex Mirror* (New York, 1975), the poem opens by announcing a potential catalogue, which it then loosely, but not anaphorically, provides: "All things seem mention of themselves / And the names which stem from them branch out to other referents."

5. See Robert Faner, *Walt Whitman and the Opera* (Carbondale, 1951), esp. ch. 5. On the Galilei and opera, see Fred Kersten, *Galileo and the 'Invention' of Opera: A Study in the Phenomenology of Consciousness* (Dordrecht, 1997). Kersten is writing in difficult Husserlian terms, but his book is important because it gives a formal basis for understanding opera as *Gesamtkunstwerk*—the composite of many dimensions of aesthetic effect—and hence a formal basis of explaining Whitman's feeling for the operatic aggregate form. I am grateful to Christine Skarda for drawing my attention to Kersten. One could easily show that opera is the most experimental of all Western art forms.

6. Walt Whitman, "Italian Music in Dakota," *Autumn Rivulets*, *NTN*, 400. Composers here are Bellini (*Somnambula* and *Norma*) and Donizetti (*Poliuto*), masters of bel canto, notable for its fioritura style, from which Whitman gets some of his ideas about his poetic of the aria and the recitative.

7. A central passage in *The New Science of Giambattista Vico*, tr. Thomas Bergin and Max Fisch, 3rd ed. (Ithaca, 1968), book two. Numerous articles in *New Vico Studies*, ed. by Donald Verene, and formerly by the late, much beloved, now greatly missed Giorgio Tagliacozzo, will indicate the scope of application for Vico's concept of a general poetics. My own contribution is *"Dipintura*: The Visual Icon of Historicism in Vico," in *Colors of the Mind: Conjectures on Thinking in Literature* (Cambridge, Mass., 1991), 147–65.

8. I owe this point to my learned friend Mitchell Meltzer, who is generally interested in more theoretical or visionary matters.

9. Whitman, *A Backward Glance*, *LA*, 662. Pragmatism is here too broad a reading of "science," since Whitman clearly explored the latter in what for him were the available

avenues of "popular science." The topic calls for further research as to the paradox of any modern science becoming a "popular" interest, for this means much to American expansion as a function of engineering skills. The United States is the only country to have literally grown up along with the development of modern technology—Britain, by contrast, was already full grown by the seventeenth century, despite all sorts of internal political strife. Imperialism plays a central role in the resourcing of this technological development, but the United States is unusual in that technology has molded our whole way of life, from the beginning—just consider Mark Twain's riverboats, or the new agricultural machinery and its relation to very large plowed and harvested lands, or the cotton gin, not to mention the engineered machines of electronic power. The main point is the coterminous character of these advances. In American history they are not overlays; they are the armatures, to use Ashbery's word.

10. Whitman, *Democratic Vistas*, *LA*, 942.

11. Ibid., *LA*, 952.

12. Ibid., *LA*, 958.

13. Whitman (ibid., *LA*, 990–91) castigates "the blind fury of parties, infidelity, entire lack of first-class captains and leaders, added to the meanness and vulgarity of the ostensible masses." Alluding here to *Lycidas*, he is yet entirely modern, aligning the vulgarity of the new masses with their industrial condition—this is 1871—"the labor question, beginning to open like a yawning gulf, rapidly widening every year." What would he say today, thinking of what he calls "scrofulous wealth?" Not to mention the "wily person in office?" This is a dubious time, and he would have hated the moneyed hypocrisy of it, as subversive and treasonous.

14. Ibid., *LA*, 956 ff.; he also says that the machinery of modern society "can no more be stopp'd than the tides, or the earth in its orbit."

15. Ibid., *LA*, 988.

16. Ibid., *LA*, 991.

17. Ibid., *LA*, 992.

18. Charles Eliot Norton, review of *Leaves*, Sept. 1855, in *A Century of Whitman Criticism*, ed. E. H. Miller (Bloomington, 1969), 2.

19. William Dean Howells, review of *Leaves*, Nov. 1855, in ibid., 7.

20. See *A Century*, 13–18, for Henry James's review of *Drum Taps*, Nov. 1865. The review reveals more about its author than about its subject, as contrasted with the Howells piece, which is a remarkable evocation of Whitman's art. Fred Kaplan, *Henry James: The Imagination of Genius* (New York, 1992), 498–99, tells the moving story of James in later years reading Whitman's poems aloud to the company at Edith Wharton's house: "his voice filled the room like an organ adagio," she said. He crooned "Out of the Cradle" "in a mood of subdued ecstasy." Hearing James read aloud "from his soul," Wharton was less surprised to hear him also say that he considered Whitman "the greatest of American poets.

21. Edward Pessen, *Jacksonian America*, rev. ed. (Urbana, Il., 1985), 194. An essential condition of historical understanding is thus stated by Pessen: "The complexity of truth suggests that at times in history, personality prevails over ideology, petty and subjective motives account for the behavior of mighty men, entire nations are turned this way or that by actions more accidental than designed. Significant issues *were* touched on by every act of the Jackson administration. But they are not exclusively the great issues of class, property, distribution of wealth, or social status" (290). The remarks immediately

following in my own text are taken from another expert work on the Jacksonian era, by Robert V. Remini. See his lectures, *The Legacy of Andrew Jackson: Essays on Democracy, Indian Removal and Slavery* (Baton Rouge, 1988), 24. Few presidents have aroused more heated opinions, and I focus deliberately on Jackson's part in the legacy of universal suffrage. An equal voting right is more often an ideal than a fact, but as I develop the grammar of the Whitman phrase, I insist that the idea of universal suffrage makes all the difference to the way Whitman wrote.

22. *Letters of George Gissing to Eduard Bertz*, ed. A. C. Young (London, 1961), 163.

23. Sean Wilentz, *Chants Democratic: New York City and the Rise of the American Working Class, 1788–1850* (New York, 1984), 115–16.

24. By altering "parcel" to "particle," Emerson gives to his *Nature*, ch. I the note of science, all the brighter since this belongs to a nature "uplifted into infinite space." At this moment Emerson is an astronomer, but as scientist, despite his enthusiasm over the modern Jardin des Plantes, he rather resembles a Presocratic cosmologist.

25. See Marcel Proust, *A la recherche du temps perdu*, vol. I, *A l'ombre des jeunes filles en fleurs* (Paris, Pléiade ed.), 529, 531, 536; vol. II, 47, 584; vol. III, passim, as indexed under "Noms de Personnes," 1279. In C. K. Scott Moncrieff, *Remembrance of Things Past*, tr., ed., and retranslated by Terence Kilmartin and Andreas Mayor (New York, 1981), vol. III, 242, 256, 260, 262–63, 380–82, and throughout *Time Regained*, e.g., 899–903, where the power of the musical phrase (and its visual equivalents in painting and the novel) is explored as the stimulus to memory.

26. Whitman, "A Broadway Pageant," sec. 2., lines 61–65, *NTN*, 245.

27. Leo Spitzer, "*Explication de Texte* Applied to Walt Whitman's Poem 'Out of the Cradle Endlessly Rocking'" (1949), in *A Century of Whitman Criticism*, ed. E. H. Miller (Bloomington, 1969), 273–84. Paul Claudel's method of "chaotic enumeration" accords with Spitzer's study of environing context in *Classical and Christian Ideas of World Harmony: Prolegomena to an Interpretation of the Word Stimmung*," ed. Anna G. Hatcher (Baltimore, 1963), and is specified in "Interpretation of an Ode by Paul Claudel," in *Linguistics and Literary History* (Princeton, 1948), 193–236; reptd. in Leo Spitzer: *Representative Essays*, ed. A. K. Forcione et al. (Stanford, 1988), 273–326.

28. "Sea Surface Full of Clouds" in Wallace Stevens, *Collected Poems* (New York, 1964), 100. "The macabre of the water glooms / In an enormous undulation fled," comes at the end of sec. II.

29. I link environmental thought with a paradox of *Walden*, discovered there by Stanley Cavell, *The Senses of Walden* (San Francisco, 1981), 54: "that what is most intimate is furthest away." See Cavell, *The Claim of Reason*, parts II and IV. Also, *In Quest of the Ordinary: Lines of Skepticism and Romanticism* (Chicago, 1988), especially the Tanner Lecture (1986) on "The Uncanniness of the Ordinary," 153–80, and "Postscript A. Skepticism and a Word Concerning Deconstruction," 130–36, with Postscripts B and C also concerning metaphoric usage in relation to the "unnatural" (146–47). Emerson's essay on Montaigne is subtitled, "Or, Skeptic."

30. Whitman, "A Thought," *NTN*, 704.

31. Ezra Greenspan, ed., *The Cambridge Companion to Walt Whitman* (Cambridge, 1995), "Some Remarks on the Poetics of 'Participle-loving Whitman,'" 92–109. See the sensitive reading of "When lilacs last," by Helen Vendler, in *Textual Analysis Some Readers Reading*, ed. Mary Ann Caws (New York, 1986), 132–43, especially 142: "The rhythm of the death carol is not periodic. Rather, like the waves of the ocean or the verses of poetry,

it is recursive, recurrent, undulant, self-reflexive, self-perpetuating." See above in my Chapter 12, "Waves and the Troping of Poetic Form."

32. Proust, *The Guermantes Ways*, tr. Moncrieff and Kilmartin, 472.

33. Emerson, *Essays: First Series*, "Circles," in *Ralph Waldo Emerson: Essays and Lectures*, ed. Joel Porte (*LA*, 1983), 410. See Eric Wilson, *Emerson's Sublime Science* (London, 1999), 76–98 ("Electric Cosmos"), and 70–75, on "Emerson's Hermeticism." Wilson shows that the influence of Goethe's nature philosophy upon Emerson had a strong hermetic tinge, which of course marks all Romantic literature insofar as it dwells, in the tradition of Renaissance alchemy, upon "affinities" between elements and different levels of natural being. Such is very much the general tenor of Emerson's Oration for the Society of the Adelphi (1841), "The Method of Nature," where he speaks of "elective attractions" (*LA*, 118), but the Goethean notion of elective affinities runs all through the *Essays*. Electricity in this discourse is always elective; there is a general fascination, as evidenced by the popular lectures of Faraday, with the mutual attraction of positive and negative charges, a fascination that rewrites the dialectic notions of logical polarities and their interaction in Hegelian terms. The North and South Poles are now electrified.

34. Whitman, *Specimen Days*, LA, 850–68, under the title "An Egotistical 'Find,'" 855–56. See W. C. Harris on Whitman and the stress of Union: *Arizona Quarterly*, 56, no. 1 (2000), 29–61.

35. The reader should consult Bloom's essay, "Whitman's Image of Voice: To the Tally of My Soul," in *Walt Whitman*, ed. Harold Bloom (New York, 1985), 127–42; also, Bloom, "Freud and the Poetic Sublime," in *Poetics of Influence*, ed. John Hollander (New Haven, 1988), for background to the Longinean tradition as it relates to Bloom's Freudian, Kabbalistic, and Gnostic theory of the American Sublime.

36. Harold Rosenberg, *The Tradition of the New* (New York, 1961), part 4, "The Herd of Independent Minds." (A parallel work would be J. L. Borges' satire, *The Chronicles of Bustos Domecq*.) Rosenberg's 1969 *Artworks and Packages* (Chicago, 1982), "Lights! Lights!" discusses the shift from Happenings to Environments in modern art. See also the notice (133) of Louise Nevelson's work, "Atmosphere and Environment I."

37. Abraham Davidson, *The Eccentrics and Other American Visionary Painters* (New York, 1978), 134. In this important passage Davidson distinguishes between the "normal" visionaries among his painters and those sharing Whitman's "cosmic" vision as it establishes an American scale of "vista," the sense of extending *chora* shared by painters like Ryder and especially Blakelock, who go out into the study of light itself, thus avoiding the "spookiness" of the normalizing of vision.

38. "Our Real Culmination," in Whitman, *Complete Prose Works*, LA, 1074.

39. Edwin Markham, *The Man with the Hoe and Other Poems* (New York, 1899). The eloquence of this ekphrastic poem is unexpected, but then we encounter a similar expressive power in other poems, such as "The Whirlwind Road,"—I felt the Mystery the Muses fear" (line 8). In the 1899 Doubleday and McClure edition, Markham shared copyright with his original publisher and employer/distributor; the co-holder was the *San Francisco Examiner*. The volume's frontispiece was an engraving of its original, and the title poem was "Written after Seeing Millet's World-Famous Painting." "World-Famous" is P. T. Barnum talk, and it fits Markham's generally middle-brow sublimity.

40. *Artist as Critic: The Critical Writings of Oscar Wilde*, ed. Richard Ellmann (New York, 1969), 125.

HAROLD BLOOM

Afterthought

1

There are three crucial components in Emerson's American religion: the God within; solitude; the best and oldest part of the self, which goes back before creation. What will the poems of that religion have in common with Dante or with the holy George Herbert?

Let me juxtapose Walt Whitman with his contemporary, Gerard Manley Hopkins, who admired the little of the American bard he had read, but declined to read any more because he feared the identity he sensed between Whitman and himself, a bond both homoerotic and rhythmic. Writing to the poet Robert Bridges on 18 October 1882, Hopkins seeks to deny Whitman's influence (rather weakly) and then declares:

> I always knew in my heart Walt Whitman's mind to be more like my own than any other man's living. As he is a very great scoundrel this is not a pleasant confession. And this also makes me the more desirous to read him and the more determined that I will not.

To characterize the ministering angel of the Washington D.C. hospitals during the Civil War as "a very great scoundrel" is sublimely absurd, even if you are a Jesuit priest and an Oxford gentleman. Our father the old man Walt Whitman was a greater poet than Father Hopkins, and of a religion beyond Hopkins's understanding. G.K. Chesterton, before he converted to the Church of Rome, gave a more accurate sense of the poet of the American religion: "... we have not yet begun to get to the beginning of Whitman. The egoism of which men accuse him is that sense of human divinity which no one has felt since Christ."

Hopkins, I suspect, read more widely in Whitman than he cared to admit. "That Nature Is a Heracletian Fire and of the Comfort of the Resurrection," written in 1888, echoes "The Sleepers," with "heaven-roysterers, in gay-gangs" taking me back to "Onward we move! a gay gang of blackguards," as though the Jesuit renders tribute to the very great scoundrel who was certainly one of his forerunners. After the birth of the United States, we produced no devotional poets of high merit. Emerson's briefly inspired disciple Jones Very celebrates only the God within, and while Eliot, Auden, and Robert Lowell are included in this book because of their confessional stances of devotion, they do not, in my own critical judgment, equal Hopkins and Christina Rossetti, let alone John Donne, George Herbert, Henry Vaughan, and Richard Crashaw.

2

So implicit and universal is the American religion, that some of its poets can be unaware that they incarnate and celebrate it. Setting aside Emerson himself and our two grandest voices, Whitman and Dickinson, why should poems by such skeptics as Robert Frost, Wallace Stevens, John Wheelwright, Elizabeth Bishop, and May Swenson be regarded as religious? Hart Crane, who professed no Christian doctrine, became the American equivalent of St. John of the Cross in the Proem, "To Brooklyn Bridge." A. R. Ammons, John Ashbery, and James Merrill, the strongest poets in my generation, have nothing conventional in their respective spiritualities, but Ammons and Ashbery bring us back to Emerson, Whitman, and Dickinson, while Merrill transmutes Yeats, Stevens and Auden into creatures largely his own.

Any distinction between sacred and secular literature is finally a political judgment, and therefore irrelevant in the realms of the aesthetic. The United States, already a plutocracy, flickers these days towards theocracy. A theocratic America doubtless will distinguish between sacred and secular utterances, but Whitmanian democracy fuses them in the divinity of the self, which is our native understanding of the Resurrection as an escape from history, that is to say, from European time. The Resurrection is not a mediated event for American Religionists, whether they be Independent Baptists, Mormons, or Emersonians. The ancient Gnostics said that *first* Jesus resurrected, and *then* he died. Our singer of *Song of Myself* records a similar career. William James became the psychologist of the American Religion, and found in Whitman the archetype of healthy-mindedness. To recover the Whitman of William James, and of Henry James after *he* had weathered his early savagery against the divine Walt, is to recover not only the greatest American poet but the grandest of American personae, "Walt Whitman, one of the roughs, an American."

To recover that Whitman, we need to break down forever that useless distinction between sacred and secular literature, a distinction purely political. By vote of Congress, L. Ron Hubbard, a bad science-fiction writer, composed a sacred text in his *Dianetics*, the tax-exempt Scientology's scripture, fit inspiration for such visionaries as John Travolta and Tom Cruise. We need not await any Congressional acclaim of *Leaves of Grass*. The thrice-blessèd Trent Lott of Mississippi has proclaimed that homoeroticism is indistinguishable from kleptomania. Walt Whitman must be spied upon lest he run off with the senatorial spoons, or the Congressional tarts. D. H. Lawrence told us that the Americans were not worthy of their Whitman, but that was before the Sage of Nottingham was chased out of the canon by the heroic *feminista* Kate Millett, who assured us that Lawrence would deny human females their orgasms. A brief textual comparison of Lawrence's *The Plumed Serpent* with Kate Millett's *Sexual Politics* should persuade even the most militant of *feministas* that no one had taught Millett how to read. Rather clearly, the Lawrence-like Mexican general Cipriano is attempting to teach his bride, the Frieda-like Kate, the pragmatics of tantric mutual *coitus reservatus*, rather than a Fascistic technique in which he comes and she does not.

It ought not to be need saying, but in this age of politically correct "sex workers" and of "animal companions," I am now obliged to defend the poet Walt Whitman from accusations of "racism" made against the man Walt Whitman in his long decline, after his great poetic decade of 1855-1865. There is a precise analogue in William Wordsworth, who declined from his great decade of 1797-1807 into a Tory government official composing sonnet-sequences in favor of capital punishment, thus fitting himself to be poet laureate of our grand state of Texas, which exults in its non-stop executions, a useful supplement to the pious Tom DeLay's agile gerrymanderings. After 1865, the sane and sacred Whitman burned out. He had nursed one too many dying young soldier, and had discovered that in elegizing Lincoln he had elegized his own poetic vocation. The stroke-ridden Good Gray Poet began to fear labor unions and emancipated blacks, but what has that to do with the poet of 1855-1865?

Walt Whitman, in that decade, wrote the authentic literature for the New World. I do not fear being called hyperbolical, since the Critical Sublime is precisely that. How great a writer was Whitman? No one since Whitman, not Henry James nor Marcel Proust, not James Joyce nor Jorge Luis Borges, nor anyone you can hope to name, is nearly as vital and as vitalizing as the visionary poet of *Leaves of Grass*. D. H. Lawrence was fiercely ambivalent towards his crucial precursor, but he at last got it right in the final version of *Studies in Classical American Literature*. Feeling himself to be more Whitman than Whitman himself could be, Lawrence thus took on the role of Christ to Walt's John the Baptist, but actually became St. Paul to Whitman's Christ. Here though is the best and most poignant prose tribute yet made to the artist-seer of *Leaves of Grass*:

> Whitman, the great poet, has meant so much to me. Whitman, the one man breaking a way ahead. Whitman, the one pioneer. And only Whitman. No English pioneers, no French. No European pioneer-poets. In Europe the would-be pioneers are mere innovators. The same in America. Ahead of Whitman, nothing. Ahead of all poets, pioneering into the wilderness of unopened life, Whitman. Beyond him, none. His wide, strange camp at the end of the great high-road. And lots of new little poets camping on Whitman's camping ground now. But none going really beyond. Because Whitman's camp is at the end of the road, and on the edge of the precipice. Over the precipice, blue distances, and the blue hollow of the future. But there is no way down. It is a dead end.
>
> Pisgah. Pisgah sights. And Death. Whitman like a strange, modern, American Moses. Fearfully mistaken. And yet the great leader.
>
> The essential function of art is moral. Not aesthetic, not decorative, not pastime and recreation. But moral. The essential function of art is moral.
>
> But a passionate, implicit morality, not didactic. A morality which changes the blood, rather than the mind. Changes the blood first. The mind follows later, in the wake.
>
> Now Whitman was the great moralist. He was a great leader. He was a great changer of the blood in the veins of men.

Matching Lawrence's praise of the sublime Walt in eloquence, Stevens actually was more accurate in giving us Whitman as precisely anti-apocalyptic, rather than Lawrence's proclaimer of finalities:

In the far South the sun autumn is passing
Like Walt Whitman walking along a ruddy shore.
He is singing and chanting the things that are part of him,
The worlds that were and will be, death and day.
Nothing is final, he chants. No man shall see the end.
His beard is of fire and his staff is a leaping flame.

Our prime shaman of the American Religion affirms the Blessing of more life. Death, for Walt Whitman, was an innocence of the earth, and no false sign or symbol of malice.

3

I do not find it useful to define Whitman's religion apart from his poetry, anymore than I trust any social pronouncements in his prose, whether published or not. His sexual orientation, in the poetry, seems to me more Onanistic than homoerotic. It is a paradox that Henry James, massively reticent in his novels, stories, and other writings, particularly in regard to his own homosexuality, may have experienced more actual erotic fulfillment than did the personally shy prophet of "adhesiveness." Still, shamans traditionally have been androgynous, and of Whitman's poetic mastery of archaic techniques of ecstasy I entertain no doubts.

To discover an American achievement equal to Whitman's, I judge you need to fuse two brothers of absolute genius, William and Henry James. Since William composed *Varieties of Religious Experience* and *The Will to Believe*, no one would dispute his eminence as the prime philosopher-psychologist of our very original national religion. Our greatest American novelist scarcely seems a religious writer, let alone an occultist like the Balzac whom he so vastly admired. Yet the ghostly tales perpetually remind us that the Master excelled at speculative connections, even in his major fictions. Relations, as Frances Wilson has noted, stop nowhere for the James family, who were occultly linked, as befitted the children of a Swedenborgian father. The idea of death is as richly ordered by the James brothers as by Whitman, yet they evade his baroque elaborations, though both of them loved his *Lilacs* elegy for Lincoln.

William James had a less dialectical relation to Emerson than Henry enjoyed, while Whitman's debt to Emerson was so vast that he tried eventually to deny it. Henry James' American heroines are Emersonians, but oddly that was true also in *The Scarlet Letter* and *The Marble Faun*. T.S. Eliot happily praised Henry James for possessing a Vision of Evil that Emerson refused to honor, but Eliot was mistaken in his Christianization of James, just as Eliot's disciple Cleanth Brooks erred in baptizing the fictions of William Faulkner. Eliot's Vision of Evil was gratified best by Christopher Marlowe's *The Jew of Malta*. I wish Eliot had left some comments on Henry James' keenly appreciative account of the Yiddish old East Side in the superb *American Scene*, the Master's return to what had been *his* New York City. In his own way Henry James, like Whitman, contained multitudes.

Again like Whitman, the Master of American prose fiction had a visionary sense of the uncertain borders between the living and the dead, just as both apprehended the wavering line between maleness and femaleness. Emerson had no interest in either demarcation; you can name this healthy-mindedness, though part of my statement is now so politically incorrect as to seem outrageous. Clearly (I would hope) I intend no offence, since Whitman and Henry James merely remain much our greatest imaginative writers. William James, like his father and brother, had something to intimate about a possible life-after-death, but as a psychologist ventured no particular insights into homoeroticism.

Sinuously, Henry did, particularly in *The Sacred Fount*, which shows an affinity with Whitman's distrust of heterosexual marriage. Shamanistic spirituality has little to do with healing marriages, and the author of the grandest American novels and tales was hardly a shaman. Walt Whitman, in an original way, was precisely that during his great decade of 1855 through 1865. He came as medicine, and found himself most truly and most strange in the Civil War hospitals of Washington D.C. Henry James, consciously imitating Whitman, visited the British wounded of World War I, during his closing years, but not very effectively. We cannot think of the Master as the Good Gray Novelist.

4

Books have been written on Whitman's relation to various nineteenth-century American quackeries, but throughout my more than a half-century as a literary critic I have rejected all historicisms, Old or New. No one has ventured to answer my persistent question: "How can any societal over-determination account for the phenomenon of any solitary genius?" Emerson memorably addressed himself to the Question of Genius; all a New

Historicist can do is shrug and label Genius a High Romantic myth. In my old age, I refuse to be bored, and what now passes for ongoing scholarly criticism of Walt Whitman is sublimely tiresome. When I teach Robert Browning, a great poet now absurdly neglected, I would feel absurd were I to begin by telling my students that this wonderful dramatic monologist was fiercely heterosexual. What does it matter that Henry James and Walt Whitman were homoerotic, or to use the going lingo, gay or queer? I begin to lose any last shreds of toleration for anyone who believes that aesthetic splendor, wisdom, and cognitive power cannot be recognized except by criteria of gender, social class, skin pigmentation, ethnic origin, and sexual orientation. The divine Oscar Wilde, who as Borges observed was always right, told us: "All bad poetry is sincere."

Walt Whitman wrote six major great poems, the crown of American literature: *Song of Myself*, "The Sleepers," "Crossing Brooklyn Ferry," "As I Ebb'd with the Ocean of Life," "Out of the Cradle Endlessly Rocking," and "When Lilacs Last in the Dooryard Bloom'd." There are about twenty other shorter poems or fragments of roughly equal eminence, but only three or four of these were composed after 1865, and Whitman died in 1892.

In his strongest poems, Whitman is a new kind of religious bard, virtually indescribable even in his own terms. Discursive contradictions between creeds and creedlessness, God and man, oblivion and immortality melt away in Walt's creative furnace, as they did in William Blake's or Victor Hugo's. I begin to feel that Gershom Scholem was accurate when he told me that Whitman, who certainly never heard of the Kabbalah, conceived of the Divine Reality as the later Kabbalists did. Like the *Ein-Sof*, the Kabbalah's revision of Yahweh, Whitman creates and ruins worlds even as he draws in his breath. John Hollander, describing Whitman's rhetoric, pragmatically invokes Lurianic Kabbalah while perhaps being unaware of the invocation: "When he announces his experiences, containments, and incorporations, he is frequently enacting a contraction and withdrawal." I would add that Walt is most like Yahweh when in effect he warns: "I will be absent wherever and whenever I will be absent." Our great American master of his own real presence, Whitman is endlessly elusive and evasive. Yahweh is not there when you need him, and so I do not trust him or like him, and I wish he would go away, though he won't. Whitman is there on the page, or in my chanting memory, and yet is not his highest art the real absence?

These days we live not in the great poem of Whitmanian democracy, but in an America that fuses plutocracy and theocracy. Tocqueville toured the United States in the 1830s, a generation before *Leaves of Grass*, and concluded that American Christianity, while more democratic than not, nevertheless restrained the national imagination. He could not have anticipated Emerson and Whitman, who freed imagination and discarded Christianity. This American Renaissance, participated in also by Hawthorne, Melville, and Thoreau, flourished from 1850 to 1860, and then yielded to the Civil War, which seems to me is still being fought against the rest of us by the old Confederacy, now the solid Republican South of Reagan and the Bushes. Tocqueville could not have anticipated the Christian Right, whose alliance with Wall Street may be permanent in this ongoing age of worldwide religious warfare. In his cosmic optimism, Whitman also could not foresee our bad time, though he rightly feared that the Union had survived at too high a cost.

What is the center of Whitmanian religion? Clearly, it is Walt Whitman himself as the Divine, post-Christian yet a messiah, another son of a carpenter who also is a son of God. There actually was a rather literal-minded Whitman cult, which fortunately ebbed and vanished with the end of World War I in 1919. Though the enterprise was absurd and useless, it serves as another reminder that the reader never can really know what is literal and what is figurative in Whitman. Perhaps nothing, including Walt himself, *was* literal, though I suspect they were only sparsely literalized, if at all. You can call Whitman a mythmaker, or merely a liar, but a great poet creates permanent fictions, and "Walt Whitman" remains the largest literary fact we have, reducing to pigmies such fictive entities as "Norman Mailer" and that Dr. Doolittle-like pushme-pullyou, the "Ginsberg-Kerouac." Usurpation rarely can be duplicated in a nation's literary history. Like Goethe, Victor Hugo, Shakespeare, Dante, and Homer, Whitman has a way of occupying all of imaginative space. These half-dozen writers are mortal gods, though only Goethe, Hugo, and Whitman seem to have asserted such status.

5

Being a god is rather hard work, though Goethe and Hugo never waned, while Whitman did, but Goethe sensibly did not fight against Napoleon. Victor Hugo gallantly raised the morale of the Paris Commune, particularly devoting himself, despite his advanced years, to gratifying the female communards. Whitman, too middle-aged to fight for the Union, became the heroic ministering angel of the Washington hospitals. By then his divinity had left him, and his magnificent elegy for President Lincoln became implicitly an elegy for his ebbing Incarnation, as poet and as God. I go on judging this as the greatest of American poems, but Whitman himself was irritated whenever anyone called it his best. William and Henry James loved it in part because their preternaturally shared consciousness is echoed by the poem's fusion of Lincoln and Whitman. I suggest that Walt's divine apotheosis lasted five years, from 1854 through 1859, when it attained a crescendo in "Sun-Down Poem," later retitled "Crossing Brooklyn Ferry." In the winter of 1859-60, Whitman evidently suffered a homoerotic crisis, perhaps akin to T. S. Eliot's brief moment with Jean Verdenal: "The awful daring of a moment's surrender / Which an age of prudence can never retract." The Whitmanian debacle gave him the two superb *Sea-Drift* elegies, "Out of the Cradle Endlessly Rocking " and "As I Ebb'd with the Ocean of Life," but to find the Divine Walt, we need to center upon *Song of Myself*, the American epic proper, in which the God of the United States achieved decisive self-recognition.

Late in life, Whitman set down in prose notes his recollections of the great Quaker preacher Elias Hicks, who broke with the Philadelphia Quakers in 1829, and led his followers back to the Inner Light vision of George Fox. Walt's paternal grandfather and Walter Whitman Sr. were among these followers, and so in a sense was the American Bard himself, who fused his Emersonian revelations of the God within into an amalgam of Concord Gnosticism with Hicksite Quakerism. Of Hicks, Whitman observed: "He is the most *democratic* of the religionists—the prophets." Partly Native American, partly African American, Hicks, like the Whitmans, was working-class and devoted his life to dissident Quaker circuit-riding. Taken first at the age of ten to hear Hicks preach, Walt revived the spirit of Elias in the final passage of *Song of Myself*, section 5:

> Swiftly arose and spread around me the peace and knowledge that
>   pass all the argument of the earth,
> And I know that the hand of God is the promise of my own,
> And I know that the spirit of God is the brother of my own,
> And that all the men ever born are also my brothers, and the
>   women my sisters and lovers,
> And that a kelson of the creation is love,
> And limitless are leaves stiff or drooping in the fields,
> And brown ants in the little wells beneath them,
> And mossy scabs of the worm fence, heap'd stones, elder, mullein
>   and poke-weed.

The directness of this testimony is Hicksite Quakerian, but the final three lines are the purest Whitman, who refuses any hierarchy of being, and who celebrates weeds as though they were flowers. His central metaphor necessarily is "leaves of grass." John Hollander deftly indicated the multiple ambiguities of that "of": are the "leaves" pages of books? Are they figurations for the fresh green of Whitmanian poems? Or are they Sibylline leaves, wind-blown oracles? Primarily they must refer to what Wallace Stevens, with highly conscious belatedness termed "the fiction of the leaves," sad emblems for the ends of particular human lives in Homer, Virgil, Dante, Milton, Shelley and Whitman himself. The "grass" then would be that of all flesh harvested by death in the prophet Isaiah, the Psalms of David, and the New Testament. Hollander adds "leavings," departures in song for other realms. I myself suspect, since Whitman learned the printer's trade in a newspaper office, that the leaves are also printer's sheets and the grass throw-away-stuff employed to fill up blank pages. This vertigo of metaphor is central to Whitman as the American bardic Christ, self-anointed to strike up the cognitive and spiritual music for the New World.

6

Walt Whitman wrote the poems of our climate, as Wallace Stevens ruefully (in certain moods) concluded. How could it have been otherwise? Here was the American Adam, early in the morning, fusing Man, god, and the Gnostic and Hermetic Angel Christ, as he is called by the Sufis. As this amalgam, Walt is like the auroras or Northern Lights described by Wordsworth as "here, there, and everywhere at once." When the daunting illuminations flash upon the beach-walking Stevens in *The Auroras of Autumn*, the aging poet attempts to defend his waning autonomy by unnaming the lights, but they will not be destroyed: "he opens the door of his house / On flames." Whitman, strongest of American bards, met the challenge of dazzling and tremendous sunrise by affirming that, now and always, he could send forth sunrise from himself. There are multitudes of poets contained in the large Walt, and one of them refuses to be subdued by natural appearances.

Angus Fletcher recently has found in Whitman the master of the Environment Poem, an American version of the Picturesque. I would prefer to call *Song of Myself* precisely the Anti-Environment Poem, despite Thoreau's enthusiasm for what in 1856 he knew as the "Sun-Down Poem," later renamed as "Crossing Brooklyn Ferry." What is urgent for Walt is the *crossing*, Emerson's metaphor for darting to a new aim. The shores of America matter most to Whitman as points-of-departure for the outward voyage. But to where? There is only the grand fourfold: night, death, the mother, and the sea. All of these constitute the unknown nature of which

Walt's soul is composed. What the Gnostics called the spark or *pneuma*, the breath of being, Whitman terms the me myself or the real me. That leaves only his supreme fiction, "Walt Whitman, one of the roughs, an American," the prime subject throughout *Song of Myself*.

This psychic cartography is so original that we as yet have not assimilated it, but the study of Whitman's great decade of poetry scarcely has begun, and indeed goes backwards at this moment, when even professional scholars of literature have never learned how to read a poem. Whitman hoped to give us chants democratic, but at his strongest he composed chants elitist: esoteric, difficult, evasive, profoundly poignant, and immersed in a new spirituality we only start to notice. He dared to write a New Bible for Americans, who remain obsessed with the old one, though they cannot read it.

Chronology

1819	Born Walter Whitman on May 31 near Huntington, Long Island to Louisa Van Velsor and Walter Whitman, a carpenter and house-builder; both parents follow the radical Quaker, Elias Hicks.
1823	Family moves to Brooklyn, where Whitman attends public school until 1830.
1830	Works as office boy to lawyers and to a doctor.
1831	Apprenticed as printer's devil to the *Patriot*, a Democratic newspaper, and then to the *Star*.
1835	Works as a printer in New York City.
1836	Teaches in various Long Island schools.
1838	Publishes and edits a new weekly, the *Long-Islander*, from Huntington, then works on the Jamaica-based *Democrat*. Writes early poems and sketches.
1840	Helps campaign for Martin Van Buren, then returns to teaching.
1841	Works as compositor for the *New World* in New York City, and as a Democratic activist.
1842	Works for several newspapers in New York City and publishes stories, sketches, and *Franklin Evans*, a temperance novel.
1845	Returns to Brooklyn to work for the *Star*, and then moves on to the *Daily Eagle*.

1848	Moves briefly to New Orleans to work as a newspaper editor. Returns to New York to edit the *Brooklyn Freeman*. Actively supports the Free Soil Movement.
1853	Writes notebooks that will form the embryo of *Leaves of Grass*.
1855	Self-publishes *Leaves of Grass* in early July; the book is comprised of twelve untitled poems, including "Song of Myself" and "The Sleepers." Father dies on July 11. Ralph Waldo Emerson writes to Whitman hailing *Leaves of Grass* as the "most extraordinary piece of wit and wisdom America has yet contributed" on July 21.
1856	Publishes second edition of *Leaves of Grass*, to which he adds "Crossing Brooklyn Ferry." The second edition includes Emerson's letter and Whitman's extraordinary reply to it. Henry David Thoreau and Bronson Alcott visit Whitman in Brooklyn.
1857	Edits Brooklyn *Times*.
1858	Undergoes period of depression lasting from late 1858 well into 1859.
1860	Publishes third edition of *Leaves of Grass* in Boston with the publishing house of Thayer and Eldridge, adding "Calamus" poems and poems later titled "Out of the Cradle Endlessly Rocking" and "As I Ebb'd with the Ocean of Life." Visits Emerson while in Boston to read proofs.
1861	Returns to journalism while visiting the sick and war-wounded at New York Hospital.
1862	Departs for Virginia battle front in December to find wounded brother George.
1863	Visits wounded soldiers in military hospitals in and around Washington, D.C.
1865	Dismissed from clerkship at Department of the Interior, perhaps because of the scandal of the third edition of *Leaves of Grass*. Writes "When Lilacs Last in the Dooryard Bloom'd" during the summer, in reaction to the death of Abraham Lincoln, and publishes it in October in *Drum-Taps and Sequel*. Meets Peter Doyle, then aged eighteen.
1867	Publishes fourth edition of *Leaves of Grass*.
1870	Publishes fifth edition of *Leaves of Grass* and *Democratic Vistas*.

1873	Suffers paralytic stroke in January. Mother dies in May. Moves to brother George's house in Camden, New Jersey, in June.
1879	Travels in American West.
1880	Travels in Canada.
1881	Meets with Emerson for the last time in Concord, Massachusetts.
1882	Receives Oscar Wilde in Camden. *Leaves of Grass* is banned in Boston, but is reprinted in Philadelphia, where *Specimen Days and Collect* is published.
1884	Moves out of brother's house and into one of his own in Camden.
1888	Suffers severe paralytic stroke.
1891	Publishes *Goodbye My Fancy* and final "deathbed" edition of *Leaves of Grass*.
1892	Dies on March 26 in Camden.

Contributors

HAROLD BLOOM is Sterling Professor of the Humanities at Yale University. He is the author of 30 books, including *Shelley's Mythmaking* (1959), *The Visionary Company* (1961), *Blake's Apocalypse* (1963), *Yeats* (1970), *A Map of Misreading* (1975), *Kabbalah and Criticism* (1975), *Agon: Toward a Theory of Revisionism* (1982), *The American Religion* (1992), *The Western Canon* (1994), and *Omens of Millennium: The Gnosis of Angels, Dreams, and Resurrection* (1996). *The Anxiety of Influence* (1973) sets forth Professor Bloom's provocative theory of the literary relationships between the great writers and their predecessors. His most recent books include *Shakespeare: The Invention of the Human* (1998), a 1998 National Book Award finalist, *How to Read and Why* (2000), *Genius: A Mosaic of One Hundred Exemplary Creative Minds* (2002), *Hamlet: Poem Unlimited* (2003), *Where Shall Wisdom be Found* (2004), and *Jesus and Yahweh: The Names Divine* (2005). In 1999, Professor Bloom received the prestigious American Academy of Arts and Letters Gold Medal for Criticism. He has also received the International Prize of Catalonia, the Alfonso Reyes Prize of Mexico, and the Hans Christian Andersen Bicentennial Prize of Denmark.

D.H. LAWRENCE was equally powerful as novelist, poet, and visionary polemicist. His poetry, at its later best, is profoundly Whitmanian, as are his greatest novels, *The Rainbow* and *Women in Love*.

KENNETH BURKE was among the most eminent American literary theorists and critics of the twentieth century. His crucial books are *A Grammar of Motives* and *The Rhetoric of Religion*.

R.W.B. LEWIS taught English at Yale University. His books include *The American Adam* and distinguished studies of Hart Crane and Edith Wharton.

KERRY C. LARSON is Senior Associate Dean of the Rackham Graduate School at the University of Michigan, where he also teaches in the English Department. He is the author of numerous articles and essays on American literature and also *Whitman's Drama of Consensus*.

DAVID BROMWICH is Housum Professor of English at Yale University. His books include *Hazlitt: The Mind of the Critic*, *Disowned by Memory: Wordsworth's Poetry of the 1790's*, and *Skeptical Music*.

MARK BAUERLEIN is Professor of English at Emory University. His publications include *Literary Criticism: An Autopsy*, *The Pragmatic Mind: Explorations in the Psychology of Belief*, and *Negrophobia: A Race Riot in Atlanta, 1906*.

JOHN HOLLANDER teaches in the English Department at Yale University. America's preeminent poet-critic, Hollander is the author of *The Figure of Echo*, *Rhyme's Reason*, *Melodious Guile*, and *The Gazer's Spirit*.

HELEN VENDLER teaches English at Harvard University. Her many distinguished works of criticism include *Shakespeare's Sonnets*, *Coming of Age as a Poet*, *The Breaking of Style*, and studies of Herbert, Keats, Yeats, and Stevens.

ANGUS FLETCHER is a distinguished professor emeritus at the City University of New York Graduate School. He is the author of *The Prophetic Moment: An Essay on Spenser*, *Allegory: The Theory of a Symbolic Mode*, and *Colors of the Mind: Conjectures on Thinking in Literature*.

Bibliography

Allen, Gay Wilson. *The Solitary Singer*. New York: New York University Press, 1967.

———. *The New Walt Whitman Handbook*. New Yori: New York University Press, 1975.

Altieri, Charles. "Spectacular Antispectacle: Ecstasy and Nationality in Whitman and His Heirs." *American Literary History* 11 (Spring 1999): 34–62.

Arvin, Newton. *Whitman*. New York: Macmillan, 1938.

Aspiz, Harold. *Walt Whitman and the Body Beautiful*. Urbana: University of Illinois Press, 1980.

Asselineau, Roger. *The Evolution of Walt Whitman*. 2 vols. Cambridge: Harvard University Press, 1960 and1962.

Auclair, Tracy. "The Language of Drug-Use in Whitman's 'Calamus' Poems." *Papers on Language and Literature* 40 (Summer 2004): 227–59.

Bauerlein, Mark. *Whitman and the American Idiom*. Baton Rouge: Louisiana University Press, 1991.

Beach, Christopher. "Walt Whitman, Literary Culture, and the Discourse of Distinction." *Walt Whitman Quarterly Review* 12 (Fall 1992): 73–85.

Black, Stephen. *Whitman's Journey into Chaos*. Princeton: Princeton University Press, 1975.

Blasing, Mutlu Konuk. *American Poetry: The Rhetoric of Its Forms*. New Haven: Yale University Press, 1987.

Bloom, Harold. *Agon*. New York: Oxford University Press, 1982.

———. *A Map of Misreading*. New York: Oxford University Press, 1975.

———. *Poetry and Repression*. New Haven: Yale University Press, 1976.

———, ed. *Walt Whitman: Selected Poems*. New York: Library of America, 2003.

Boggs, Colleen Glenney. "Specimens of Translation in Walt Whitman's Poetry." *Arizona Quarterly* 58 (Autumn 2002): 33–56.

Borges, Jorge Luis. "The Achievements of Walt Whitman." *Texas Quarterly* 5 (1962): 43–48.

Bromwich, David. "A Simple Separate Person" in *A Choice of Inheritance: Self and Community from Edmund Burke to Robert Frost*. Cambridge: Harvard University Press, 1989.

Carlisle, E.G. *The Uncertain Self: Whitman's Drama of Identity*. East Lansing: Michigan State University Press, 1973.

Caviello, Peter. "Intimate Nationality: Anonymity and Attachment in Whitman." *American Literature* 73 (March 2001): 85–119.

Chase, Richard. *Walt Whitman Reconsidered*. New York: William Sloane Associates, 1955.

Clarke, Graham. *Walt Whitman: The Poem as Private History* New York: Vision Press, 1991.

Crawley, Thomas. *The Structure of Leaves of Grass*. Austin: University of Texas Press, 1970.

Davenport, Guy. *The Geography of the Imagination*. New York: Pantheon Books, 1981.

Donoghue, Denis. "Leaves of Grass and American Culture." *Sewanee Review* (Summer 2003): 347–374.

Duffey, Bernard. *Poetry in America: Expression and Its Values in the Times of Bryant, Whitman, and Pound*. Durham: Duke University Press, 1978.

Erkkila, Betsy. *Whitman the Political Poet*. New York: Oxford University Press, 1989.

Fletcher, Angus. *A New Theory for American Poetry*. Cambridge: Harvard University Press, 2004.

Hindus, Milton, ed. *Leaves of Grass: One Hundred Years After*. Stanford: Stanford University Press, 1955.

———, ed. *Walt Whitman: The Critical Heritage*. New York: Barnes and Noble, 1971.

Hollis, C Carroll. "Whitman and the American Idiom." *Quarterly Journal of Speech* 43 (1957): 408–20.

Hollander, John. *The Work of Poetry*. New York: Columbia University Press, 1997.

Hutchinson, George B. *The Ecstatic Whitman: Literary Shamanism and the Crisis of the Union*. Columbus: Ohio State University Press, 1986.

Irwin, John T. *American Hieroglyphics: The Symbol of Egyptian Hieroglyphics in the American Renaissance* New Haven: Yale University Press, 1980.

Kaplan, Justin. *Walt Whitman: A Life*. New York: Simon and Schuster, 1980.

Killingsworth, M. Jimmie. *Whitman's Poetry of the Body: Sexuality, Politics, and the Text*. Chapel Hill: University of North Carolina Press, 1989.

Kuebrich, David. *Minor Prophecy: Walt Whitman's New American Religion*. Bloomington: Indiana University Press, 1989.

Larson, Kerry C. *Whitman's Drama of Consensus*. Chicago: University of Chicago Press, 1988.

Lawson, Andrew. "'Spending for Vast Returns': Sex, Class, and Commerce in the First Leaves of Grass." *American Literature* 75 (June 2003): 335–365.

Lewis, R.W.B., ed. *The Presence of Walt Whitman*. New York: Columbia University Press, 1962.

———. *Trials of the Word: Essays in American Literature and the Humanistic Tradition*. New Haven: Yale University Press, 1965.

Lipking, Lawrence. *The Life of the Poet: Beginning and Ending Poetic Careers*. Chicago: University of Chicago Press, 1982.

Loving, Jerome. *Emerson, Whitman and the American Muse*. Chapel Hill: University of North Carolina Press, 1982.

Marki, Ivan. *The Trial of the Poet: An Interpretation of the First Edition of Leaves of Grass*. New York: Columbia University Press, 1975.

Maslan, Mark. "Whitman, Sexuality, and Poetic Authority." *Raritan* 17 (Spring 1998): 98–119.

Matthiessen, F. O. *American Renaissance*. New York: Oxford University Press, 1941.

Miller, Edwin Haviland. *Walt Whitman's Poetry: A Psychological Journey*. New York: New York University Press, 1969.

———, ed. *A Century of Whitman Criticism*. Bloomington: Indiana University Press, 1969.

Miller, James E., Jr. *The American Quest for a Supreme Fiction: Whitman's Legacy in the Personal Epic*. Chicago: University of Chicago Press, 1979.

———. *A Critical Guide to Leaves of Grass*. Chicago: University of Chicago Press, 1957.

————. *Whitman's "Song of Myself": Origin, Growth, Meaning*. New York: Dodd, Mead, 1964.

Molesworth, Charles. "Whitman's Political Vision." *Raritan* 12 (Summer 1992): 98–112.

Moon, Michael. *Disseminating Whitman: Revision and Corporeality in Leaves of Grass*. Cambridge: Harvard University Press, 1991.

Mulcaire, Terry. "Publishing Intimacy in Leaves of Grass." *English Literary History* 60 (Summer 1993): 471–501.

Murphy, Francis, ed. *Walt Whitman*. Harmondsworth: Penguin, 1969.

Newfield, Christopher. "Democracy and Male Homoeroticism." *The Yale Journal of Criticism* 6 (Fall 1993): 29–62.

Pearce, Roy Harvey. *The Continuity of American Poetry*. Princeton: Princeton University Press, 1961.

Pease, Donald. "Blake, Crane, Whitman, and Modernism: A Poetics of Pure Possibility." *PMLA* 96 (1981): 64–85.

———— and Walter Benn Michaels. *The American Renaissance Reconsidered*. Baltimore: Johns Hopkins University Press, 1985.

Price, Kenneth. *Whitman and Tradition: The Poet in His Century*. New Haven: Yale University Press, 1990.

Rubin, Joseph Jay. *The Historic Whitman*. University Park: Pennsylvania State University Press, 1973.

Stovall, Floyd. *The Foreground of Leaves of Grass*. Charlottsville: University Press of Virginia, 1974.

Strom, Susan. "'Face to Face': Whitman's Biblical References in 'Crossing Brooklyn Ferry.'" *Walt Whitman Review* 24 (1978): 7–16.

Symonds, John Addington. *Walt Whitman: A Study*. New York: AMS Press, 1968.

Thomas, M. Wynn. *The Lunar light of Whitman's Poetry*. Cambridge: Harvard University Press, 1987.

Trilling, Lionel. "Sermon on a Text from Whitman." *Nation* 160 (1945): 215–40.

Vendler, Helen. "Poetry and the Mediation of Value: Whitman on Lincoln." *Michigan Quarterly Review* 39 (Winter 2000): 1–18.

————. "Whitman's 'When Lilacs Last in the Dooryard Bloom'd,'" in Mary Ann Caws, ed. *Textual Analysis: Some Readers Reading*. New York: Modern Language Association of America, 1986.

Waggoner, Hyatt. *American Poets and Poetry*. New York: Harcourt, 1968.

Waskow, Howard. *Whitman: Explorations in Form*. Chicago: University of Chicago Press, 1966.

Wilhite, Keith. "His Mind Was Full of Absences: Whitman and the Scene of Writing." *English Literary History* 71 (Winter 2004): 921–48.

Zweig, Paul. *Walt Whitman: The Making of the Poet*. New York: Basic, 1984.

Acknowledgments

"Whitman" by D.H. Lawrence. From *Studies in Classic American Literature*. © 1923 by Thomas Seltzer, Inc., renewed 1950 by Frieda Lawrence. © 1961 by The Estate of the late Mrs. Frieda Lawrence. Used by permission of Viking Penguin, a division of Penguin Group (USA) Inc.

"Policy Made Personal" by Kenneth Burke. From *Leaves of Grass, One Hundred Years After*, Milton Hiindus, ed. pp. 74–108. © 1955 by the Board of Trustees of the Leland Stanford Jr. University, renewed 1983. All rights reserved. Used with the permission of Stanford University Press, www.sup.org.

"Walt Whitman: Always Going Out & Coming In" by R.W.B. Lewis. From *Trials of the Wod: Essays in American Literature & The Humanistic Tradition*. pp. 3–35. © 1965 by Yale University Press. Originally published in *Major Writers of America*, Perry Miller, ed. © 1962 Harcourt.

"Whitmen's Image of Voice: To the Tally of My Soul" by Harold Bloom. From *Agon: Towards a Theory of Revisionism*. © 1983 by Oxford University Press, Inc. Used by permission of Oxford University Press, Inc.

"Native Models" by K.C. Larson. From *Whitman's Drama of Consensus*. pp. 106–131. © The University of Chicago Press.

"A Simple Separate Person" by David Bromwich. From *A Choice of Inheritance: Self and Community from Edmund Burke to Robert Frost*. pp. 160–169. © 1989 by the President and Fellow of Harvard College. Reprinted by permission.

"Reading" reprinted by permission of Louisiana State University Press from *Whitman & the American Idiom* by Mark Bauerlein. © 1991 by Louisiana State University Press.

"Whitman's Difficult Availability" by John Hollander. From *The Work of Poetry*. Pp. 177–189. © 1997 by Columbia University Press.

"Poetry and the Mediation of Value: Whitman on Lincoln" by Helen Vendler. From *Michigan Quarterly Review* 39, no. 1 (Winter 2000): 1–18. © Helen Vendler.

"The Whitman Phrase" by Angus Fletcher. From *A New Theory of American Poetry: Democracy, the Environment, and the Future of Imagination*. pp. 94–116. © 2004 by the President and Fellow of Harvard College. Reprinted by permission.

Index